C-3880　　CAREER EXAMINATION SERIES

*This is your
PASSBOOK for...*

Associate Fraud Investigator

*Test Preparation Study Guide
Questions & Answers*

COPYRIGHT NOTICE

This book is SOLELY intended for, is sold ONLY to, and its use is RESTRICTED to individual, bona fide applicants or candidates who qualify by virtue of having seriously filed applications for appropriate license, certificate, professional and/or promotional advancement, higher school matriculation, scholarship, or other legitimate requirements of education and/or governmental authorities.

This book is NOT intended for use, class instruction, tutoring, training, duplication, copying, reprinting, excerption, or adaptation, etc., by:

1) Other publishers
2) Proprietors and/or Instructors of "Coaching" and/or Preparatory Courses
3) Personnel and/or Training Divisions of commercial, industrial, and governmental organizations
4) Schools, colleges, or universities and/or their departments and staffs, including teachers and other personnel
5) Testing Agencies or Bureaus
6) Study groups which seek by the purchase of a single volume to copy and/or duplicate and/or adapt this material for use by the group as a whole without having purchased individual volumes for each of the members of the group
7) Et al.

Such persons would be in violation of appropriate Federal and State statutes.

PROVISION OF LICENSING AGREEMENTS – Recognized educational, commercial, industrial, and governmental institutions and organizations, and others legitimately engaged in educational pursuits, including training, testing, and measurement activities, may address request for a licensing agreement to the copyright owners, who will determine whether, and under what conditions, including fees and charges, the materials in this book may be used them. In other words, a licensing facility exists for the legitimate use of the material in this book on other than an individual basis. However, it is asseverated and affirmed here that the material in this book CANNOT be used without the receipt of the express permission of such a licensing agreement from the Publishers. Inquiries re licensing should be addressed to the company, attention rights and permissions department.

All rights reserved, including the right of reproduction in whole or in part, in any form or by any means, electronic or mechanical, including photocopying, recording, or by any information storage and retrieval system, without permission in writing from the Publisher.

Copyright © 2024 by
National Learning Corporation

212 Michael Drive, Syosset, NY 11791
(516) 921-8888 • www.passbooks.com
E-mail: info@passbooks.com

PUBLISHED IN THE UNITED STATES OF AMERICA

PASSBOOK® SERIES

THE *PASSBOOK® SERIES* has been created to prepare applicants and candidates for the ultimate academic battlefield – the examination room.

At some time in our lives, each and every one of us may be required to take an examination – for validation, matriculation, admission, qualification, registration, certification, or licensure.

Based on the assumption that every applicant or candidate has met the basic formal educational standards, has taken the required number of courses, and read the necessary texts, the *PASSBOOK® SERIES* furnishes the one special preparation which may assure passing with confidence, instead of failing with insecurity. Examination questions – together with answers – are furnished as the basic vehicle for study so that the mysteries of the examination and its compounding difficulties may be eliminated or diminished by a sure method.

This book is meant to help you pass your examination provided that you qualify and are serious in your objective.

The entire field is reviewed through the huge store of content information which is succinctly presented through a provocative and challenging approach – the question-and-answer method.

A climate of success is established by furnishing the correct answers at the end of each test.

You soon learn to recognize types of questions, forms of questions, and patterns of questioning. You may even begin to anticipate expected outcomes.

You perceive that many questions are repeated or adapted so that you can gain acute insights, which may enable you to score many sure points.

You learn how to confront new questions, or types of questions, and to attack them confidently and work out the correct answers.

You note objectives and emphases, and recognize pitfalls and dangers, so that you may make positive educational adjustments.

Moreover, you are kept fully informed in relation to new concepts, methods, practices, and directions in the field.

You discover that you are actually taking the examination all the time: you are preparing for the examination by "taking" an examination, not by reading extraneous and/or supererogatory textbooks.

In short, this PASSBOOK®, used directedly, should be an important factor in helping you to pass your test.

ASSOCIATE FRAUD INVESTIGATOR

DUTIES

Associate Fraud Investigators perform supervision and/or work of complex difficulty and responsibility in the investigations of reported or suspected fraud activities in social benefit programs, or in the investigation of reported or suspected violations of tax laws and organized tax fraud activities; perform related work.

TEST

The multiple-choice test may include questions on principles of supervision such as planning, organizing and monitoring work; principles and techniques of investigation; knowledge of the civil and criminal justice systems; comprehension and preparation of written materials; dealing effectively with the public; standards of proper employee ethical conduct and other related areas.

HOW TO TAKE A TEST

I. YOU MUST PASS AN EXAMINATION

A. *WHAT EVERY CANDIDATE SHOULD KNOW*

Examination applicants often ask us for help in preparing for the written test. What can I study in advance? What kinds of questions will be asked? How will the test be given? How will the papers be graded?

As an applicant for a civil service examination, you may be wondering about some of these things. Our purpose here is to suggest effective methods of advance study and to describe civil service examinations.

Your chances for success on this examination can be increased if you know how to prepare. Those "pre-examination jitters" can be reduced if you know what to expect. You can even experience an adventure in good citizenship if you know why civil service exams are given.

B. *WHY ARE CIVIL SERVICE EXAMINATIONS GIVEN?*

Civil service examinations are important to you in two ways. As a citizen, you want public jobs filled by employees who know how to do their work. As a job seeker, you want a fair chance to compete for that job on an equal footing with other candidates. The best-known means of accomplishing this two-fold goal is the competitive examination.

Exams are widely publicized throughout the nation. They may be administered for jobs in federal, state, city, municipal, town or village governments or agencies.

Any citizen may apply, with some limitations, such as the age or residence of applicants. Your experience and education may be reviewed to see whether you meet the requirements for the particular examination. When these requirements exist, they are reasonable and applied consistently to all applicants. Thus, a competitive examination may cause you some uneasiness now, but it is your privilege and safeguard.

C. *HOW ARE CIVIL SERVICE EXAMS DEVELOPED?*

Examinations are carefully written by trained technicians who are specialists in the field known as "psychological measurement," in consultation with recognized authorities in the field of work that the test will cover. These experts recommend the subject matter areas or skills to be tested; only those knowledges or skills important to your success on the job are included. The most reliable books and source materials available are used as references. Together, the experts and technicians judge the difficulty level of the questions.

Test technicians know how to phrase questions so that the problem is clearly stated. Their ethics do not permit "trick" or "catch" questions. Questions may have been tried out on sample groups, or subjected to statistical analysis, to determine their usefulness.

Written tests are often used in combination with performance tests, ratings of training and experience, and oral interviews. All of these measures combine to form the best-known means of finding the right person for the right job.

II. HOW TO PASS THE WRITTEN TEST

A. NATURE OF THE EXAMINATION

To prepare intelligently for civil service examinations, you should know how they differ from school examinations you have taken. In school you were assigned certain definite pages to read or subjects to cover. The examination questions were quite detailed and usually emphasized memory. Civil service exams, on the other hand, try to discover your present ability to perform the duties of a position, plus your potentiality to learn these duties. In other words, a civil service exam attempts to predict how successful you will be. Questions cover such a broad area that they cannot be as minute and detailed as school exam questions.

In the public service similar kinds of work, or positions, are grouped together in one "class." This process is known as *position-classification*. All the positions in a class are paid according to the salary range for that class. One class title covers all of these positions, and they are all tested by the same examination.

B. FOUR BASIC STEPS

1) Study the announcement

How, then, can you know what subjects to study? Our best answer is: "Learn as much as possible about the class of positions for which you've applied." The exam will test the knowledge, skills and abilities needed to do the work.

Your most valuable source of information about the position you want is the official exam announcement. This announcement lists the training and experience qualifications. Check these standards and apply only if you come reasonably close to meeting them.

The brief description of the position in the examination announcement offers some clues to the subjects which will be tested. Think about the job itself. Review the duties in your mind. Can you perform them, or are there some in which you are rusty? Fill in the blank spots in your preparation.

Many jurisdictions preview the written test in the exam announcement by including a section called "Knowledge and Abilities Required," "Scope of the Examination," or some similar heading. Here you will find out specifically what fields will be tested.

2) Review your own background

Once you learn in general what the position is all about, and what you need to know to do the work, ask yourself which subjects you already know fairly well and which need improvement. You may wonder whether to concentrate on improving your strong areas or on building some background in your fields of weakness. When the announcement has specified "some knowledge" or "considerable knowledge," or has used adjectives like "beginning principles of..." or "advanced ... methods," you can get a clue as to the number and difficulty of questions to be asked in any given field. More questions, and hence broader coverage, would be included for those subjects which are more important in the work. Now weigh your strengths and weaknesses against the job requirements and prepare accordingly.

3) Determine the level of the position

Another way to tell how intensively you should prepare is to understand the level of the job for which you are applying. Is it the entering level? In other words, is this the position in which beginners in a field of work are hired? Or is it an intermediate or advanced level? Sometimes this is indicated by such words as "Junior" or "Senior" in the class title. Other jurisdictions use Roman numerals to designate the level – Clerk I, Clerk II, for example. The word "Supervisor" sometimes appears in the title. If the level is not indicated by the title, check the description of duties. Will you be working under very close supervision, or will you have responsibility for independent decisions in this work?

4) Choose appropriate study materials

Now that you know the subjects to be examined and the relative amount of each subject to be covered, you can choose suitable study materials. For beginning level jobs, or even advanced ones, if you have a pronounced weakness in some aspect of your training, read a modern, standard textbook in that field. Be sure it is up to date and has general coverage. Such books are normally available at your library, and the librarian will be glad to help you locate one. For entry-level positions, questions of appropriate difficulty are chosen -- neither highly advanced questions, nor those too simple. Such questions require careful thought but not advanced training.

If the position for which you are applying is technical or advanced, you will read more advanced, specialized material. If you are already familiar with the basic principles of your field, elementary textbooks would waste your time. Concentrate on advanced textbooks and technical periodicals. Think through the concepts and review difficult problems in your field.

These are all general sources. You can get more ideas on your own initiative, following these leads. For example, training manuals and publications of the government agency which employs workers in your field can be useful, particularly for technical and professional positions. A letter or visit to the government department involved may result in more specific study suggestions, and certainly will provide you with a more definite idea of the exact nature of the position you are seeking.

III. KINDS OF TESTS

Tests are used for purposes other than measuring knowledge and ability to perform specified duties. For some positions, it is equally important to test ability to make adjustments to new situations or to profit from training. In others, basic mental abilities not dependent on information are essential. Questions which test these things may not appear as pertinent to the duties of the position as those which test for knowledge and information. Yet they are often highly important parts of a fair examination. For very general questions, it is almost impossible to help you direct your study efforts. What we can do is to point out some of the more common of these general abilities needed in public service positions and describe some typical questions.

1) General information

Broad, general information has been found useful for predicting job success in some kinds of work. This is tested in a variety of ways, from vocabulary lists to questions about current events. Basic background in some field of work, such as sociology or economics, may be sampled in a group of questions. Often these are principles which have become familiar to most persons through exposure rather than through formal training. It is difficult to advise you how to study for these questions; being alert to the world around you is our best suggestion.

2) Verbal ability

An example of an ability needed in many positions is verbal or language ability. Verbal ability is, in brief, the ability to use and understand words. Vocabulary and grammar tests are typical measures of this ability. Reading comprehension or paragraph interpretation questions are common in many kinds of civil service tests. You are given a paragraph of written material and asked to find its central meaning.

3) Numerical ability

Number skills can be tested by the familiar arithmetic problem, by checking paired lists of numbers to see which are alike and which are different, or by interpreting charts and graphs. In the latter test, a graph may be printed in the test booklet which you are asked to use as the basis for answering questions.

4) Observation

A popular test for law-enforcement positions is the observation test. A picture is shown to you for several minutes, then taken away. Questions about the picture test your ability to observe both details and larger elements.

5) Following directions

In many positions in the public service, the employee must be able to carry out written instructions dependably and accurately. You may be given a chart with several columns, each column listing a variety of information. The questions require you to carry out directions involving the information given in the chart.

6) Skills and aptitudes

Performance tests effectively measure some manual skills and aptitudes. When the skill is one in which you are trained, such as typing or shorthand, you can practice. These tests are often very much like those given in business school or high school courses. For many of the other skills and aptitudes, however, no short-time preparation can be made. Skills and abilities natural to you or that you have developed throughout your lifetime are being tested.

Many of the general questions just described provide all the data needed to answer the questions and ask you to use your reasoning ability to find the answers. Your best preparation for these tests, as well as for tests of facts and ideas, is to be at your physical and mental best. You, no doubt, have your own methods of getting into an exam-taking mood and keeping "in shape." The next section lists some ideas on this subject.

IV. KINDS OF QUESTIONS

Only rarely is the "essay" question, which you answer in narrative form, used in civil service tests. Civil service tests are usually of the short-answer type. Full instructions for answering these questions will be given to you at the examination. But in case this is your first experience with short-answer questions and separate answer sheets, here is what you need to know:

1) Multiple-choice Questions

Most popular of the short-answer questions is the "multiple choice" or "best answer" question. It can be used, for example, to test for factual knowledge, ability to solve problems or judgment in meeting situations found at work.

A multiple-choice question is normally one of three types—
- It can begin with an incomplete statement followed by several possible endings. You are to find the one ending which *best* completes the statement, although some of the others may not be entirely wrong.
- It can also be a complete statement in the form of a question which is answered by choosing one of the statements listed.

- It can be in the form of a problem – again you select the best answer.

Here is an example of a multiple-choice question with a discussion which should give you some clues as to the method for choosing the right answer:

When an employee has a complaint about his assignment, the action which will *best* help him overcome his difficulty is to
  A. discuss his difficulty with his coworkers
  B. take the problem to the head of the organization
  C. take the problem to the person who gave him the assignment
  D. say nothing to anyone about his complaint

In answering this question, you should study each of the choices to find which is best. Consider choice "A" – Certainly an employee may discuss his complaint with fellow employees, but no change or improvement can result, and the complaint remains unresolved. Choice "B" is a poor choice since the head of the organization probably does not know what assignment you have been given, and taking your problem to him is known as "going over the head" of the supervisor. The supervisor, or person who made the assignment, is the person who can clarify it or correct any injustice. Choice "C" is, therefore, correct. To say nothing, as in choice "D," is unwise. Supervisors have and interest in knowing the problems employees are facing, and the employee is seeking a solution to his problem.

2) True/False Questions

The "true/false" or "right/wrong" form of question is sometimes used. Here a complete statement is given. Your job is to decide whether the statement is right or wrong.

SAMPLE: A roaming cell-phone call to a nearby city costs less than a non-roaming call to a distant city.

This statement is wrong, or false, since roaming calls are more expensive.

This is not a complete list of all possible question forms, although most of the others are variations of these common types. You will always get complete directions for answering questions. Be sure you understand *how* to mark your answers – ask questions until you do.

V. RECORDING YOUR ANSWERS

Computer terminals are used more and more today for many different kinds of exams.
For an examination with very few applicants, you may be told to record your answers in the test booklet itself. Separate answer sheets are much more common. If this separate answer sheet is to be scored by machine – and this is often the case – it is highly important that you mark your answers correctly in order to get credit.
An electronic scoring machine is often used in civil service offices because of the speed with which papers can be scored. Machine-scored answer sheets must be marked with a pencil, which will be given to you. This pencil has a high graphite content which responds to the electronic scoring machine. As a matter of fact, stray dots may register as answers, so do not let your pencil rest on the answer sheet while you are pondering the correct answer. Also, if your pencil lead breaks or is otherwise defective, ask for another.

Since the answer sheet will be dropped in a slot in the scoring machine, be careful not to bend the corners or get the paper crumpled.

The answer sheet normally has five vertical columns of numbers, with 30 numbers to a column. These numbers correspond to the question numbers in your test booklet. After each number, going across the page are four or five pairs of dotted lines. These short dotted lines have small letters or numbers above them. The first two pairs may also have a "T" or "F" above the letters. This indicates that the first two pairs only are to be used if the questions are of the true-false type. If the questions are multiple choice, disregard the "T" and "F" and pay attention only to the small letters or numbers.

Answer your questions in the manner of the sample that follows:

32. The largest city in the United States is
    A. Washington, D.C.
    B. New York City
    C. Chicago
    D. Detroit
    E. San Francisco

1) Choose the answer you think is best. (New York City is the largest, so "B" is correct.)
2) Find the row of dotted lines numbered the same as the question you are answering. (Find row number 32)
3) Find the pair of dotted lines corresponding to the answer. (Find the pair of lines under the mark "B.")
4) Make a solid black mark between the dotted lines.

VI. BEFORE THE TEST

Common sense will help you find procedures to follow to get ready for an examination. Too many of us, however, overlook these sensible measures. Indeed, nervousness and fatigue have been found to be the most serious reasons why applicants fail to do their best on civil service tests. Here is a list of reminders:

- Begin your preparation early – Don't wait until the last minute to go scurrying around for books and materials or to find out what the position is all about.
- Prepare continuously – An hour a night for a week is better than an all-night cram session. This has been definitely established. What is more, a night a week for a month will return better dividends than crowding your study into a shorter period of time.
- Locate the place of the exam – You have been sent a notice telling you when and where to report for the examination. If the location is in a different town or otherwise unfamiliar to you, it would be well to inquire the best route and learn something about the building.
- Relax the night before the test – Allow your mind to rest. Do not study at all that night. Plan some mild recreation or diversion; then go to bed early and get a good night's sleep.
- Get up early enough to make a leisurely trip to the place for the test – This way unforeseen events, traffic snarls, unfamiliar buildings, etc. will not upset you.
- Dress comfortably – A written test is not a fashion show. You will be known by number and not by name, so wear something comfortable.

- Leave excess paraphernalia at home – Shopping bags and odd bundles will get in your way. You need bring only the items mentioned in the official notice you received; usually everything you need is provided. Do not bring reference books to the exam. They will only confuse those last minutes and be taken away from you when in the test room.
- Arrive somewhat ahead of time – If because of transportation schedules you must get there very early, bring a newspaper or magazine to take your mind off yourself while waiting.
- Locate the examination room – When you have found the proper room, you will be directed to the seat or part of the room where you will sit. Sometimes you are given a sheet of instructions to read while you are waiting. Do not fill out any forms until you are told to do so; just read them and be prepared.
- Relax and prepare to listen to the instructions
- If you have any physical problem that may keep you from doing your best, be sure to tell the test administrator. If you are sick or in poor health, you really cannot do your best on the exam. You can come back and take the test some other time.

VII. AT THE TEST

The day of the test is here and you have the test booklet in your hand. The temptation to get going is very strong. Caution! There is more to success than knowing the right answers. You must know how to identify your papers and understand variations in the type of short-answer question used in this particular examination. Follow these suggestions for maximum results from your efforts:

1) Cooperate with the monitor

The test administrator has a duty to create a situation in which you can be as much at ease as possible. He will give instructions, tell you when to begin, check to see that you are marking your answer sheet correctly, and so on. He is not there to guard you, although he will see that your competitors do not take unfair advantage. He wants to help you do your best.

2) Listen to all instructions

Don't jump the gun! Wait until you understand all directions. In most civil service tests you get more time than you need to answer the questions. So don't be in a hurry. Read each word of instructions until you clearly understand the meaning. Study the examples, listen to all announcements and follow directions. Ask questions if you do not understand what to do.

3) Identify your papers

Civil service exams are usually identified by number only. You will be assigned a number; you must not put your name on your test papers. Be sure to copy your number correctly. Since more than one exam may be given, copy your exact examination title.

4) Plan your time

Unless you are told that a test is a "speed" or "rate of work" test, speed itself is usually not important. Time enough to answer all the questions will be provided, but this does not mean that you have all day. An overall time limit has been set. Divide the total time (in minutes) by the number of questions to determine the approximate time you have for each question.

5) Do not linger over difficult questions

If you come across a difficult question, mark it with a paper clip (useful to have along) and come back to it when you have been through the booklet. One caution if you do this – be sure to skip a number on your answer sheet as well. Check often to be sure that you have not lost your place and that you are marking in the row numbered the same as the question you are answering.

6) Read the questions

Be sure you know what the question asks! Many capable people are unsuccessful because they failed to *read* the questions correctly.

7) Answer all questions

Unless you have been instructed that a penalty will be deducted for incorrect answers, it is better to guess than to omit a question.

8) Speed tests

It is often better NOT to guess on speed tests. It has been found that on timed tests people are tempted to spend the last few seconds before time is called in marking answers at random – without even reading them – in the hope of picking up a few extra points. To discourage this practice, the instructions may warn you that your score will be "corrected" for guessing. That is, a penalty will be applied. The incorrect answers will be deducted from the correct ones, or some other penalty formula will be used.

9) Review your answers

If you finish before time is called, go back to the questions you guessed or omitted to give them further thought. Review other answers if you have time.

10) Return your test materials

If you are ready to leave before others have finished or time is called, take ALL your materials to the monitor and leave quietly. Never take any test material with you. The monitor can discover whose papers are not complete, and taking a test booklet may be grounds for disqualification.

VIII. EXAMINATION TECHNIQUES

1) Read the general instructions carefully. These are usually printed on the first page of the exam booklet. As a rule, these instructions refer to the timing of the examination; the fact that you should not start work until the signal and must stop work at a signal, etc. If there are any *special* instructions, such as a choice of questions to be answered, make sure that you note this instruction carefully.

2) When you are ready to start work on the examination, that is as soon as the signal has been given, read the instructions to each question booklet, underline any key words or phrases, such as *least, best, outline, describe* and the like. In this way you will tend to answer as requested rather than discover on reviewing your paper that you *listed without describing*, that you selected the *worst* choice rather than the *best* choice, etc.

3) If the examination is of the objective or multiple-choice type – that is, each question will also give a series of possible answers: A, B, C or D, and you are called upon to select the best answer and write the letter next to that answer on your answer paper – it is advisable to start answering each question in turn. There may be anywhere from 50 to 100 such questions in the three or four hours allotted and you can see how much time would be taken if you read through all the questions before beginning to answer any. Furthermore, if you come across a question or group of questions which you know would be difficult to answer, it would undoubtedly affect your handling of all the other questions.

4) If the examination is of the essay type and contains but a few questions, it is a moot point as to whether you should read all the questions before starting to answer any one. Of course, if you are given a choice – say five out of seven and the like – then it is essential to read all the questions so you can eliminate the two that are most difficult. If, however, you are asked to answer all the questions, there may be danger in trying to answer the easiest one first because you may find that you will spend too much time on it. The best technique is to answer the first question, then proceed to the second, etc.

5) Time your answers. Before the exam begins, write down the time it started, then add the time allowed for the examination and write down the time it must be completed, then divide the time available somewhat as follows:
   - If 3-1/2 hours are allowed, that would be 210 minutes. If you have 80 objective-type questions, that would be an average of 2-1/2 minutes per question. Allow yourself no more than 2 minutes per question, or a total of 160 minutes, which will permit about 50 minutes to review.
   - If for the time allotment of 210 minutes there are 7 essay questions to answer, that would average about 30 minutes a question. Give yourself only 25 minutes per question so that you have about 35 minutes to review.

6) The most important instruction is to *read each question* and make sure you know what is wanted. The second most important instruction is to *time yourself properly* so that you answer every question. The third most important instruction is to *answer every question*. Guess if you have to but include something for each question. Remember that you will receive no credit for a blank and will probably receive some credit if you write something in answer to an essay question. If you guess a letter – say "B" for a multiple-choice question – you may have guessed right. If you leave a blank as an answer to a multiple-choice question, the examiners may respect your feelings but it will not add a point to your score. Some exams may penalize you for wrong answers, so in such cases *only*, you may not want to guess unless you have some basis for your answer.

7) Suggestions
   a. Objective-type questions
      1. Examine the question booklet for proper sequence of pages and questions
      2. Read all instructions carefully
      3. Skip any question which seems too difficult; return to it after all other questions have been answered
      4. Apportion your time properly; do not spend too much time on any single question or group of questions

5. Note and underline key words – *all, most, fewest, least, best, worst, same, opposite,* etc.
6. Pay particular attention to negatives
7. Note unusual option, e.g., unduly long, short, complex, different or similar in content to the body of the question
8. Observe the use of "hedging" words – *probably, may, most likely,* etc.
9. Make sure that your answer is put next to the same number as the question
10. Do not second-guess unless you have good reason to believe the second answer is definitely more correct
11. Cross out original answer if you decide another answer is more accurate; do not erase until you are ready to hand your paper in
12. Answer all questions; guess unless instructed otherwise
13. Leave time for review

b. Essay questions
1. Read each question carefully
2. Determine exactly what is wanted. Underline key words or phrases.
3. Decide on outline or paragraph answer
4. Include many different points and elements unless asked to develop any one or two points or elements
5. Show impartiality by giving pros and cons unless directed to select one side only
6. Make and write down any assumptions you find necessary to answer the questions
7. Watch your English, grammar, punctuation and choice of words
8. Time your answers; don't crowd material

8) Answering the essay question

Most essay questions can be answered by framing the specific response around several key words or ideas. Here are a few such key words or ideas:

M's: manpower, materials, methods, money, management
P's: purpose, program, policy, plan, procedure, practice, problems, pitfalls, personnel, public relations

a. Six basic steps in handling problems:
1. Preliminary plan and background development
2. Collect information, data and facts
3. Analyze and interpret information, data and facts
4. Analyze and develop solutions as well as make recommendations
5. Prepare report and sell recommendations
6. Install recommendations and follow up effectiveness

b. Pitfalls to avoid
1. *Taking things for granted* – A statement of the situation does not necessarily imply that each of the elements is necessarily true; for example, a complaint may be invalid and biased so that all that can be taken for granted is that a complaint has been registered

2. *Considering only one side of a situation* – Wherever possible, indicate several alternatives and then point out the reasons you selected the best one
3. *Failing to indicate follow up* – Whenever your answer indicates action on your part, make certain that you will take proper follow-up action to see how successful your recommendations, procedures or actions turn out to be
4. *Taking too long in answering any single question* – Remember to time your answers properly

IX. AFTER THE TEST

Scoring procedures differ in detail among civil service jurisdictions although the general principles are the same. Whether the papers are hand-scored or graded by machine we have described, they are nearly always graded by number. That is, the person who marks the paper knows only the number – never the name – of the applicant. Not until all the papers have been graded will they be matched with names. If other tests, such as training and experience or oral interview ratings have been given, scores will be combined. Different parts of the examination usually have different weights. For example, the written test might count 60 percent of the final grade, and a rating of training and experience 40 percent. In many jurisdictions, veterans will have a certain number of points added to their grades.

After the final grade has been determined, the names are placed in grade order and an eligible list is established. There are various methods for resolving ties between those who get the same final grade – probably the most common is to place first the name of the person whose application was received first. Job offers are made from the eligible list in the order the names appear on it. You will be notified of your grade and your rank as soon as all these computations have been made. This will be done as rapidly as possible.

People who are found to meet the requirements in the announcement are called "eligibles." Their names are put on a list of eligible candidates. An eligible's chances of getting a job depend on how high he stands on this list and how fast agencies are filling jobs from the list.

When a job is to be filled from a list of eligibles, the agency asks for the names of people on the list of eligibles for that job. When the civil service commission receives this request, it sends to the agency the names of the three people highest on this list. Or, if the job to be filled has specialized requirements, the office sends the agency the names of the top three persons who meet these requirements from the general list.

The appointing officer makes a choice from among the three people whose names were sent to him. If the selected person accepts the appointment, the names of the others are put back on the list to be considered for future openings.

That is the rule in hiring from all kinds of eligible lists, whether they are for typist, carpenter, chemist, or something else. For every vacancy, the appointing officer has his choice of any one of the top three eligibles on the list. This explains why the person whose name is on top of the list sometimes does not get an appointment when some of the persons lower on the list do. If the appointing officer chooses the second or third eligible, the No. 1 eligible does not get a job at once, but stays on the list until he is appointed or the list is terminated.

X. HOW TO PASS THE INTERVIEW TEST

The examination for which you applied requires an oral interview test. You have already taken the written test and you are now being called for the interview test – the final part of the formal examination.

You may think that it is not possible to prepare for an interview test and that there are no procedures to follow during an interview. Our purpose is to point out some things you can do in advance that will help you and some good rules to follow and pitfalls to avoid while you are being interviewed.

What is an interview supposed to test?

The written examination is designed to test the technical knowledge and competence of the candidate; the oral is designed to evaluate intangible qualities, not readily measured otherwise, and to establish a list showing the relative fitness of each candidate – as measured against his competitors – for the position sought. Scoring is not on the basis of "right" and "wrong," but on a sliding scale of values ranging from "not passable" to "outstanding." As a matter of fact, it is possible to achieve a relatively low score without a single "incorrect" answer because of evident weakness in the qualities being measured.

Occasionally, an examination may consist entirely of an oral test – either an individual or a group oral. In such cases, information is sought concerning the technical knowledges and abilities of the candidate, since there has been no written examination for this purpose. More commonly, however, an oral test is used to supplement a written examination.

Who conducts interviews?

The composition of oral boards varies among different jurisdictions. In nearly all, a representative of the personnel department serves as chairman. One of the members of the board may be a representative of the department in which the candidate would work. In some cases, "outside experts" are used, and, frequently, a businessman or some other representative of the general public is asked to serve. Labor and management or other special groups may be represented. The aim is to secure the services of experts in the appropriate field.

However the board is composed, it is a good idea (and not at all improper or unethical) to ascertain in advance of the interview who the members are and what groups they represent. When you are introduced to them, you will have some idea of their backgrounds and interests, and at least you will not stutter and stammer over their names.

What should be done before the interview?

While knowledge about the board members is useful and takes some of the surprise element out of the interview, there is other preparation which is more substantive. It *is* possible to prepare for an oral interview – in several ways:

1) Keep a copy of your application and review it carefully before the interview

This may be the only document before the oral board, and the starting point of the interview. Know what education and experience you have listed there, and the sequence and dates of all of it. Sometimes the board will ask you to review the highlights of your experience for them; you should not have to hem and haw doing it.

2) Study the class specification and the examination announcement

Usually, the oral board has one or both of these to guide them. The qualities, characteristics or knowledges required by the position sought are stated in these documents. They offer valuable clues as to the nature of the oral interview. For example, if the job involves supervisory responsibilities, the announcement will usually indicate that knowledge of modern supervisory methods and the qualifications of the candidate as a supervisor will be tested. If so, you can expect such questions, frequently in the form of a hypothetical situation which you are expected to solve. NEVER go into an oral without knowledge of the duties and responsibilities of the job you seek.

3) Think through each qualification required

Try to visualize the kind of questions you would ask if you were a board member. How well could you answer them? Try especially to appraise your own knowledge and background in each area, *measured against the job sought*, and identify any areas in which you are weak. Be critical and realistic – do not flatter yourself.

4) Do some general reading in areas in which you feel you may be weak

For example, if the job involves supervision and your past experience has NOT, some general reading in supervisory methods and practices, particularly in the field of human relations, might be useful. Do NOT study agency procedures or detailed manuals. The oral board will be testing your understanding and capacity, not your memory.

5) Get a good night's sleep and watch your general health and mental attitude

You will want a clear head at the interview. Take care of a cold or any other minor ailment, and of course, no hangovers.

What should be done on the day of the interview?

Now comes the day of the interview itself. Give yourself plenty of time to get there. Plan to arrive somewhat ahead of the scheduled time, particularly if your appointment is in the fore part of the day. If a previous candidate fails to appear, the board might be ready for you a bit early. By early afternoon an oral board is almost invariably behind schedule if there are many candidates, and you may have to wait. Take along a book or magazine to read, or your application to review, but leave any extraneous material in the waiting room when you go in for your interview. In any event, relax and compose yourself.

The matter of dress is important. The board is forming impressions about you – from your experience, your manners, your attitude, and your appearance. Give your personal appearance careful attention. Dress your best, but not your flashiest. Choose conservative, appropriate clothing, and be sure it is immaculate. This is a business interview, and your appearance should indicate that you regard it as such. Besides, being well groomed and properly dressed will help boost your confidence.

Sooner or later, someone will call your name and escort you into the interview room. *This is it.* From here on you are on your own. It is too late for any more preparation. But remember, you asked for this opportunity to prove your fitness, and you are here because your request was granted.

What happens when you go in?

The usual sequence of events will be as follows: The clerk (who is often the board stenographer) will introduce you to the chairman of the oral board, who will introduce you to the other members of the board. Acknowledge the introductions before you sit down. Do not be surprised if you find a microphone facing you or a stenotypist sitting by. Oral interviews are usually recorded in the event of an appeal or other review.

Usually the chairman of the board will open the interview by reviewing the highlights of your education and work experience from your application – primarily for the benefit of the other members of the board, as well as to get the material into the record. Do not interrupt or comment unless there is an error or significant misinterpretation; if that is the case, do not hesitate. But do not quibble about insignificant matters. Also, he will usually ask you some question about your education, experience or your present job – partly to get you to start talking and to establish the interviewing "rapport." He may start the actual questioning, or turn it over to one of the other members. Frequently, each member undertakes the questioning on a particular area, one in which he is perhaps most competent, so you can expect each member to participate in the examination. Because time is limited, you may also expect some rather abrupt switches in the direction the questioning takes, so do not be upset by it. Normally, a board member will not pursue a single line of questioning unless he discovers a particular strength or weakness.

After each member has participated, the chairman will usually ask whether any member has any further questions, then will ask you if you have anything you wish to add. Unless you are expecting this question, it may floor you. Worse, it may start you off on an extended, extemporaneous speech. The board is not usually seeking more information. The question is principally to offer you a last opportunity to present further qualifications or to indicate that you have nothing to add. So, if you feel that a significant qualification or characteristic has been overlooked, it is proper to point it out in a sentence or so. Do not compliment the board on the thoroughness of their examination – they have been sketchy, and you know it. If you wish, merely say, "No thank you, I have nothing further to add." This is a point where you can "talk yourself out" of a good impression or fail to present an important bit of information. Remember, *you close the interview yourself*.

The chairman will then say, "That is all, Mr. _____, thank you." Do not be startled; the interview is over, and quicker than you think. Thank him, gather your belongings and take your leave. Save your sigh of relief for the other side of the door.

How to put your best foot forward

Throughout this entire process, you may feel that the board individually and collectively is trying to pierce your defenses, seek out your hidden weaknesses and embarrass and confuse you. Actually, this is not true. They are obliged to make an appraisal of your qualifications for the job you are seeking, and they want to see you in your best light. Remember, they must interview all candidates and a non-cooperative candidate may become a failure in spite of their best efforts to bring out his qualifications. Here are 15 suggestions that will help you:

1) Be natural – Keep your attitude confident, not cocky

If you are not confident that you can do the job, do not expect the board to be. Do not apologize for your weaknesses, try to bring out your strong points. The board is interested in a positive, not negative, presentation. Cockiness will antagonize any board member and make him wonder if you are covering up a weakness by a false show of strength.

2) Get comfortable, but don't lounge or sprawl

Sit erectly but not stiffly. A careless posture may lead the board to conclude that you are careless in other things, or at least that you are not impressed by the importance of the occasion. Either conclusion is natural, even if incorrect. Do not fuss with your clothing, a pencil or an ashtray. Your hands may occasionally be useful to emphasize a point; do not let them become a point of distraction.

3) Do not wisecrack or make small talk

This is a serious situation, and your attitude should show that you consider it as such. Further, the time of the board is limited – they do not want to waste it, and neither should you.

4) Do not exaggerate your experience or abilities

In the first place, from information in the application or other interviews and sources, the board may know more about you than you think. Secondly, you probably will not get away with it. An experienced board is rather adept at spotting such a situation, so do not take the chance.

5) If you know a board member, do not make a point of it, yet do not hide it

Certainly you are not fooling him, and probably not the other members of the board. Do not try to take advantage of your acquaintanceship – it will probably do you little good.

6) Do not dominate the interview

Let the board do that. They will give you the clues – do not assume that you have to do all the talking. Realize that the board has a number of questions to ask you, and do not try to take up all the interview time by showing off your extensive knowledge of the answer to the first one.

7) Be attentive

You only have 20 minutes or so, and you should keep your attention at its sharpest throughout. When a member is addressing a problem or question to you, give him your undivided attention. Address your reply principally to him, but do not exclude the other board members.

8) Do not interrupt

A board member may be stating a problem for you to analyze. He will ask you a question when the time comes. Let him state the problem, and wait for the question.

9) Make sure you understand the question

Do not try to answer until you are sure what the question is. If it is not clear, restate it in your own words or ask the board member to clarify it for you. However, do not haggle about minor elements.

10) Reply promptly but not hastily

A common entry on oral board rating sheets is "candidate responded readily," or "candidate hesitated in replies." Respond as promptly and quickly as you can, but do not jump to a hasty, ill-considered answer.

11) Do not be peremptory in your answers

A brief answer is proper – but do not fire your answer back. That is a losing game from your point of view. The board member can probably ask questions much faster than you can answer them.

12) Do not try to create the answer you think the board member wants

He is interested in what kind of mind you have and how it works – not in playing games. Furthermore, he can usually spot this practice and will actually grade you down on it.

13) Do not switch sides in your reply merely to agree with a board member

Frequently, a member will take a contrary position merely to draw you out and to see if you are willing and able to defend your point of view. Do not start a debate, yet do not surrender a good position. If a position is worth taking, it is worth defending.

14) Do not be afraid to admit an error in judgment if you are shown to be wrong

The board knows that you are forced to reply without any opportunity for careful consideration. Your answer may be demonstrably wrong. If so, admit it and get on with the interview.

15) Do not dwell at length on your present job

The opening question may relate to your present assignment. Answer the question but do not go into an extended discussion. You are being examined for a *new* job, not your present one. As a matter of fact, try to phrase ALL your answers in terms of the job for which you are being examined.

Basis of Rating

Probably you will forget most of these "do's" and "don'ts" when you walk into the oral interview room. Even remembering them all will not ensure you a passing grade. Perhaps you did not have the qualifications in the first place. But remembering them will help you to put your best foot forward, without treading on the toes of the board members.

Rumor and popular opinion to the contrary notwithstanding, an oral board wants you to make the best appearance possible. They know you are under pressure – but they also want to see how you respond to it as a guide to what your reaction would be under the pressures of the job you seek. They will be influenced by the degree of poise you display, the personal traits you show and the manner in which you respond.

ABOUT THIS BOOK

This book contains tests divided into Examination Sections. Go through each test, answering every question in the margin. We have also attached a sample answer sheet at the back of the book that can be removed and used. At the end of each test look at the answer key and check your answers. On the ones you got wrong, look at the right answer choice and learn. Do not fill in the answers first. Do not memorize the questions and answers, but understand the answer and principles involved. On your test, the questions will likely be different from the samples. Questions are changed and new ones added. If you understand these past questions you should have success with any changes that arise. Tests may consist of several types of questions. We have additional books on each subject should more study be advisable or necessary for you. Finally, the more you study, the better prepared you will be. This book is intended to be the last thing you study before you walk into the examination room. Prior study of relevant texts is also recommended. NLC publishes some of these in our Fundamental Series. Knowledge and good sense are important factors in passing your exam. Good luck also helps. So now study this Passbook, absorb the material contained within and take that knowledge into the examination. Then do your best to pass that exam.

EXAMINATION SECTION

EXAMINATION SECTION
TEST 1

DIRECTIONS: Each question or incomplete statement is followed by several suggested answers or completions. Select the one that BEST answers the question or completes the statement. *PRINT THE LETTER OF THE CORRECT ANSWER IN THE SPACE AT THE RIGHT.*

1. Which of the following statements concerning the questioning of a witness by an investigator is VALID?   1.____

    A. The investigator should insist on *yes* and *no* answers from a witness because such responses insure accurate answers.
    B. The investigator should ask questions which suggest answers in order to speed the flow of information from the witness.
    C. Long and complicated questions should be used to impress the witness with the perceptiveness and intelligence of the investigator, thus insuring the cooperation of the witness.
    D. The investigator may be able to distinguish between honest mistakes and intended misrepresentations made by a witness by rewording his queries and by asking additional questions.

2. Following are three statements concerning interviewing and investigative practice: 2.____
    I. In order to improve his ability to interview persons successfully, the investigator should evaluate his performance during and after each interview
    II. An investigator who has detected evasiveness in the statements of a subject should write off these remarks as of little value to his investigation, and need not attempt to substantiate them
    III. In order to gain a psychological advantage over a difficult witness in an interview, it would be good practice for an investigator to ask the subject to sit in a chair other than the one the subject has selected

    Which of the following CORRECTLY classifies the above statements into those which are correct and those which are not?

    A. III is correct, but I and II are not.
    B. I is correct, but II and III are not.
    C. I and III are correct, but II is not.
    D. II and III are correct, but I is not.

3. An investigator, following a subject under surveillance, boards the same bus that the subject has just entered. If the subject suddenly jumps off before it starts, the investigator should   3.____

    A. stay on the bus, get off at the next stop, and wait for the next bus
    B. attempt to get off the bus before it starts
    C. stay on the bus, get off the next stop, and take another bus or taxi back to the original stop
    D. assume that he has been spotted and discontinue any further attempts to follow the subject

4. The technique of taking a written statement of the information the investigator obtains from a witness and then having the witness sign the statement is   4.____

A. *useful,* because a written statement presented to the court is more acceptable than oral testimony from that witness
B. *not useful,* because the witness will be intimidated
C. *useful,* because the witness may forget or change his version of what happened at a later time
D. *not useful,* because it delays the investigator's handling of the case

5. For evidence to be admissible in court, it must be 5.____

   A. relevant but not necessarily material
   B. material and relevant
   C. of sufficient weight to influence any judicial decision or determination
   D. of sufficient weight to be material

6. Which of the following statements BEST describes the term *judicial notice?* 6.____
   The

   A. act by which a court recognizes the truth of certain facts without the formal presentation of evidence
   B. method by which a court notifies an individual that he is indicted
   C. process by which notice of court action is given to the general public
   D. communication of notice of court action, orally or in writing, directly to the affected person or the party to be charged

7. Assume that you are a supervising investigator interviewing a witness to alleged 7.____
   employee corruption. In replying to a question on bribe-taking, the subject shifts to a totally unrelated topic.
   Of the following, the BEST way to determine why the witness seems to be evading the question is to pursue the questioning

   A. *aggressively,* chiefly because the subject is probably an unwilling accomplice to misconduct
   B. *aggressively,* chiefly because the subject is probably protecting a fellow employee
   C. *tactfully,* chiefly because the subject is probably unaware of any wrongdoing
   D. *tactfully,* chiefly because the subject is probably withholding information that embarrasses him

8. An investigator usually develops positive or negative rapport with individuals he interviews. 8.____
   When this occurs, the investigator should

   A. control the nature and intensity of the relationship
   B. direct his total attention to finishing the interview
   C. develop a passive, professional attitude toward the interviewee
   D. appear personally friendly to eliminate any negative feelings the interviewee may have

9. Which of the following techniques is MOST effective in detecting erasures on a document? 9.____

   A. Look for an abrupt change in the style of writing
   B. Examine the spacing of letters to see whether there has been crowding

C. Hold the document approximately edgewise to a light, close to the edge of the light's shade, and look for damaged paper fibers
D. Fume the document with the chemical vapors of gallo-tannate or nigrosine acid, which react with ink's residue

10. At times, an investigator may ask a subject for samples of his handwriting for purposes of comparison with a questioned document.
When taking such samples, which of the following procedures should be AVOIDED?

   A. Placing the subject in a quiet place under minimal acceptable observation
   B. Having the subject write something other than a list of signatures
   C. Having the subject copy written or printed material
   D. Removing each sample before the next one is started

11. Which of the following can PROPERLY be classified as *secondary* evidence?

   A. Altered time sheets of accused employees
   B. Eyewitness testimony regarding time and leave abuses
   C. Official payroll roster records
   D. Photocopies of forged checks

12. Following are three statements describing possible characteristics of fraudulent checks:
   I. The first endorsement is clearly signed, matches the payee's name on the front, and appears right above the second endorsement
   II. The name of the bank on which the check is drawn and its location are abbreviated on the face of the check
   III. The digit and written amount of the check correspond exactly, and the payer's account number is inked over

   Which of the following CORRECTLY classifies the above statements into those that describe characteristics generally peculiar to fraudulent checks and those that do not?

   A. I and II are characteristic, but III is not.
   B. I is a characteristic, but II and III are not.
   C. II and III are characteristic, but I is not.
   D. III is a characteristic, but I and II are not.

13. Following are four statements concerning communication between an investigator and an informant:
   I. Meetings between an investigator and an informant should be held at the investigator's office
   II. The proper name of the informant should not be used when telephoning
   III. The investigator's organization should not be identified in any correspondence with the informant
   IV. The circumstances surrounding meetings between the investigator and an informant should be repeated to establish a pattern

   Which one of the following choices CORRECTLY classifies the above statements into those which are valid and those which are not valid as procedures for handling communications with an informant?

   A. I and II are valid, but III and IV are not valid.
   B. II and III are valid, but I and IV are not valid.
   C. III is valid, but I, II, and IV are not valid.
   D. IV is valid, but I, II, and III are not valid.

14. Of the following, the IMMEDIATE objective of an investigator, while speaking on the telephone to an anonymous person who is voluntarily offering information, should be to

    A. form an estimate of the informant's reliability
    B. decide on the motives and interests of the informer
    C. draw out all relevant information before the informer hangs up
    D. compare this information with that obtained from other sources

15. Supervising investigators are often called upon to provide subordinate investigators with on-the-job training. Following are three statements concerning the administration of on-the-job training:
    I. The supervisor selected to provide training must be an outstanding performer of the job he is teaching.
    II. The supervisor should have access to information about the training needs of the investigators he is to train.
    III. The subordinate investigators should be assigned to the work stations in which they will ultimately be employed.

    Which of the following CORRECTLY classifies the above statements into those that are appropriate practices and those that are not?

    A. I is appropriate, but II and III are not.
    B. III is appropriate, but I and II are not.
    C. I and III are appropriate, but II is not.
    D. II and III are appropriate, but I is not.

16. Assume you are training a group of new investigators and that one member of the group is a slower learner than the others.
    Of the following, the BEST way to handle this situation is to

    A. adapt your instruction speed to the rate of the slowest learner in order to reduce the possibility of frustrating him
    B. instruct at the level that is best suited to the majority of the group and give the slow learner individual help after the regular training sessions
    C. teach at the level at which you are most comfortable and handle problems as you become aware of them
    D. adjust your instruction speed to that of the slowest learner and provide him with extra remedial exercises or practice work

17. The one of the following that is a DISADVANTAGE of the conference approach to training investigators is that

    A. each investigator's ideas are critically evaluated by the other group members
    B. the informal atmosphere prevents the development of close relationships among investigators
    C. group members have time to reflect only on their own contributions and not on those of other investigators
    D. many investigators lack the skills or discipline to benefit from such training

18. Standard methods for performing various investigative tasks are useful MAINLY because they

    A. permit the supervisor to reduce the total time he spends on planning
    B. eliminate the need for monitoring costs
    C. enable the supervisor to spend less time on routine and detail
    D. reduce the number of forms needed to complete the tasks

19. Assume that, in one agency, the average number of absences per employee varies greatly from one investigative unit to another but the physical working conditions and type of work performed are similar in each of these units.
    Of the following, the MOST probable cause of the differences in the amount of absenteeism is the

    A. educational background of the employees
    B. number of female employees in the agency
    C. attitudes of the supervisors
    D. existence of an agency medical unit

20. In order to learn their job properly, newly hired investigators must receive an indication from their supervisors of the quality of their performance. The one of the following techniques that provides the MOST constructive *feedback* from supervisors to their subordinates is

    A. praising all aspects of subordinates' performance
    B. pointing out to subordinates that mistakes may result in poor probationary reports
    C. drawing the subordinates' attention to how close their performance is to the expected level of performance
    D. preparing written critiques for study by subordinates

21. Of the following, the BEST way for a supervisor to reduce absenteeism within his unit is to

    A. inform subordinates that all excuses due to illness will be referred to the personnel officer
    B. discuss with individual employees the reasons for their absences
    C. assign less desirable work to those absent most often
    D. recommend that employees who are absent most often be transferred to other units

22. Of the following, the MOST important factor in determining whether a supervisor is a success or a failure as a manager is his ability to

    A. do all work assigned to his unit better than his subordinates can
    B. make suggestions which are acceptable to top management
    C. train employees for various responsibilities
    D. delegate work so that it is performed effectively

Questions 23-25.

DIRECTIONS: Below is a report consisting of 15 numbered sentences, some of which are not consistent with the principles of good report writing. Answer Questions 23 through 25 SOLELY on the basis of the information contained in the report and your knowledge of investigative principles and practices.

To: Tom Smith, Administrative Investigator
From: John Jones, Supervising Investigator

1. On January 7, I received a call from Mrs. H. Harris of 684 Sunset Street, Brooklyn.
2. Mrs. Harris informed me that she wanted to report an instance of fraud relating to public assistance payments being received by her neighbor, Mrs. I Wallace.
3. I advised her that such a subject would best be discussed in person.
4. I then arranged a field visitation for January 10 at Mrs. Harris' apartment, 684 Sunset Street, Brooklyn.
5. On January 10, I discussed the basis for Mrs. Harris' charge against Mrs. Wallace at the former's apartment.
6. She stated that her neighbor is receiving Aid to Dependent Children payments for seven children, but that only three of her children are still living with her.
7. In addition, Mrs. Harris also claimed that her husband, whom she reported to the authorities as missing, usually sees her several times a week.
8. After further questioning, Mrs. Harris admitted to me that she had been quite friendly with Mrs. Wallace until they recently argued about trash left in their adjoining hall corridor.
9. However, she firmly stated that her allegations against Mrs. Wallace were valid and that she feared repercussions for her actions.
10. At the completion of the interview, I assured Mrs. Harris of the confidentiality of her statements and that an attempt would be made to verify her allegations.
11. As I was leaving Mrs. Harris' apartment, I noticed a man, aged approximately 45, walking out of Mrs. Wallace's apartment.
12. I followed him until he entered a late model green Oldsmobile and sped away.
13. On January 3, I returned to 684 Sunset Court, having determined that Mrs. Wallace is receiving assistance as indicated by Mrs. Harris.
14. However, upon presentation of official identification Mrs. Wallace refused to admit me to her apartment or grant an interview.
15. I an therefore referring this matter to you for further instructions.

John Jones
Supervising Investigator

23. The one of the following statements that clearly lacks vital information is statement
 A. 8   B. 10   C. 12   D. 14

24. Which of the following sentences from the report is ambiguous? Sentence
 A. 2   B. 3   C. 7   D. 10

25. Which of the following sentences contains information contradicting other data in the above report? Sentence
 A. 3   B. 8   C. 10   D. 13

KEY (CORRECT ANSWERS)

1. D
2. C
3. A
4. C
5. B

6. A
7. D
8. A
9. C
10. C

11. D
12. C
13. B
14. C
15. D

16. B
17. D
18. C
19. C
20. C

21. B
22. D
23. C
24. C
25. D

———

EXAMINATION SECTION
TEST 1

DIRECTIONS: Each question or incomplete statement is followed by several suggested answers or completions. Select the one that BEST answers the question or completes the statement. *PRINT THE LETTER OF THE CORRECT ANSWER IN THE SPACE AT THE RIGHT.*

1. Assume you are supervising a group of investigators. Your unit is assigned a rush job requiring a special skill and overtime work.
   Of the following, the MOST appropriate method of choosing the investigator to do this job is to

   A. assign the investigator who has the special skill required for the job
   B. ask an investigator who has previously indicated a willingness to work overtime
   C. call for a volunteer to perform this work
   D. offer the job to the investigator who is next in line to work overtime

2. Formal training programs can help remedy specific problems in an investigative unit. The one of the following that is NOT an intended result of such training programs is to

   A. eliminate the need for on-the-job training for new investigators
   B. help reduce the amount of overtime paid
   C. minimize the number of grievances made by investigators
   D. develop a pool of trained investigators needed for agency expansion

3. Periodic evaluation of subordinates' performance on the job serves all of the following purposes EXCEPT to

   A. point out weaknesses in performance to subordinates so that attempts can be made to eliminate them
   B. identify capable subordinates and insure that they are promoted
   C. indicate those subordinates who deserve training for greater responsibilities
   D. identify those subordinates who have exceptional ability

4. All of the following are proper objectives in the investigation of outside complaints about agency personnel EXCEPT the protection of the

   A. integrity and reputation of the staff
   B. public interest in identifying wrongdoers
   C. organization from liability resulting from unjust claims
   D. accused employees from disciplinary action

5. Assume that one of your subordinates had had a minor accident while performing a surveillance. In spite of your repeated demands, the subordinate refuses to prepare an accident report because he was only slightly injured. Of the following actions, it would be BEST in this situation for you to

   A. contact your superior to discuss disciplinary action
   B. have the employee file an affidavit absolving you of any responsibility for his injury
   C. ask the employee to submit a doctor's note to you on the extent of his injury
   D. call a meeting of subordinate personnel to discuss this situation

6. The one of the following that is likely to provide subordinates with the GREATEST satisfaction on the job is

   A. compensation for overtime production
   B. challenging and interesting work
   C. compensation proportional to the amount of work produced
   D. minimum responsibility for the completion of work

7. An employee is GENERALLY considered guilty of insubordination when he

   A. refuses to obey a supervisor's order with which he disagrees
   B. declines to carry out a directive he genuinely believes will cause him personal injury
   C. uses foul or abusive language among other work group members
   D. reports to work late after being warned not do do so

8. The one of the following that is GENERALLY characteristic of the more effective supervisors is that they

   A. specify every detail of the work to be done
   B. give subordinates leeway in the methods they use to complete their work
   C. supervise more closely than the less effective supervisors
   D. tend to be production-centered rather than employee-centered

9. If workers participate in planning, making important decisions, and the like, the supervisor will lose prestige and his authority will deteriorate.
   This statement is

   A. *true* because people have little respect for a leader who seeks their advice
   B. *true* because a supervisor must establish a firm command over his subordinates to be effective
   C. *false* because a skillful supervisor works with his subordinates to establish a goal and then works to reach it
   D. *false* because a supervisor gains prestige only by making all important decisions himself

10. As a supervisor, you note that while one of your subordinates does what he is told to do, he seems disinterested and lacks motivation in performing his work.
    Of the following, the BEST action for you to take to motivate this employee would be to

    A. transfer him to a more active unit
    B. give him less desirable work
    C. give him more responsibility
    D. assign him to work with a more experienced employee

11. Newly appointed supervisors will often assume responsibility for work which could be handled by their subordinates.
    Of the following, the MOST likely result of such a practice would be that the

    A. supervisor will gain the confidence of his subordinates
    B. subordinates' sense of initiative and responsibility will diminish
    C. supervisor will note an increase in the job satisfaction of his subordinates
    D. subordinates will have more time to learn more complex job skills

12. In order to accomplish the work of his unit MOST effectively, a supervisor of investigators should   12._____

    A. do the important work himself
    B. assign complete responsibility for the completion of work only to his more productive subordinates
    C. judiciously delegate authority to make decisions to his subordinates
    D. give sensitive and responsible work only to his most competent investigators

13. Assume, as a supervisor, you are approached by one of the investigators in your unit with what you consider to be a minor grievance.   13._____
    Of the following, the BEST way to handle this situation is to

    A. postpone taking any action since the passage of time usually resolves minor grievances
    B. try to resolve the problem immediately before it gets out of hand
    C. tell the investigator not to be concerned with minor grievances
    D. thank the investigator for calling the grievance to your attention and await further developments

14. Following are three guidelines a supervisor might follow in handling criticism by a superior: 14._____
    I. Consider the source of criticism before taking any action.
    II. Try to react calmly to criticism that is not justified.
    III. Analyze carefully only the criticism that requires a response.
    Which of the following CORRECTLY classifies the above guidelines into those which are valid and those which are not valid?

    A. I is valid, but II and III are not.
    B. I and II are valid, but III is not.
    C. II and III are valid, but I is not.
    D. III is valid, but I and II are not.

15. Assume that a supervisor notices that several of his subordinates, who are normally punctual, have been late for work quite often during the last few months.   15._____
    Which one of the following actions should the supervisor take FIRST in dealing with this problem?

    A. Refer the matter to the personnel staff of his agency.
    B. Schedule counseling sessions on the need for being prompt.
    C. Review his own supervision to determine whether it has been adequate.
    D. Inform the subordinates that exact records of their latenesses are being kept.

16. Following are three statements concerning principles of delegation: 16._____
    I. Supervisors should not be held accountable for work that has been delegated to their subordinates.
    II. Subordinates should normally have only one line supervisor.
    III. When subordinates are given authority that is limited by factors such as departmental rules, their responsibility is also limited.
    Which of the following BEST classifies the above statements into those that are valid and those that are not valid?

A. I is valid, but II and III are not.
B. II is valid, but I and III are not.
C. I and II are valid, but III is not.
D. II and III are valid, but I is not.

17. Following are six steps that should be taken in the course of report preparation:
    I. Outlining the material for presentation in the report.
    II. Analyzing and interpreting the facts
    III. Analyzing the problem
    IV. Reaching conclusions
    V. Writing, revising, and rewriting the final copy
    VI. Collecting data

    According to the principles of good report writing, the CORRECT order in which these steps should be taken is

    A. VI, III, II, I, IV, V
    B. III, VI, II, IV, I, V
    C. III, VI, II, I, IV, V
    D. VI, II, III, IV, I, V

17.___

18. Following are three statements concerning written reports:
    I. Clarity is generally more essential in oral reports than in written reports.
    II. Short sentences composed of simple words are generally preferred to complex sentences and difficult words.
    III. Abbreviations may be used whenever they are customary and will not distract the attention of the reader.

    Which of the following choices CORRECTLY classifies the above statements into those which are valid and those which are not valid?

    A. I and II are valid, but III is not valid.
    B. I is valid, but II and III are not valid.
    C. II and III are valid, but I is not valid.
    D. III is valid, but I and II are not valid.

18.___

19. In order to produce a report written in a style that is both understandable and effective, an investigator should apply the principles of unity, coherence, and emphasis. The one of the following which is the BEST example of the principle of coherence is

    A. interlinking sentences so that thoughts flow smoothly
    B. having each sentence express a single idea to facilitate comprehension
    C. arranging important points in prominent positions so they are not overlooked
    D. developing the main idea fully to insure complete consideration

19.___

20. Following are three statements concerning public relations in a city agency:
    I. Public relations in an agency should be the sole responsibility of a trained public relations professional
    II. Public relations involves every contact the agency has with the public, whether the contact is in person or by letter or telephone
    III. The public should be told by the agency what it is going to do and how it is going to do it before hearing a version from other sources which may be distorted

    Which of the following choices CORRECTLY classifies the above statements into those which are correct and those which are not?

20.___

A. I and II are correct, but III is not.
B. I is correct, but II and III are not.
C. II is correct, but I and III are not.
D. II and III are correct, but I is not.

21. Communication, both written and oral, is essential to the functioning of any organization. Written communication is generally more appropriate than oral communication when the information being transmitted 21.____

    A. concerns a small group of people
    B. has long-term significance
    C. is only of minimal importance
    D. is concise and simple to comprehend

22. Subordinates are MOST likely to accept changes in their work plans and schedules when their supervisor 22.____

    A. advises them that such changes must be implemented because they have been ordered by management
    B. gives them some background to help them understand the need for the changes
    C. tells them that even though he disagrees with the changes, they must be adhered to
    D. informs them he will follow up to determine how effective such changes are

Questions 23-25.

DIRECTIONS: Below is a report consisting of 15 numbered sentences, some of which are not consistent with the principles of good report writing. Questions 23 through 25 are to be answered SOLELY on the basis of the information contained in the report and your knowledge of investigative principles and practices.

To: Tom Smith, Administrative Investigator
From: John Jones, Senior Investigator

1. On January 7, I received a call from Mrs. H. Harris of 684 Sunset Street, Brooklyn.
2. Mrs. Harris informed me that she wanted to report an instance of fraud relating to public assistance payments being received by her neighbor, Mrs. I. Wallace.
3. I advised her that such a subject would best be discussed in person.
4. I then arranged a field visitation for January 10 at Mrs. Harris' apartment, 684 Sunset Street, Brooklyn.
5. On January 10, I discussed the basis for Mrs. Harris' charge against Mrs. Wallace at the former's apartment.
6. She stated that her neighbor is receiving Aid to Dependent Children payments for seven children, but that only three of her children are still living with her.
7. In addition, Mrs. Harris also claimed that her husband, whom she reported to the authorities as missing, usually sees her several times a week.
8. After further questioning, Mrs. Harris admitted to me that she had been quite friendly with Mrs. Wallace until they recently argued about trash left in their adjoining hall corridor.
9. However, she firmly stated that her allegations against Mr. Wallace were valid and that she feared repercussions for her actions.

10. At the completion of the interview, I assured Mrs. Harris of the confidentiality of her statements and that an attempt would be made to verify her allegations.
11. However, upon presentation of official identification, Mrs. Wallace refused to admit me to her apartment or grant an interview.
12. As I was leaving Mrs. Harris' apartment, I noticed a man, aged approximately 45, walking out of Mrs. Wallace's apartment.
13. I followed him until he entered a late model green Oldsmobile Cutlass, license plate #238DAB, and sped away.
14. On January 15, I returned to 684 Sunset Street, having determined that Mrs. Wallace is receiving assistance as indicated by Mrs. Harris.
15. I am, therefore, referring this matter to you for further instructions.

                                                            John Jones
                                                            Senior Investigator

23. The one of the following that indicates the MOST logical order for statements 11 through 15 is

    A. 11, 12, 13, 14, 15   B. 13, 14, 11, 12, 15
    C. 11, 13, 14, 12, 15   D. 12, 13, 14, 11, 15

24. Which of the following sentences from the report is ambiguous?
Sentence

    A. 2   B. 7   C. 8   D. 9

25. Of the following, based on the above report and your knowledge of investigative practice, it is MOST likely that investigator Jones failed to obtain the desired information from Mrs. Wallace because

    A. she was aware of Mrs. Harris' allegations
    B. she was fearful of personal injury
    C. he was not operating under cover
    D. he had not made a prior arrangement for the visit

KEY (CORRECT ANSWERS)

1.	A	11.	B
2.	A	12.	C
3.	B	13.	B
4.	D	14.	B
5.	A	15.	C
6.	B	16.	B
7.	A	17.	B
8.	B	18.	C
9.	C	19.	A
10.	C	20.	D

21. B
22. B
23. D
24. B
25. C

EXAMINATION SECTION
TEST 1

DIRECTIONS: Each question or incomplete statement is followed by several suggested answers or completions. Select the one that BEST answers the question or completes the statement. *PRINT THE LETTER OF THE CORRECT ANSWER IN THE SPACE AT THE RIGHT.*

1. In handling a case, an investigator should summarize the facts he has gathered and the observations he has made about the family and incorporate this material into a formal social study of the family.
   Of the following, the CHIEF advantage of such a practice is that it will provide a(n)

   A. picture of the family on the basis of which evaluations and plans can be made
   B. easily accessible listing of the factors pertaining to eligibility
   C. simple and uniform method of recording the family's social history
   D. opportunity for the investigator to record his evaluation of the family's situation

   1.____

2. An applicant for assistance tells the investigator that he has always supported himself by doing odd jobs.
   While attempting to verify the applicant's history of past maintenance, it is MOST important for the investigator to determine, in addition,

   A. how the applicant was able to obtain a sufficient number of odd jobs to support himself
   B. what skills the applicant had that enabled him to obtain these jobs
   C. why the applicant never sought or kept a steady job
   D. whether such jobs are still available as a source of income for the applicant

   2.____

3. For an investigator to make a collateral contact with a client's legally responsible relative when that relative is herself receiving assistance is

   A. *advisable,* mainly because the relative may be able to assist the client with needed services
   B. *inadvisable,* mainly because the relative is in receipt of assistance and cannot assist the client financially
   C. *advisable,* mainly because the worker may obtain information concerning the relative's eligibility for assistance
   D. *inadvisable,* because any information concerning the relative can be obtained from other sources

   3.____

4. An applicant for assistance tells the investigator that her bank savings are exhausted.
   While a bank clearance can verify her statement, it is still important for the investigator to see her bank book CHIEFLY in order to

   A. determine when the account was first opened and the amount of the initial deposit
   B. correlate withdrawals and deposits with the applicant's story of past management
   C. learn if the applicant had closed this account in order to open an account in another bank
   D. verify that the last withdrawal was made before the applicant applied for assistance

   4.____

5. It has been suggested that all investigators be kept currently informed about general departmental actions taken, changes in other departmental work units, and new developments of general interest in their department.
For a department to put this suggestion into effect is, generally,

   A. *inadvisable;* investigators should perform the duties specifically assigned to them and not get involved in matters that do not concern them directly
   B. *advisable;* investigators may often need to know such information in order to coordinate their work properly with that of other work units
   C. *inadvisable;* changes in other work units have little effect on the work performed by investigators not assigned to these units
   D. *advisable;* broad knowledge of the activities in any agency tends to improve work skills

6. Although there is a normal distinction between the successive ranks of supervision in an agency, the greatest distinction and change in rank occurs, however, when an investigator becomes a supervisor.
This is true CHIEFLY because the supervisor

   A. must be better informed than his investigators in all aspects
   B. must learn to assume new and more complex duties
   C. becomes responsible for the first time for the job performance of members of the investigation staff
   D. has greater responsibility and authority than the investigators under his supervision

7. When an experienced supervisory investigator does not agree personally with some of the procedurally correct objectives and directions of his supervisor, it would be MOST correct for him to

   A. continue to supervise his unit in accordance with the supervisor's directions
   B. direct his workers to follow the supervisor's directions, but indicate the weaknesses therein and be somewhat more lenient in the supervision of these duties
   C. seek to change the supervisor's directions through use of grievance procedures
   D. develop his own methods and apply them to the work of his unit on a trial basis

8. It has been said that the success or failure of the work of his unit rests on the supervisor.
If the supervisor wants to stimulate growth among his investigators, it would generally be BEST for him to

   A. set an easy pace for his investigators so that they will not become confused because of having to learn too much too rapidly
   B. set the pace for his investigators so that the job is never too easy but is a constant challenge calling for more and better work
   C. spot check the investigators' records at irregular intervals in order to determine whether they are performing their duties properly
   D. see to it that the broad objectives and goals of the department are periodically communicated and interpreted to his investigators

9. The effectiveness of the work of a unit of investigators depends in a large measure on that unit's will to work.
The BEST of the following methods for the supervisor to employ in order to increase the will of the members of the unit to work is for the unit supervisor to

A. allow each investigator to proceed at his own pace
B. be constantly on guard for any laxity among his investigators
C. provide comfortable working facilities for his investigators
D. clearly discuss with his investigators the functions and objectives of the agency

10. For a supervisor to encourage his investigators to think about the reasons for a policy is   10.____

   A. *advisable,* mainly because the investigators are then more likely to apply the policy appropriately
   B. *inadvisable,* mainly because the investigators may then apply the policy too flexibly
   C. *advisable,* mainly because the investigators then feel that they have participated in policy making
   D. *inadvisable,* mainly because the investigators may interpret the policy incorrectly if they misunderstand its meaning

11. A supervisor who plans his work properly and who has no difficulty in meeting deadlines   11.____
    insists that his new investigators pattern their activities after his in every detail.
    This method is

   A. *undesirable,* chiefly because such compliance can cause antagonism and hamper the investigators' growth
   B. *undesirable,* chiefly because this method cannot work as successfully for the new investigators
   C. *desirable,* chiefly because the supervisor's methods have proved successful and will eliminate waste
   D. *desirable,* chiefly because the untrained investigator needs guidelines to follow

12. Of the following, the MOST important reason for obtaining information in an initial investigation regarding financial maintenance of the applicant prior to the application for assistance is to   12.____

   A. comply with the provisions in the Social Welfare Law requiring that a record be made of the financial history of applicants for public assistance
   B. determine if the applicant may be expected to handle properly public assistance grants in the form of money
   C. determine the way in which the present situation differs from the past
   D. show the applicant that the department is interested in his past and present circumstances and may be expected to maintain this interest in the future

13. An applicant for assistance who has legally responsible relatives is informed by the   13.____
    investigator of the responsibility of such relatives to contribute to the applicant's support.
    The applicant requests permission to discuss the matter privately with these relatives prior to any contact by the department.
    In this case, it would be ADVISABLE for the investigator to

   A. *agree* to the request because the applicant is entitled to an opportunity to prepare the relatives for the coming official contact
   B. *agree* to the request because the applicant is in a better position than the investigator to uncover any concealment of assets by his relatives
   C. *refuse* the request because it might give the applicant and his relatives opportunity to devise means of avoiding or minimizing the existing responsibility
   D. *refuse* the request because the applicant is not likely to be able to give a proper interpretation to the relatives of their responsibility

14. The findings of a medical examination of a client who has claimed to be unemployable because of physical illness are that the client is employable. When told of these findings, the client reiterates that she is too ill to work.
    In this case, the BEST of the following actions for the investigator to take FIRST is to

    A. discuss the situation with the client in an attempt to discover what reasons she may have for not wanting to accept employment
    B. make arrangements for a psychiatric examination of the client
    C. request that a second medical examination of the client be made by another doctor
    D. tell the client that the case will be closed unless she accepts employment

15. An investigator is told by a relative of a recipient that the recipient has won $6000 in a lottery and is soon to receive the prize money.
    Of the following, the BEST action for the investigator to take FIRST is to

    A. close the case since the recipient did not notify the department of his winnings and since he now has enough money on which to live and pay his bills
    B. discuss the situation with the recipient, planning with him the future management of his funds
    C. let the recipient know that the use of relief money for gambling is illegal and that the police department must be notified of the facts in the case
    D. see that legal steps are taken to recover for services rendered to the client by the department.

16. When told at an interview with the investigator that he must agree to give to the department a lien on his real estate property, a client assumes a resistant attitude.
    Of the following, it would usually be BEST for the investigator to

    A. discuss with the client the laws governing the giving of such liens and the purposes to be served by his giving the lien
    B. drop the matter, hoping to meet with less resistance at some future time
    C. tell the client that this is not a matter for discussion, that he must either agree to the lien or the case will be closed
    D. terminate the interview, telling the client that he may return when he is willing to discuss the means of providing the department with the lien

17. An investigator refers to his supervisor an applicant for assistance who has refused to supply certain information which is regularly asked of applicants. The applicant complains that he is being asked to supply private and personal information about himself that has nothing to do with his application for assistance and that the investigator has treated him with discourtesy.
    The BEST of the following courses of action for the supervisor to take is to

    A. apologize for any appearance of discourtesy but insist that the applicant supply him with the information that had been sought
    B. apologize for any appearance of discourtesy, explain the need for the information that has been requested, and ask the applicant to supply it to the investigator
    C. explain that the investigator is doing a difficult job under difficult conditions and instruct the applicant to cooperate with him
    D. explain why the information is needed and state that no assistance will be forthcoming unless it is supplied

18. At an interview, in order to secure as efficiently as possible the information necessary to determine whether an applicant for assistance is eligible, investigators should generally be instructed to

    A. allow the applicant to explain his problem without interrupting him and then ask him to answer a previously prepared list of detailed questions covering necessary information
    B. confine the interview to a set of detailed questions prepared in advance by the investigator except that new questions may be added on the basis of leads provided by the answers to previous questions
    C. permit the applicant to explain his problems, using questions to keep the applicant from wandering from the subject and to bring out necessary information not covered by him in his narrative
    D. supply the applicant with a set of written questions immediately prior to the interview and confine the interview to a discussion of these questions

19. Assume that a client believes that his case has been unfairly closed, in spite of the fact that the investigator has explained the pertinent rules to him.
    It would be MOST proper, at this point, for the investigator to refer this client to

    A. an assistant to the commissioner at the central office
    B. an official of the state
    C. the supervisor in charge
    D. the supervisor in charge of the unit

20. An investigator is told by a client who is a resident of a nursing home that he is being neglected and not receiving proper care in the home.
    The investigator should

    A. discuss the situation with the proprietor of the nursing home
    B. investigate the situation on subsequent visits to determine the validity of the complaint
    C. report the matter to the medical social worker upon return to his center
    D. write a memorandum to the central nursing home service reporting the situation

21. Modern thinking and research on the efficient conduct of business has developed concepts of democratic supervision and human relations.
    Proper application of these concepts in dealing with investigators USUALLY results in

    A. a reduction in the use of formal discipline
    B. an increase in the use of formal discipline
    C. discarding discipline imposed from without to be completely replaced by self-imposed discipline
    D. elimination of formal discipline in favor of informal discipline

22. At the first interview between a supervisor and a newly appointed investigator, GREATEST care should be taken to

    A. build toward a satisfactory personal relationship even if some other objectives of the interview must be postponed
    B. cover a predetermined list of specific objectives so as to make a further orientation interview unnecessary

C. create an image of a forceful, determined supervisor whose wishes cannot be imposed by a subordinate without great risk
D. create an impression of efficiency and control of operation free from interpersonal relationships

23. In teaching the job to an investigator recently assigned to a unit, many teaching methods must be used.
In general, however, the BEST way for the supervisor to train such an investigator is by having him

   A. do the job under proper supervision
   B. listen to lectures
   C. observe the work of other investigators
   D. study written material

24. A recently appointed investigator has reached the stage in learning his job where he is just beginning to be able to make decisions, although he still makes numerous mistakes and frequently does not know how to handle a situation.
When the supervisor finds that the investigator has handled a certain situation in an acceptable manner, but not in the best manner, it would be BEST for the supervisor to

   A. explain to the investigator how he could have handled the situation better
   B. indicate approval of the way the situation was handled and explain how it could have been handled better
   C. say nothing about the situation
   D. show dissatisfaction with the way the situation was handled and explain how it could have been handled better

25. A supervisor has a job to be done of a type usually done by an investigator. The job is an important and recurring one, but not urgent at the moment. He knows that it would take more time to tell the investigator how to do the job than to do it himself, and that it would take still more time to make the investigator understand the situation, decide how to handle it, and then get the job done.
In such a case, it would generally be BEST for the supervisor to

   A. assign the job to the investigator without explaining it
   B. do the job himself
   C. explain the situation and help the investigator to decide how to handle it
   D. tell the investigator exactly what to do

KEY (CORRECT ANSWERS)

1.	A	11.	A
2.	D	12.	C
3.	A	13.	A
4.	B	14.	A
5.	B	15.	B
6.	C	16.	A
7.	A	17.	B
8.	B	18.	C
9.	D	19.	D
10.	A	20.	D

21. A
22. A
23. A
24. B
25. C

———

TEST 2

DIRECTIONS: Each question or incomplete statement is followed by several suggested answers or completions. Select the one that BEST answers the question or completes the statement. *PRINT THE LETTER OF THE CORRECT ANSWER IN THE SPACE AT THE RIGHT.*

1. In order to improve the work of an experienced investigator who usually does average work, the one of the following actions which it would generally be BEST for the supervisor to take is to

    A. allow the investigator to be self-directed and unsupervised except where there is a large outlay of money involved
    B. apply strict discipline to any signs of laxness or inattention to duty
    C. carefully list and document every error made by the investigator and inform him of them
    D. use praise as a device to motivate the investigator to do better work

    1.___

2. The one of the following guiding principles to which a supervisor should give MOST consideration when it becomes necessary to discipline an investigator is that

    A. rules should be applied in a fixed and inflexible manner
    B. the discipline should be applied for the purpose of improving the morale of all his investigators
    C. the main benefit to be derived from disciplining one offender is to deter other potential offenders
    D. the nature of the discipline should be such as to improve the future work of the offender

    2.___

3. A unit supervisor notices one of his investigators reading a novel at his desk during working hours. This is the first time that this has happened. The investigator is an experienced employee who does above-average work.
For the unit supervisor to ignore the situation is GENERALLY

    A. *wise*, since it is never desirable to penalize a good employee because of any single incident
    B. *unwise*, since it may be interpreted by the staff as condoning inattention to work
    C. *wise*, since democratic supervision allows employees leeway to apportion their workday as they see fit
    D. *unwise*, since it is necessary to take strong action at the first sign of insubordination

    3.___

4. When investigators in a particular unit are guilty of infractions, it is the practice of the unit supervisor to give necessary warnings or reprimands in a jocular manner. This practice is GENERALLY

    A. *unwise*, because humorous or jocular aspects should be kept from relationships between supervisors and investigators
    B. *unwise*, because it leaves the investigator unsure of the true intent or extent of the discipline
    C. *wise*, because it makes the investigator realize that there is no personal animosity involved
    D. *wise*, because it reduces the severity of the warning or reprimand

    4.___

5. An experienced investigator complains to his unit supervisor that the latter's continual very close supervision of his work is unnecessary and annoying. The unit supervisor is a recently appointed supervisor.
In this case, it would generally be BEST for the unit supervisor to

   A. ask the investigator to explain his complaint further, telling him that it will receive consideration, and then re-evaluate his supervisory practices, seeking advice from his own supervisor if necessary
   B. assure the investigator that there had been no intention of singling him out but that, as a subordinate, he will have to get used to new supervisory methods employed by new, wide-awake supervisors
   C. explain to the investigator that it is the job of the unit supervisor to supervise him and that he should understand his role and be able to overcome his annoyance
   D. promise the investigator that the annoying supervisory methods will be discontinued but remind him that the unit supervisor must be respected and looked to for assistance, training, and supervision

5._____

6. A unit supervisor becomes aware that one of his investigators has a personal problem which is causing the subordinate considerable concern and is beginning to affect his work.
Of the following, the action which it would generally be BEST for the unit supervisor to take is to

   A. ignore the matter but, if the investigator brings the matter up, politely tell him that it is not proper for a unit supervisor to discuss personal problems of subordinates
   B. make the investigator aware that he may discuss personal problems with his unit supervisor who will offer whatever assistance he can, compatible with the duties of his job
   C. refer the matter to his own supervisor
   D. indicate that he would like to help solve the problem and insist that the investigator provide full details

6._____

7. An investigator who has many personal problems frequently introduces one or more of them into the discussion at conferences with his unit supervisor. He talks of them at some length.
It would generally be BEST for the unit supervisor to

   A. discuss the problems with the investigator and, as a helping person, assist with their solution
   B. explain that he would like to help solve the problems but that the repeated introduction of them in conferences is interfering with the work of the unit
   C. inform the investigator that his personal problems should not be brought to the office and that it would be improper for the unit supervisor to try to help with them
   D. listen silently to the exposition of the problems made by the investigator and then return to the business at hand without commenting on the problem

7._____

8. For the investigator to understand the culture of a family is important CHIEFLY because the

   A. client tends to react to the situation largely in ways derived from attitudes learned at home

8._____

B. needs of the entire family cannot be satisfied unless the individual needs of each member are satisfied first
C. client can be treated more effectively when considered as a member of a cultural group rather than a separate individual
D. family can be understood much more readily if the dominant individual motivating it is understood first

9. Emphasis in the practice of casework has shifted from merely providing the client with a practical service, to involving the client in using the service or treatment.
This statement implies MOST NEARLY that, at present,

   A. casework will attempt to help the client only when it is felt that he will profit from the service
   B. casework is no longer deeply involved in assisting the client in a direct and realistic way
   C. the most important change in casework today has been its shift from helping the client in a practical way to planning for him in a theoretical way
   D. the caseworker or investigator attempts to mobilize the client to active participation in decision-making

10. In all casework practice, whether it be in an agency or in an institution, the properly prepared case history record is of great importance in the treatment of the client and his problem CHIEFLY because it

    A. gives the supervisory and administrative casework staff reviewing the case a keener understanding of the general sociological and psychological causes underlying dependency and other factors which make it necessary for clients to seek casework assistance
    B. furnishes the agency or institution involved in the case with a factual record as a basis for determining whether or not continuing treatment of the client is justified
    C. assists the caseworkers or investigators involved in the case by providing them, on a continuous basis, with a clear picture of the various factors underlying the client's problems and of what has been done to help resolve the situation
    D. provides the caseworker or investigator responsible for the case with the basic facts which will enable her to determine whether the client is really trying to help himself or whether he is passing his responsibility on to the caseworker or investigator

11. When comparing the narrative form with the summary form of a casework recording, the narrative form is usually the BEST way to record

    A. objective material obtained from investigations of the client's statements, while the summary form is best to record worker's detailed observations of client's reactions to his present problem
    B. both social data and eligibility material, while the summary form is best to record material dealing with feelings, attitudes and client-worker relationships
    C. material relating to prognosis, treatment given, and the results obtained, while the summary form is best to record a verbatim report of primary evidence obtained from personal worker-client contacts
    D. material dealing with feelings, attitudes, and client-worker relationships, while the summary form is best to record both social data and eligibility material

12. A problem in recording is to decide how much detail to have in a case record. The case history should GENERALLY include

    A. a more detailed description of the client's reaction to practical matters than to psychological conflicts
    B. a verbatim account of worker-client interaction in significant interviews and a detailed description of the client's feelings toward the treatment plan
    C. only as much data, whether it be sociological or psychological, as will enable the worker to understand the client, the problem to be solved, and the main factors in its solution
    D. the full details of the client's personality development and emotional relationships regardless of the type or complexity of the problem

13. Interviewing is always directed to the client and his situation.
    The one of the following which is the MOST accurate statement with respect to the proper focus of an interview is that the

    A. investigator limits the client to concentration on objective data
    B. client is generally permitted to talk about facts and feelings with no direction from the investigator
    C. main focus in interviews is on feelings rather than facts
    D. investigator is responsible for helping the client focus on any material which seems to be related to his problems or difficulties

14. Assume that you are conducting a training program for the investigators under your supervision. At one of the sessions, you discuss the problem of interviewing a dull and stupid client who gives a slow and disconnected case history.
    The BEST of the following interviewing methods for you to recommend in such a case in order to ascertain the facts is for the investigator to

    A. ask the client leading questions requiring *yes* or *no* answers
    B. request the client to limit his narration to the essential facts so that the interview can be kept as brief as possible
    C. review the story with the client, patiently asking simple questions
    D. tell the client that unless he is more cooperative, he cannot be helped to solve his problem

15. A recent development in interviewing procedure, known as multiple-client interviewing, consists of interviews of the entire family at the same time. However, this may not be an effective method in certain situations.
    Of the following, the situation in which the standard individual interview would be PREFERABLE is when

    A. family members derive consistent and major gratification from assisting each other in their destructive responses
    B. there is a crucial family conflict to which the members are reacting
    C. the family is overwhelmed by interpersonal anxieties which have not been explored
    D. the investigator wants to determine the pattern of family interaction to further his diagnostic understanding

16. The one of the following which is the CHIEF value of verbatim recording of all or a portion of an important interview is the possibility it offers for

    A. careful study and clarification of psychological goals in treatment
    B. a prompt solution to the problem by preservation, in an orderly and concise fashion of the full psychological and economic picture of the client's situation
    C. quick determination of the more obvious social goals and offering of concrete services by presentation of the essential facts
    D. supervision of experienced investigators by showing the emotional overtones, subtle reactions, and intricate investigator-client interchanges

17. Experts in the field of casework recording generally agree that the kind of material for which the narrative form of recording is MOST suitable is

    A. material that deals with feelings, attitudes, and client-investigator relationships, because this style permits the use of primary evidence in the form of verbal material and behavior observed in the interview
    B. social data, including eligibility material and family background history, because it can then be presented in a chronological, orderly fashion to enable the investigator to select the desired facts
    C. personal facts concerning the individual's personality patterns and their growth and development, because they can be seen in an orderly progression from primal immaturity until their ultimate stage of completion
    D. selectively chosen and documented material essential to a quicker and clearer understanding of the various ramifications of the case by a new investigator when responsibility for handling the client is reassigned

18. A case record includes relevant social and psychological facts about the client, the nature of his request, his feeling about his situation, his attitude towards the agency and his use of and reaction to treatment.
    In addition, it should always contain

    A. routine history
    B. complete details of personality development and emotional relationships
    C. detailed process accounts of all contacts
    D. data necessary for understanding the problem and the factors important in arriving at a solution

19. The CHIEF basis for the inability of a troubled client to express his problem clearly to the investigator is that the client

    A. sees his problem in complex terms and does not think it possible to give the investigator the whole picture
    B. has erected defenses against emotions that seem to him inadmissible or intolerable
    C. cannot describe how he feels about his problem
    D. views the situation as unlikely to be solved and is blocked in self-expression

20. In aggressive casework, when an investigator visits a multi-problem family, he should begin by

    A. arranging individual interviews with the children
    B. outlining the steps to be taken in the solution of their problems

C. inviting the family to visit the agency so that a normal casework situation may be created
D. explaining what points of risk or danger exist in their situation and inviting an expression of their feelings

21. The job of the supervisory investigator may be considered in part an administrative one CHIEFLY because it

   A. requires administrative training or experience
   B. involves a direct relationship with the executive office of the department
   C. entails responsibility for staff development
   D. calls for planning, organizing, and coordinating

22. If a supervisory investigator discovers that the amount of the grant in a particular case is inaccurate, he should

   A. make the necessary adjustments and assign another investigator to the case
   B. caution all investigators in the unit to be more careful in the future
   C. assume that the investigator's computation was correct when it was made
   D. arrange to have the investigator review the budget with the client and make the necessary adjustments

23. If, in the process of investigating eligibility for assistance, discrepancies occur between the applicant's statement of his situation and that given by a relative interviewed, the investigator should USUALLY

   A. accept the relative's statement since the relative has less interest in falsifying the facts
   B. return to the client for clarification of the situation
   C. immediately discount the relative's statement since he may be motivated by his legal responsibility for supporting the applicant
   D. point out the discrepancies to the relative and ask him for any explanation he can give

24. In evaluating the adequacy of an individual's income, an investigator should place PRIMARY emphasis on

   A. its value in relation to the average income
   B. the source of the income
   C. its relation to the earning capacity of the individual
   D. its purchasing power

25. The length of residence required to make a person eligible for the various forms of public assistance available in the United States

   A. is the same in all states but is different among public assistance programs in a given state
   B. is the same in all states and among different public assistance programs in a given state
   C. is the same in all states for different categories
   D. varies among states and among different public assistance programs in a given state

KEY (CORRECT ANSWERS)

1. D
2. D
3. B
4. B
5. A

6. B
7. B
8. A
9. D
10. C

11. D
12. C
13. D
14. C
15. A

16. A
17. A
18. D
19. B
20. D

21. D
22. D
23. B
24. D
25. D

TEST 3

DIRECTIONS: Each question or incomplete statement is followed by several suggested answers or completions. Select the one that BEST answers the question or completes the statement. *PRINT THE LETTER OF THE CORRECT ANSWER IN THE SPACE AT THE RIGHT.*

1. A person who knowingly brings a needy person from another state into the state for the purpose of making him a public charge is guilty of

    A. violation of the Displaced Persons Act
    B. violation of the Mann Act
    C. a felony
    D. a misdemeanor

    1.____

2. An aged person who is unable to produce immediate proof of age has made an application for assistance. He states that it will take about a week to obtain the necessary proof and that he does not have enough money to provide meals for himself until then.
   If it appears that he is in immediate need, he should be told that

    A. temporary assistance will be provided pending the completion of the investigation
    B. a personal loan will be made to him from a revolving fund
    C. he should arrange for a small loan from private sources
    D. he will have to produce an affidavit witnessed by two relatives who will vouch for the accuracy of his statements before any assistance can be provided

    2.____

3. If the investigator learns during an interview that the client has applied for assistance without the knowledge of her husband, even though he is a member of the same household, the investigator should

    A. appear not to notice this oversight but watch for other evidences of marital discord
    B. make no mention of this to the applicant but, before taking final action, send a note to the husband asking him to come in
    C. discuss this situation with the client and help her recognize the value of her husband's participation in the application
    D. point out to the applicant the implications of her behavior and ask for an explanation of her motives

    3.____

4. Of the sources through which an agency can seek information about the family background and economic needs of a particular client, the MOST important consists of

    A. records and documents covering the client
    B. interviews with the client's relatives
    C. the client's own story
    D. direct contacts with former employers

    4.____

5. The one of the following sources of evidence which would be MOST likely to give information needed to verify residence is

    A. family affidavits
    B. medical and hospital bills
    C. an original birth certificate
    D. rental receipts

    5.____

6. Vital statistics are a resource used by investigators to

   A. help establish eligibility through verification of births, deaths, and marriages
   B. help establish eligibility through verification of divorce proceedings
   C. secure proof of unemployment and eligibility for unemployment compensation
   D. secure indices of the cost of living in the larger cities

7. Case records should be considered confidential in order to

   A. permit investigators to make objective, rather than subjective, comments
   B. prevent recipients from comparing amounts of assistance given to other recipients
   C. keep pertinent information from other investigators
   D. protect clients and their families

8. Because the investigator generally is not trained as a psychiatrist, he should, when encountering psychiatric problems in the performance of his departmental duties,

   A. ignore such problems because they are beyond the scope of his responsibilities
   B. inform the affected persons that he recognizes their problems personally but will take no official cognizance of them
   C. ask to be relieved of the cases in which these problems are met and recommend that they be assigned to a psychiatrist
   D. recognize such problems where they exist and make referrals to the proper sources for treatment

9. Inasmuch as periodic visits to clients at home are required by the department, according to good work practice, it is MOST desirable for the investigator to

   A. visit without appointment as this gives him a chance to see the person and the house *as they really are* and forestalls changing things to create a different impression
   B. write giving an appointment time as this saves the investigator from visiting when people are not at home and helps him to plan his work more efficiently
   C. write suggesting an appointment time so that the client may be prepared for the interview and the investigator uses his time economically
   D. advise all applicants during their first interview that they will be visited periodically but will not be given definite appointments

10. Assuming that careful interpretation has been given but an applicant for assistance refuses to accede to the necessary procedures to establish his eligibility, the MOST preferable of the following courses of action for the investigator to take would be to

    A. do nothing further
    B. grant a temporary delay in the hope that the applicant will change his mind
    C. try to ascertain why the applicant feels as he does, but to respect his decision if he refuses to change his mind
    D. proceed to check on all the facts possible even though the applicant has not given his permission

11. The PRIMARY purpose in discussing with an applicant the steps in determining his eligibility and the kind of verification of facts which the agency will need is to 11.____

    A. enable the applicant to understand the basis of eligibility and participate in determining it
    B. protect the position of the agency so that there will be no comeback if the application is not granted
    C. give the applicant an opportunity to modify any statement he may have made previously
    D. promote public relations for the agency since the applicant will tell others how the agency is operating

12. Of the following, the LEAST valid reason for the maintenance of the case record is to 12.____

    A. furnish reference material for other investigators
    B. improve the quality of service to the client
    C. show how the funds are being expended
    D. reduce the complexities of the case to manageable proportions

13. A public agency will lean more on forms than a private agency in the same field of activity because 13.____

    A. forms simplify the recording responsibilities of newly appointed investigators
    B. public records are of the family agency type
    C. the governmental framework requires a greater degree of standardization
    D. more interviews and visits are made in connection with public cases

14. In spite of the need which most of us have of finding rules and procedures to guide us, we must face the difficulty at the outset that there is no such thing as a model case record. 14.____
    Of the following, the BEST justification for this statement is that

    A. records should be written to suit the case
    B. case recording should be patterned after the best models obtainable
    C. rules cannot be applied to case work because each case requires individual treatment
    D. the establishment of routine and procedures in investigatory work is an ideal which cannot be realized

15. In attempting to discover whether an applicant for aid has had any previous experience as a recipient through other agencies in the community, the investigator should 15.____

    A. check the application with the social service exchange
    B. send the fingerprints of the applicant to the Police Department
    C. consult the latest records of the department
    D. ask the applicant to submit a notarized statement to the effect that such aid has not been received from any other source

16. Suppose a client whom you are investigating has borrowed $250 in order to purchase an evening gown for one of her children who is being graduated from high school. She is planning to repay the loan at the rate of ten dollars a week and presents verification of this transaction as well as the purchase. 16.____
    As an investigator, you would be complying with the BEST casework principles by

A. telling the client her grant will be reduced in view of her ability to manage on ten dollars less each week
B. telling the client that she must never do this again
C. explaining to the client how her action will make it more difficult for the family to get along on their limited grant
D. suggesting that she return the dress and repay the borrowed money in this way

17. An investigator determined, while investigating an applicant for Medical Assistance for the Aged, that the applicant's income and resources are over and above the limits permitted under the Medical Assistance for the Aged program. However, the applicant's medical needs seem to be extensive, and the applicant insists that he cannot pay for his needed medical care.
    The investigator should

    A. accept the case for Medical Assistance for the Aged in the normal manner and await a determination of the cost of the medical care in order to determine if there is actually a budget deficit
    B. have the cost of the medical care determined prior to making any decision as to acceptance or rejection of the case
    C. handle the case exactly as he would the case of an applicant for any other type of assistance who does not have a budget deficit
    D. reject the case for Medical Assistance for the Aged until the applicant can obtain verification of the cost of his needed medical care

17.____

18. Of the following, the choice of method to be used in the supervisory process should be influenced MOST by the

    A. number and type of cases carried by each investigator
    B. emotional maturity of the investigator
    C. number of investigators supervised and their past experience
    D. subject matter to be learned and the long range goals of supervision

18.____

19. In an evaluation conference with an investigator, the BEST approach for the supervisor to take is to

    A. help the investigator to identify his strengths, as a basis for working on his weaknesses
    B. identify the investigator's weaknesses and help him overcome them
    C. allow the investigator to identify his weaknesses first and then suggest ways of overcoming them
    D. discuss the investigator's weaknesses but emphasize his strengths

19.____

20. Assume that an investigator is discouraged about the progress of his work and feels that it is futile to attempt to cope with many of his cases.
    Of the following, it would be BEST for the supervisor to

    A. suggest to the investigator that such feelings are inappropriate for a professional worker
    B. tell the investigator that he must seek professional help in order to overcome these feelings
    C. reduce the investigator's caseload and give him cases that are less complex
    D. review with the investigator several of his cases in which there were obvious accomplishments

20.____

21. The supervisor is responsible for providing the investigator with the following means of support, with the EXCEPTION of

    A. interest and advice on his personal problems
    B. instruction on community resources
    C. inspiration for carrying out the work of the agency
    D. understanding his strengths and limitations

21.____

22. When an investigator frequently takes the initiative in asking questions and discussing problems during a supervisory conference, this is probably an indication that the

    A. supervisor is not sufficiently interested in the investigator
    B. conference is a positive learning experience for the investigator
    C. worker is hostile and resists supervision
    D. supervisor's position of authority is in question

22.____

23. When a supervisor finds that one of his investigators cannot accept criticism, of the following, it would be BEST for the supervisor to

    A. have the investigator transferred to another supervisor
    B. warn the investigator of disciplinary proceedings unless his attitude changes
    C. have the investigator suspended after explaining the reason
    D. explore with the investigator his attitude toward authority

23.____

24. Of the following, the condition which the inexperienced investigator is LEAST likely to be aware of, without the guidance of the supervisor, is

    A. when he is successful in helping a client
    B. when he is not making progress in helping a client
    C. that he has a personal bias toward certain clients
    D. that he feels insecure because of lack of experience

24.____

25. The supervisor should provide an inexperienced investigator with controls as well as freedom MAINLY because controls will

    A. enable him to set up his own controls sooner
    B. put him in a situation which is closer to the realities of life
    C. help him to use authority in handling a casework problem
    D. give him a feeling of security and lay the foundation for future self-direction

25.____

KEY (CORRECT ANSWERS)

1.	D	11.	A
2.	A	12.	D
3.	C	13.	C
4.	C	14.	A
5.	D	15.	A
6.	A	16.	C
7.	D	17.	A
8.	D	18.	D
9.	C	19.	A
10.	C	20.	D

21. A
22. B
23. D
24. C
25. D

EXAMINATION SECTION
TEST 1

DIRECTIONS: Each question or incomplete statement is followed by several suggested answers or completions. Select the one that BEST answers the question or completes the statement. *PRINT THE LETTER OF THE CORRECT ANSWER IN THE SPACE AT THE RIGHT.*

1. Which of the following is the BEST way to get an accurate account of an incident?
   A. Interview those involved immediately
   B. Interview those involved as soon as possibility
   C. Wait until you review the official reports and then interview those involved as soon as possible
   D. Carefully observe a videotaped simulation

2. While conducting investigations, it is necessary to pay close attention to nonverbal communication.
   This would include all of the following EXCEPT
   A. analyzing each individual's behavior as it arises
   B. paying attention to the person's tone of voice
   C. viewing the nonverbal messages as indicators
   D. noting discrepancies between verbal and nonverbal messages

3. While conducting an interview, it is MOST important to
   A. ignore your own values and past experiences
   B. utilize your own values and past experiences in recording information
   C. explain your own values to those you are interviewing
   D. be aware of your own values and experiences and of how they might influence the interview

4. Of the following, which is the BEST way to question a witness?
   A. Ask pointed questions   B. Talk in a clipped manner
   C. Talk aimlessly   D. Ask random questions

5. You are interviewing an uncooperative person.
   Of the following, the FIRST thing you should do in this situation is to
   A. try various appeal to win the person over to a cooperative attitude
   B. try to ascertain the reason for noncooperation
   C. promise the person that all data will be kept confidential
   D. alter the interviewing technique

6. Which of the following is the BEST way to make a witness feel at ease?
   A. Reassure him or her of the importance of the situation
   B. Tell the witness that any comments he or she makes will be of no use if the witness is too nervous

C. Allow the witness a little extra time to collect his or her thoughts
D. Maintain a friendly attitude

7. Which of the following behaviors would be the WORST to display during an investigative interview?
   A. Being unfocused
   B. Displaying uncertainty about some departmental regulations
   C. Acting biased
   D. Acting like you are overloaded with work

8. Investigations should be conducted with all of the following EXCEPT
   A. objectivity
   B. speed
   C. subjectivity
   D. thoroughness

9. When trying to help someone focus during an interview, it is BEST to
   A. use an open-ended question
   B. offer to reschedule at a time when the person is better prepared
   C. ask the person being interviewed to summarize the situation
   D. use a close-ended question

10. There are usually four stages during an interview: preparation, opening, conducting, and closing.
    All of the following are steps included in the closing stage of an interview EXCEPT
    A. verifying information
    B. stating the continuing responsibilities, if any, of the person being interviewed
    C. summarizing
    D. describing any additional steps that may need to be taken

11. During an employment interview, which of the following questions can legally be asked?
    A. What is your nationality?
    B. Are you at least 18 years of age?
    C. Do you wish to be addressed as Miss, Mrs. or Ms.?
    D. Do you have a disability?

12. As you continue talking with a man you are interviewing, you have the feeling that some of his answers to earlier questions were not totally correct. You think that he might have been afraid or confused earlier, but that the interview has now put him in a more comfortable frame of mind.
    In order to test the reliability of information received from the earlier questions, the BEST thing for you to do now is to ask new questions that
    A. allow him to explain why he deliberately gave you false information
    B. would yield the same information but are worded differently
    C. put pressure on him so that he personally wants to clear up the facts in his earlier answers
    D. indicate to him that you are aware of is deceptiveness

13. When investigating a situation, it is MOST important that those whom you have questioned 13.____
    A. feel that you are unbiased
    B. feel comfortable around you
    C. feel confident in your abilities
    D. admire your investigative skills

14. All of the following are examples of flight defenses EXCEPT 14.____
    A. rationalization
    B. talking about problems excessively
    C. using threatened language
    D. withdrawing

15. Assume that you have been assigned to conduct a follow-up interview with a primary witness whom you would like to have testify at an important hearing. Under these circumstances, it is MOST important to 15.____
    A. do your best to ensure that the witness remains cooperative
    B. conduct the matter in secret
    C. allow the witness to determine where and when the interview takes place
    D. conduct the interview as soon as possible to ensure a strong case

16. You are interviewing someone who is under a great deal of stress. He is talking continuously an rambling, making it difficult for you to obtain the information you need. 16.____
    In order to make the interview more successful, it would be BEST for you to
    A. interrupt him and ask him specific questions in order to get the information you need
    B. tell him that his rambling is causing you a lot of problems
    C. let him continue talking for as long as he wishes
    D. ask him to get to the point because you need to interview others

17. When an investigator first arrives at the scene of an incident, it is MOST important for him or her to be sure that 17.____
    A. all of the witnesses are telling the truth
    B. no additional physical evidence is destroyed
    C. all of the witnesses agree with each other about what they observed
    D. the witnesses do not become angry

18. All of the following statements about nonverbal communication are true EXCEPT: 18.____
    A. Nonverbal communication is easily controlled
    B. Much of the meaning of a message is transmitted through nonverbal behavior
    C. Nonverbal behaviors can reveal hidden agendas
    D. Nonverbal signals can help the interviewer determine if the person being interviewed is confused but unwilling to admit it

19. For state agencies, a properly conducted investigation might do any of the following EXCEPT 19.____
    A. discover the cause of a workplace accident
    B. uncover tax fraud or unfair labor practices by an employer

C. provide a supervisor with effective supervisory methods
D. uncover information critical to determining the outcome of an employee grievance

20. In interviewing, the practice of verbally anticipating the other person's answers to your questions is GENERALLY
    A. *desirable*, because it is effective and economical when interviewing large numbers of people
    B. *desirable*, because many people have language difficulties
    C. *undesirable*, because it is the right of every person to answer however he or she wishes
    D. *undesirable*, because the person being interviewed may be led to agree with the answer proposed by the interviewer even when the question is not entirely correct

KEY (CORRECT ANSWERS)

1.	A	11.	B
2.	A	12.	B
3.	D	13.	A
4.	A	14.	C
5.	B	15.	A
6.	D	16.	A
7.	C	17.	B
8.	C	18.	A
9.	D	19.	C
10.	A	20.	D

TEST 2

DIRECTIONS: Each question or incomplete statement is followed by several suggested answers or completions. Select the one that BEST answers the question or completes the statement. *PRINT THE LETTER OF THE CORRECT ANSWER IN THE SPACE AT THE RIGHT.*

1. All of the following are good examples of the volatile and vulnerable nature of evidence EXCEPT
   A. those involved may be intimidated to forget or to make up key elements of testimony
   B. physical evidence can disappear
   C. two extra copies are made of a valuable floppy disk
   D. water that caused an industrial accident can dry up

2. You find that many of the people you interview are verbally abusive and unusually hostile to you.
   Of the following, the MOST appropriate action for you to take FIRST is to
   A. review your interviewing techniques and consider whether you may be somehow provoking those you interview
   B. act in a more authoritative manner when interviewing troublesome interviewees
   C. tell those people that you will not be able to help them unless their troublesome behavior ceases
   D. disregard the troublesome behavior and proceed as you would normally

3. Of the following statements, which is the MOST accurate?
   A. Good investigative techniques are easily learned.
   B. Witnesses should be given a lot of time to collect their thoughts before being interviewed.
   C. The more standardized and thought-out the investigative procedures, the better the chance that the investigation will be successful.
   D. Statements taken from witnesses are not usually as critical to an investigation and subsequent action as some experts claim.

4. The information sought in an interview is sometimes fixed in advance by a printed form or specific instructions from an interviewer's supervisor.
   Because of this, it is IMPORTANT to
   A. use your own judgment as to whether or not these questions should be used in the interview
   B. have the form in front of you so you can read from it and not miss any important points when interviewing
   C. make a copy of the form and give it to the client to complete
   D. be thoroughly acquainted with the purpose behind each question and understand its significance

5. As an investigator, you perform field work in order to enforce state labor laws. If no set agency policy is in effect, it would MOST likely be the highest priority to investigate a report of

A. a minimum wage violation
B. nonpayment of overtime wages to an employee
C. nonpayment to a worker in an industrial homework setting
D. systematic nonpayment to farm workers

6. In order to get the maximum amount of information from someone during an interview, it is MOST important for the interviewer to communicate to the person being interviewed the feeling that the interviewer is
   A. interested in what the person has to say
   B. a figure of authority
   C. efficient in his or her work habits
   D. sympathetic to the lifestyle of the person being interviewed

7. When an initial interview is being conducted, one way of starting is to explain the purpose of the interview to the person being interviewed.
   The practice of starting the interview with such an explanation is GENERALLY
   A. *desirable*, because the person can then understand why the interview is necessary and what it should accomplish
   B. *desirable*, because it creates the rapport which is necessary to successful interviewing
   C. *undesirable*, because time will be saved if starting off directly with the questions which must be asked
   D. *undesirable*, because the interviewer should have the choice of starting an interview in the manner that he or she prefers

8. The GREATEST problem for investigators is when witnesses
   A. are so eager to cooperate that they frequently interrupt the investigator
   B. become a little bored telling and retelling what they have observed
   C. are not very willing to cooperate
   D. are eager to get back to work

9. Two important skills sometimes used during an interview are giving behavioral feedback and confronting.
   What is the key difference between the two?
   A. There is none; they are actually two different names for the same process.
   B. Confronting is threatening, but giving behavioral feedback is not.
   C. Behavioral feedback merely describes action, while confronting evaluates the consequences of behavior.
   D. Behavioral feedback requires equipment in order to test the response of the client.

10. If applied properly, *being a good listener* is a desirable technique PRIMARILY because it
    A. more easily catches the person being interviewed in misrepresentations and lies
    B. conserves the energies of the interviewer

3 (#2)

C. encourages the person being interviewed to talk about his or her personal affairs without restraint
D. is more likely to secure information which is generally reliable and complete

11. A full-scale police criminal investigation   11.____
    A. should be avoided at all costs
    B. may be warranted in some cases
    C. most likely means the agency investigator did not do his or her job properly
    D. is not necessary in state agencies

12. Which of the following are usually the MOST effective techniques for handling difficult behaviors during an interview?   12.____
    I. Focusing on nondefensive behaviors
    II. Respecting silence; letting yourself and the person you are interviewing get emotions under control
    III. Giving advice
    IV. Avoiding upsetting issues
    The CORRECT answer is:
    A. II, III   B. I, II   C. III, IV   D. I, III, IV

13. Assume that you are conducting safety and health inspections in a wide variety of settings. The supervisor at one of the sites you must periodically inspect seems very anxious during your visits and always wants you to pinpoint exactly when you will be returning for your next inspection.   13.____
    It would be BEST to
    A. assume the supervisor has something to hide, so you will double the number of inspections at the site
    B. assume nothing
    C. assume the supervisor is just slightly neurotic
    D. check to see if the supervisor has a criminal record

14. Of the following, the MOST important characteristic for an interviewer to have is   14.____
    A. personal attractiveness   B. sincerity
    C. appealing personality   D. a sense of humor

15. It is MOST likely that the longer the time before statements are taken from witnesses, the more   15.____
    A. time the witnesses will have to accurately reflect on what has occurred
    B. likely it is that the witnesses will be totally unwilling to cooperate
    C. likely it is that some distortion will occur
    D. likely it is that the witnesses will be willing to cooperate

16. The person you are interviewing is making, what you feel are, distasteful remarks. Of the following, the BEST approach would be to   16.____
    A. selectively ignore the remarks
    B. question the person about the remarks

C. confront the person
D. ask the person to stop or ask him or her to leave the interview

17. Which of the following behaviors should concern investigators the MOST? 17.____
    A. The tendency of eyewitnesses to *homogenize* what they have seen when exchanging information or chatting about the incident
    B. Eyewitnesses who are clear about minor details
    C. Eyewitnesses who are a little nervous
    D. Eyewitnesses who dislike their supervisors intensely

18. Part of your job requires the investigation of possible state sales tax fraud by organizations. 18.____
    Which of the following would MOST likely trigger a full-scale investigation?
    A. An anonymous phone call involving possible large-scale sales tax fraud by an organization
    B. A salesclerk forgets to add the sales tax to your order
    C. A new business does not have their sales tax *Certificate of Authority* prominently displayed so customers can see it
    D. The books and receipts of a large organization show that sales tax was not collected on $75 worth of merchandise

19. All of the following are inquiries that cannot be legally asked during an employment interview EXCEPT: 19.____
    A. Where were you born?
    B. Are you planning on having children?
    C. Are you able to carry out all necessary job assignments and perform them in a safe manner?
    D. In case of an emergency or accident, what is the name and address of the person to be notified?

20. When investigating a situation, you are careful when asking questions to never indicate how you think the question should be answered. 20.____
    This practice is a good idea PRIMARILY because
    A. it shows those you interview that you have confidence in their intelligence
    B. you will be more likely to get truthful answers
    C. you will not be significantly influencing the answers of those you have interviewed
    D. you will impress them with your interviewing skills

KEY (CORRECT ANSWERS)

1.	C	11.	B
2.	A	12.	B
3.	C	13.	B
4.	D	14.	B
5.	D	15.	C
6.	A	16.	A
7.	A	17.	A
8.	C	18.	A
9.	C	19.	C
10.	D	20.	C

EXAMINATION SECTION
TEST 1

DIRECTIONS: Each question or incomplete statement is followed by several suggested answers or completions. Select the one that BEST answers the question or completes the statement. *PRINT THE LETTER OF THE CORRECT ANSWER IN THE SPACE AT THE RIGHT.*

1. The BEST reason, among the following, for obtaining a written and signed statement of the testimony of a witness is that

    A. unless reduced to writing, it cannot ultimately be placed in evidence in court
    B. the witness may be unavailable at the time of a subsequent trial or may attempt to change his testimony
    C. the investigator's notes of the interview may be defective or incomplete
    D. such a written statement becomes *best evidence* whereas the investigator's report is mere hearsay.

2. When an investigator hears an important statement made by a witness and the witness is not willing to reduce the statement to writing, the MOST advisable of the following procedures for the investigator to follow is to

    A. write it himself and have the witness sign it if he is willing to do so
    B. write it himself and insist that the witness sign it
    C. write it himself, making sure the witness does not see it
    D. threaten to write it himself if the witness will not do so

3. Suppose that you are interviewing an eleven-year-old boy. The CHIEF point, among the following, for you to keep in mind is that a child, as compared with an adult, is generally

    A. more likely to attempt to conceal information
    B. a person of lower intelligence
    C. more garrulous
    D. more receptive to suggestive questions

4. Of the following, witnesses to the same event should be interviewed

    A. *together* so that each can help to refresh the recollection of the others
    B. *together* so that discrepancies in their statements can be corrected more readily
    C. *separately* since many persons refuse to speak in the presence of others
    D. *separately* to prevent the testimony of one from coloring the testimony of the others

5. When a witness is reluctant to talk because he does not like to be involved in litigation, the MOST advisable of the following procedures for the investigator is to

    A. be as gentle as possible and interrogate in the form of casual questions and conversation
    B. attempt to give the witness a new interest or motive for testifying
    C. use a device, such as the association method, to elicit the desired information
    D. proceed with sternness and determination, warning the witness of the serious consequences of his refusal

6. If a person you are interviewing in connection with a character investigation obviously is not telling the truth, the MOST advisable of the following procedures is to

   A. let him talk as much as he likes so that he may eventually contradict himself and tell the truth
   B. threaten him with criminal prosecution if he does not tell the truth
   C. administer an oath to him before he is questioned
   D. disregard his testimony entirely and question him no further

7. In the course of a routine investigation of sales tax payments, the examination of a firm's books discloses to the investigator evidence that the firm's bookkeeper may be appropriating large sums of the firm's funds to his own use.
   The investigator's BEST course of action, among the following, would be to

   A. warn the bookkeeper of his discovery but take no further action since his obligations are toward the city not the firm
   B. advise the firm of his suspicions, suggesting an audit of the books
   C. immediately report his findings to the District Attorney
   D. take no action other than to include the evidence among the findings in his report

8. Information obtained by an investigator from a very small child should be carefully evaluated because, of the following reasons, children

   A. are less observing than adults
   B. have less retentive memories
   C. easily confuse their own experiences with those of others
   D. are apt to have been coached by adults

9. In the course of an investigation of a claim for damages for personal injuries sustained by an individual, an anonymous letter is received by the investigator accusing this individual of mistreating his wife and children. The MOST advisable of the following courses of action for the investigator to pursue is

   A. as a law enforcement officer, to report the matter to the proper authorities
   B. to place less credence in the testimony given by the individual in view of this impeachment of his character
   C. to attempt to trace the letter and inquire further into the allegations made therein before submitting his report
   D. to disregard the letter since it has no direct bearing on the matter under investigation

10. In interviewing a person, *suggestive questions* should be avoided because, among the following,

    A. the answers to leading questions are not admissible in evidence
    B. an investigator must be fair and impartial
    C. the interrogation of a witness must be formulated according to his mentality
    D. they are less apt to lead to the truth

11. Among the following, it is GENERALLY desirable to interview a person outside his home or office because

    A. the presence of relatives and friends may prevent him from speaking freely
    B. a person's surroundings tend to color his testimony

C. the person will find less distraction outside his home or office
D. a person tends to dominate the interview when in familiar surroundings.

12. Even when an investigator is convinced of the honesty and truthfulness of a witness, thorough checking of all reported information with physical facts is imperative because, among the following,

    A. mere parole testimony is not accepted as legal evidence
    B. the observation of the witness may have been imperfect due to some factors which distort normal sensory perception
    C. the physical facts may have changed since they were observed by the witness
    D. an interview with a witness is merely an informal questioning conducted to learn facts

12.____

13. If the memory of a witness fails him about the time of an occurrence concerning which he is being questioned, the MOST advisable of the following procedures for the investigator to follow is to

    A. supply the data for him in his report
    B. assume the presence of a motive for concealing the information
    C. request him to make an affidavit to that effect
    D. try to give him some associated ideas to refresh his memory

13.____

14. If a person interviewed seems hesitant to talk while the investigator is taking notes, the MOST advisable of the following procedures for the investigator is to

    A. adjourn the interview until a time when it can be conducted in a place with a hidden microphone to record it
    B. secure his cooperation by explaining to the witness the importance of full and complete notes for good investigation reports
    C. complete the interview without notetaking and, at the first opportunity after the interview, reduce it to writing
    D. administer an oath to the person so that he will commit perjury by failing to tell the whole truth

14.____

15. The personal interview as a means of obtaining information about past occurrences is

    A. the most reliable and accurate method
    B. useful principally as a means of finding clues to more reliable sources of information
    C. generally as reliable as recourse to documentary sources
    D. qualitatively inferior but quantitatively superior to all other methods

15.____

16. Experiments have shown that the MOST satisfactory method, among the following, for obtaining dependable data in an interview is by employment of

    A. the free narrative method, in which the person interviewed is permitted to talk without interruption
    B. the question-and-answer method, in which the person interviewed gives information only in response to questions

16.____

C. a combination of the question-and-answer and free narrative methods, with the free narrative given first
D. a combination of the question-and-answer and free narrative methods, with the question-and-answer interview given first

17. Interviewing witnesses by the question-and-answer method, rather than allowing the witness to tell his story without interruption, will GENERALLY _____ accuracy of the report.

    A. *increase* the range but decrease the
    B. *decrease* the range but increase the
    C. *decrease* both the range and
    D. *increase* both the range and

18. Among the following, the present good health of a disabled war veteran is BEST indicated by

    A. a recently issued life insurance policy
    B. a return to his pre-war employment as a cashier
    C. his withdrawal of a civil service veteran preference claim
    D. a reduction in the amount of his pension by the Veterans Administration.

19. Among the following, a person's general good character is BEST evidenced by

    A. the absence of an F.B.I. record
    B. a Police Department good conduct certificate
    C. his school and employment records
    D. letters of recommendation he obtains from friends

20. Among the following, the signature cards of a bank might be employed as a means of verifying an individual's

    A. character   B. identity
    C. financial status   D. employment

21. Of the following, the overt item of evidence which most strongly indicates that an adult person is probably NOT a citizen is

    A. the fact he associates frequently with recently arrived aliens
    B. his lack of a birth certificate
    C. his inability to speak English
    D. the fact his parents are aliens

22. Among the following, an original birth certificate may serve as proof of age and

    A. physical condition   B. religion
    C. citizenship   D. residence

23. *Prima facie* evidence is evidence which

    A. suffices to establish a fact unless rebutted or until overcome by other evidence
    B. has not been tested or measured as to its validity
    C. shows the existence of one fact by proof of the existence of other facts from which the first may be inferred
    D. results from certain presumptions of law, which may not have a basis in fact

24. A copy, accompanied by a certificate of the proceedings necessary to be taken in order to authorize the same to be entered of record, is called a(n) _____ copy.

    A. exemplified
    B. certified
    C. true
    D. verified

25. The term *surveillance*, as used in connection with investigations, is synonymous with

    A. undercover work
    B. reconnaissance
    C. shadowing
    D. inspection

26. An investigation manual directs that all investigators' reports contain a precis. The term *precis* is synonymous with

    A. extract
    B. paraphrase
    C. synopsis
    D. conclusion

27. A sworn statement made by the person who served a summons, setting forth the place and manner of service, is called a(n) _____ of service.

    A. admission
    B. affidavit
    C. certificate
    D. acknowledgment

28. A book in which deeds are recorded in the City Registrar's Office is referred to as a

    A. text   B. folio   C. volume   D. liber

29. The system of describing persons that is GENERALLY employed by modern investigators is known as the _____ system.

    A. Bertillion
    B. Henry
    C. Moulage
    D. Portrait Parle

30. A satisfaction piece is an instrument

    A. which purports to discharge land from the lien of a mortgage
    B. by which pending litigation is settled out of court
    C. acknowledging payment of a money judgment
    D. by which a lien on personal property is discharged

31. The part of an instrument which reads: *Sworn to before me this eighteenth day of July, 2015, Joseph Smith, Notary Public, State of .....* is known as the

    A. jurat
    B. authentication
    C. certification
    D. attestation

32. An authority for the arrest of a person on a criminal charge with a view to his trial and commitment thereon is called a

    A. subpoena   B. summons   C. complaint   D. warrant

33. Entries on the block index sheets for conveyances in the city Registrar's Office are made in _____ order.

    A. alphabetical
    B. date
    C. numerical
    D. no particular

34. Generally, a summons may be served

    A. at any hour of the day or night any day of the week
    B. between sunrise and sunset on any day of the week
    C. at any hour of the day or night, any day of the week, except Sunday
    D. between sunrise and sunset on any day of the week, except Sunday

35. A party refuses to accept service of a summons when properly offered him. Among the following methods, personal service upon him could be properly made after informing him of the nature of the instrument by

    A. thrusting the summons into his lap or upon his person
    B. sending the summons to him by registered mail
    C. leaving the summons on a table before him in his presence
    D. leaving the summons with another member of his household

36. In an action against the city, personal service of the summons is made by delivering a copy thereof to the mayor,

    A. treasurer, or city clerk
    B. comptroller or city clerk
    C. treasurer or corporation counsel
    D. comptroller or corporation counsel

37. Among the following, the present home and business address of a member of the board of directors of a city bank may MOST readily be obtained from

    A. MOODY'S BANK AND FINANCE DIRECTORY
    B. POOR'S REGISTER
    C. TROW'S CITY DIRECTORY
    D. DAU'S BLUE BOOK

38. Among the following, a list of the names and addresses of various professional associations and societies in the United States would be found in the

    A. WORLD ALMANAC   B. ENCYCLOPEDIA BRITANNICA
    C. CONGRESSIONAL RECORD   D. POOR'S REGISTER

39. Workmen's Compensation claims are filed with the

    A. Comptroller
    B. State Department of Labor
    C. United States Department of Labor
    D. Municipal Compensation Board

40. The Bureau of Narcotics is part of the United States

    A. Department of Agriculture
    B. Department of Commerce
    C. Treasury Department
    D. Justice Department

DIRECTIONS: Questions 41 through 49 are to be answered on the basis of the following passage.

Assume that in an interview John Jones, the subject of an investigation, gave the following information concerning himself:

I was born on January 5, 1948 in a hospital in Manhattan. My parents resided in Brooklyn at the time. My mother was born in this country, but my father was born in England and came to this country with his parents when he was about eighteen years old. I attended P.S. 300 in Brooklyn from 1954 to 1962 and Central High School in Brooklyn from 1962 to 1966. From 1966 to 1972, I was employed as a clerk by the XYZ Corporation, which has since gone out of business and been dissolved. In 1972, I was inducted into the Army at Fort Dix, New Jersey, from Selective Service Board No. 528, Brooklyn. I served with the 1097th Infantry Regiment until my discharge on December 1, 1975. After that, I was employed as a merchant seaman on the U.S. Barclay by the Red Circle Steamship Company.

41. Among the following, Jones' birth record should be sought in the

    A. County Clerk's Office of the county in which he was born
    B. City Clerk's Office
    C. Department of Health
    D. Register's Office

42. If no record of Jones' birth is available there and he has no baptismal record, among the following, his date of birth may BEST be verified from the records of

    A. P.S. 300, Brooklyn
    B. the Board of Elections
    C. Draft Board No. 528, Brooklyn
    D. the XYZ Corporation

43. Among the following, Jones' father's citizenship can be verified through records of the

    A. Department of State
    B. Immigration and Naturalization Service
    C. Federal Bureau of Investigation
    D. U.S. Customs Service

44. If, in verifying Jones' education, it is desirable to write to the principal of Central High School, among the following, his full name and the address of the school will be found in the

    A. Brooklyn Telephone Directory
    B. NEW YORK CITY OFFICIAL DIRECTORY (THE GREEN BOOK)
    C. Civil List
    D. DIRECTORY OF AMERICAN SCHOOLS AND COLLEGES

45. Among the following, data regarding the now defunct XYZ Corporation could BEST be obtained from the records of the

    A. New York City Department of Commerce
    B. United States Department of Commerce
    C. Secretary of State of New York State
    D. Attorney General of New York State

46. Among the following, an inquiry regarding Jones' military service should be addressed to the   46._____

   A. Chairman, Selective Service Board No. 528, Brooklyn, N.Y.
   B. Adjutant General, The Pentagon, Washington, D.C.
   C. Commanding Officer, 1097th Infantry Regiment, Defense Department, Washington, D.C.
   D. Regional Office, Veterans Administration, Brooklyn, N.Y.

47. Among the following, if none of the officers of the XYZ Corporation can be located, Jones' employment with that Corporation might BEST be verified from the records of the   47._____

   A. State Department of Labor
   B. Secretary of State
   C. Social Security Administration
   D. Superintendent of Insurance

48. Among the following, data regarding Jones' financial and credit status can BEST be obtained from   48._____

   A. R.L. POLK DIRECTORY
   B. DUN AND BRADSTREET'S
   C. Municipal Credit Union
   D. Tax Department

49. If Jones did not want his present employer to know of the pending investigation, from among the following, his employment on the S.S. Barclay could be verified from the records of the   49._____

   A. U.S. Maritime Commission
   B. Bureau of Customs
   C. Port of New York Authority
   D. Department of Marine and Aviation

Questions 50-57.

DIRECTIONS: Column I lists various records or instruments. Column II lists various public offices. In the space at the right, opposite the number preceding each of the records or instruments in Column I, place the letter preceding the public office in Column II in which such record or information concerning such instrument may be obtained.

COLUMN I
50. Voting records
51. Record of deaths
52. Record of marriages performed in 2015
53. Record of marriages performed in 1953
54. Birth certificates
55. Lis pendens in a real property action
56. Will relating to real property
57. Certificate of appointment of a notary public

COLUMN II
A. County Clerk's Office
B. Surrogate's Office
C. Board of Elections
D. Department of Health

Questions 58-66.

DIRECTIONS: Column I lists various records. Column II lists various governmental departments and offices. In the space at the right, opposite the number preceding each of the records in Column I, place the letter preceding the department or office in Column II from which you would seek information regarding such record.

COLUMN I
58. Real estate tax assessment rolls
59. Compensating use tax records
60. Personal injury claims against the city
61. Licenses as Commissioner of Deed
62. Pawnbroker's license records
63. Pistol license records
64. Zoning regulations
65. Real estate mortgage records
66. Public assistance records

COLUMN II
A. Health Department
B. Comptroller's Office
C. City Register's Office
D. Department of Finance
E. Department of Licenses
F. Police Department
G. City Marshal
H. Tax Department
I. Bureau of Real Estate
J. City Clerk's Office
K. City Planning Commission
L. Welfare Department

Questions 67-74.

DIRECTIONS: Column I lists various licenses and records. Column II lists various state departments and offices. In the space at the right, opposite the number preceding each of the licenses or records in Column I, place the letter preceding the department or office in Column II from which you would seek information regarding such license or record.

COLUMN I
67. Bailbondsman's license
68. Retail liquor store permit
69. Certificate of incorporation of stock corporation
70. Real estate broker's license
71. Physician's license
72. Income tax records
73. License as private investigator
74. State criminal identification records

COLUMN II
A. Secretary of State
B. Department of Education
C. Department of Taxation and Finance
D. Department of Audit and Control
E. Alcoholic Beverage Control Division
F. Division of Parole
G. Department of Correction H. Department of Labor
H. Banking Department J. Insurance Department
I. Department of Social Services

Questions 75-80.

DIRECTIONS: Column I lists various records or instruments. Column II lists various federal departments or offices. In the space at the right, opposite the number preceding each of the records or instruments in Column I, place the letter preceding the office or department in Column II from which information regarding such record or instrument may be obtained.

COLUMN I
75. Passport records
76. Register of copyrights
77. Federal income tax records
78. Vietnam War draft records
79. Immigration visas
80. Bankruptcy petitions

COLUMN II
A. Department of State
B. Library of Congress
C. U.S. District Court
D. Social Security Administration
E. U.S. Patent Office
F. Office of Selective Service Records
G. Internal Revenue Bureau
H. Adjutant General's Office
I. Department of Justice

KEY (CORRECT ANSWERS)

1. B	21. C	41. C	61. J
2. A	22. C	42. A	62. E
3. D	23. A	43. B	63. F
4. D	24. A	44. B	64. K
5. B	25. C	45. C	65. C
6. A	26. C	46. B	66. L
7. B	27. B	47. C	67. J
8. C	28. D	48. B	68. E
9. D	29. D	49. A	69. A
10. D	30. A	50. C	70. A
11. A	31. A	51. D	71. B
12. B	32. D	52. A	72. C
13. D	33. B	53. D	73. A
14. C	34. C	54. D	74. G
15. B	35. C	55. A	75. A
16. C	36. D	56. B	76. B
17. A	37. B	57. A	77. G
18. A	38. A	58. H	78. F
19. C	39. B	59. B	79. A
20. B	40. D	60. B	80. C

EXAMINATION SECTION
TEST 1

DIRECTIONS: Each question or incomplete statement is followed by several suggested answers or completions. Select the one that BEST answers the question or completes the statement. *PRINT THE LETTER OF THE CORRECT ANSWER IN THE SPACE AT THE RIGHT.*

1. Assume that you are interviewing a witness who is telling a story crucial to your investigation. It is important that you get all the facts being related by this witness.
   In order to secure this vital information, the BEST of the following techniques is to
   A. quietly interrupt the witness's story and request him to speak with deliberation to that you can record his statement
   B. guide the witness during his recital so that all important points are validated
   C. confine your activities during the story to brief note-taking; and after the information has been secured, request a full written statement
   D. inform the witness that he must relate all the facts as truthfully and concisely as possible

2. The statement of any witness obtained by an investigator in an interview should GENERALLY be considered
   A. as a lead requiring substantiation by additional evidence
   B. accurate if the witness appears honest and is cooperative
   C. unreliable if the witness has been involved in similar investigations
   D. as a fact admissible under the rules of evidence

3. During an important interview, an investigator takes notes from time to time but very rarely looks at the subject being questioned.
   Such action on the part of the investigator is
   A. *unacceptable*, chiefly because during the actual interview an investigator should pay more attention to the witness's manner of giving the information rather than to the content of his statement
   B. *acceptable*, chiefly because data should be recorded at the earliest opportunity and important data should be noted meticulously
   C. *unacceptable*, chiefly because it inhibits the person being interviewed and is not conducive to a give-and-take discussion
   D. *acceptable*, chiefly because focusing attention on note-taking and not on the person being interviewed creates an impression of professional objectivity

4. The BEST source with which to check the credit rating of a business you are investigating is
   A. the Better Business Bureau
   B. Standard and Poor's
   C. Dun and Bradstreet, Inc.
   D. the State Attorney General's Office

5. Since he must, in the course of his investigations, interview persons with various personalities and attitudes, an investigator should GENERALLY adopt a method of interviewing that
   A. is uniformly applicable to all types so that discrepancies in the accounts of individuals may be readily detected
   B. can be adjusted to the persons whom he interviews
   C. is based on the premise that most witnesses tend to be uncooperative
   D. requires the investigator to spend as little time as possible in questioning witnesses

6. An investigator finds that X, Y, and Z are eyewitnesses to an incident under investigation. He interviews X, who gives him a complete and very detailed statement about the incident. X also informs the investigator that he has discussed the matter with Y and Z, and that each of them completely agrees with him as to what had occurred.
   Under these circumstances, it would be MOST appropriate for the investigator to
   A. interview Y and Z before assessing the value of the statements made by the three witnesses
   B. interview Y and Z and accept their versions if they both disagree with the story given by witness X
   C. interview either Y or Z and close the investigation if the statement of either witness agrees with the story given by witness X
   D. close the investigation on the basis of his interview with witness X since there is no reason to assume that Y and Z will tell a different story

7. Which one of the following is a legal requirement for the admissibility of evidence in a legal procedure?
   A. Weight   B. Sufficiency   C. Competency   D. Recency

8. Of the following diagrams, which one represents the CORRECT utilization of the ABC Method of Surveillance?
   Note: S identifies the suspect's position
         X identifies the positions of investigators
         Arrow indicates direction in which suspect is moving

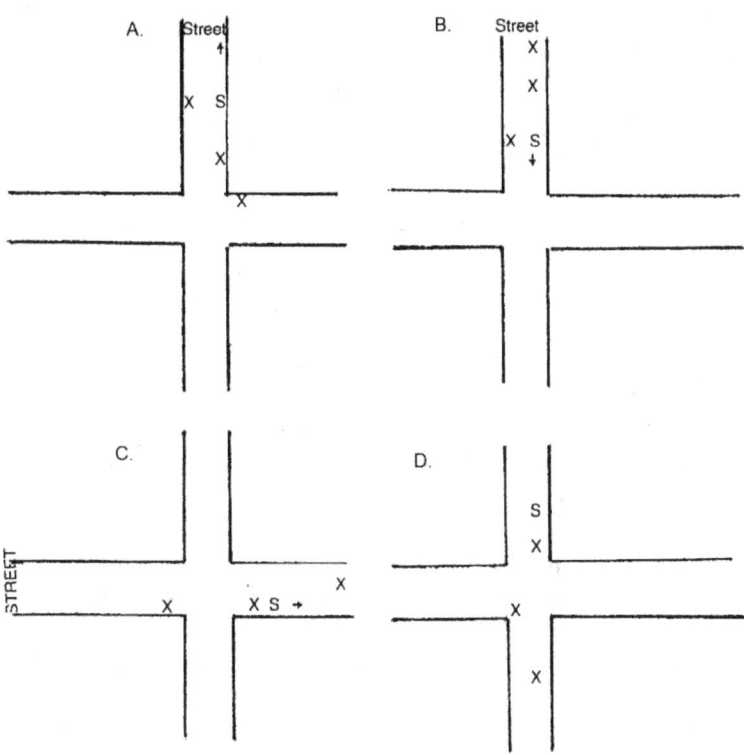

9. During an interview, an interviewee makes the following statement: *I have given the problem of getting a job a great deal of thought. I am looking primarily for an opportunity to grow and develop—to find the type of job that will provide the greatest challenge and bring out the best that is in me. Security probably ranks at the bottom of my list since I feel that I can always make a living somewhere.*
From an analysis of this statement, an investigator would be LEAST likely to conclude that the interviewee is
   A. capable of analytical thought
   B. looking for job satisfaction
   C. seeking self-improvement
   D. trying to cover for his lack of self-confidence

9._____

10. One of the more difficult tasks facing an investigator in an interview is to control the tendency of witnesses to ramble when giving information.
Of the following, the BEST technique for keeping a witness's comments pertinent is to
   A. ask questions which indicate the desired answer
   B. insist on *yes* and *no* answers to his questions
   C. construct questions that restrict the range of information which the witness can give in response
   D. ask precise questions so that the answers of the witness will necessarily be brief

10._____

11. The BASIC purpose of producing evidence in legal proceedings is to
    A. provide a permanent official record for legal action
    B. screen out confusing issues of law and fact
    C. determine the truth of a matter in issue
    D. insure that hearsay statements will be excluded

12. An investigator is handling a case involving an individual and find that the case is proving very difficult because he has run out of leads to follow up.
    Of the following, the BEST way for the investigator to deal with this case is FIRST to
    A. prepare a report of the case indicating that no further action can be taken
    B. place himself in the position of the person being investigated
    C. re-interview all those affected by the case until a new clue is revealed
    D. wait for the first break in the case which will give a substantial lead

13. Assume that you need to interview a person who is suspected of collaborating with the subject under investigation.
    Of the following, the interviewing procedure that is MOST appropriate for handling this situation is to
    A. conduct a casual interview with the person on a pretext different from the actual purpose of the interview
    B. interview the person intensively by means of the *team* method until he breaks down and gives information
    C. insist that the suspected person cooperate
    D. plan to review every statement made by the person until he realizes that no fact will be overlooked

14. Assume that two disinterested individuals had directly witnessed the same event. An investigator who interviewed them received two distinctly different versions of this event.
    Which of the following assumptions PROBABLY accounts for the difference in the two versions?
    A. The event must have consisted of so many separate happenings that no one could understand everything that occurred.
    B. Each individual was selective in his perception of the event.
    C. The interviewing technique used by the investigator was instrumental in eliciting different facts from each individual.
    D. One of the individuals wishes to cooperate with the investigator, but the other did not.

15. During interviews, a certain investigator phrases follow-up questions mentally during pauses while the subject is still answering the previous question.
    This practice is GENERALLY
    A. *desirable*, chiefly because it gives the impression that the investigator is well-acquainted with all the facts
    B. *undesirable*, chiefly because the investigator cannot know whether such questions will be appropriate

C. *desirable*, chiefly because it enables the investigator to pose new questions without significant breaks in the discussion
D. *undesirable*, chiefly because it subjects the person being interviewed to a barrage of questions

16. Generally, a professional investigator's practice of training himself to give the impression of telling the truth during court appearances is considered
    A. *desirable*, chiefly because only by such practice can he perfect his ability to give accurate testimony
    B. *undesirable*, chiefly because any deviation from the unadulterated truth by using a pretension constitutes perjury
    C. *desirable*, chiefly because such training lessens the possibility of his appearing nervous and timid while testifying, which might convey the impression that he is evasive or lying
    D. *undesirable*, chiefly because all testimony should be given in a natural manner, including hesitations, to avoid the court's suspicion that the witness has been coached

17. Assume that prior to an interview, a person makes a spontaneous declaration relating to his case in the presence of an investigator.
    According to a rule of evidence, the person's statement is GENERALLY
    A. *admissible*, only if the investigator testifies to the declaration and his testimony is corroborated by another person
    B. *inadmissible*, chiefly because it constitutes a hearsay declaration against the person's interest
    C. *admissible*, chiefly because it was not the product of the person's deliberation and reflection
    D. *inadmissible*, chiefly because the person was under duress when the exclamation was made

18. In order to break down the communication barriers between an interviewer and his subject, the interviewer should GENERALLY ask introductory questions which
    A. focus on the individual's job status
    B. can be answered in a *yes-or-no* fashion
    C. focus directly on official business
    D. are likely to be of mutual interest to the two parties

19. To introduce as evidence a set of business books prepared by a person other than the individual under investigation, preliminary evidence pertaining to the content of the books must first be established.
    Which of the following does NOT constitute a fact which must be established before such books may be admitted as evidence?
    A. entries were made in the regular course of business at or about the time of the transactions involved
    B. books have been audited and certified as correct
    C. books are the regular books used for making business entries
    D. entries in the books were made by persons required to make them in the course of their regular duties

20. A person who is suffering from a mental disability is not necessarily disqualified from testifying as a witness in a legal proceeding PROVIDED that such person
    A. has the ability to recall and describe past events pertaining to the case
    B. is not an inmate of a mental institution
    C. is attended by a qualified psychiatrist at all times while in the courtroom
    D. swears that he knows the difference between right and wrong

20.____

21. Of the following public records, which is the BEST single source of information on the personal history and background of a subject?
    A. Birth or baptismal certificate
    B. Marriage license application
    C. Discharge certificate from the military services
    D. Income tax return

21.____

22. When it is necessary to prove the contents of a written instrument concerning a matter in dispute, the *best evidence rule* provides that
    A. the contents of written instruments must be subscribed and sworn to before a notary public to be admissible in legal proceedings
    B. no evidence outside the instrument itself shall be used to alter the wording of the instrument
    C. a witness who qualifies as an expert in handwriting identification shall first testify on the genuineness of the instrument
    D. the original instrument itself must be produced in court if it is available

22.____

23. Public documents, if otherwise competent, are admissible as evidence of the facts recorded therein, without the testimony of the officers who entered the facts, CHIEFLY because
    A. public records are subject to such strict security that the entries therein cannot be altered or falsified
    B. all such documents require further corroboration before they are admissible as proof of any facts recorded therein
    C. entries in these documents are made by officers who have sworn to perform their duties in the public interest
    D. hearsay evidence may not be admitted to prove a fact in dispute without the testimony of the officer who recorded it

23.____

24. One of the following ways in which an investigator might ordinarily detect an inconsistency in an interviewee's story is by
    A. having a third party present during the interview
    B. requesting the subject to speak more slowly
    C. observing the subject's manner of dress or attire
    D. watching the subject's facial expressions and mannerisms

24.____

25. The use of small talk or conversation about extraneous topics such as sports, the weather, or current events at the start of a routine interview designed to elicit information is GENERALLY considered
    A. *desirable*, chiefly because it gives the subject a chance to relax and relieve himself of the tension that normally develops before an interview

25.____

B. un*desirable*, chiefly because it wastes the valuable time of subjects with matters that are unrelated to the purpose of the interview
C. *desirable*, chiefly because it is the only way the interviewer is able to ascertain whether he and the subject will be able to develop rapport
D. un*desirable*, chiefly because it is possible to obtain more information about the subject if he is unaware of the purpose of the interview

26. Assume that your superior assigns you to interview an individual who, he warns, seems to be highly *introverted*.
You should be aware that, during an interview, such a person is likely to
    A. hold views which are highly controversial in nature
    B. be domineering and try to control the direction of the interview
    C. resist answering personal questions regarded his background
    D. give information which is largely fabricated

27. The one of the following persons who is MOST likely to be willing to give information leading to the apprehension of a suspect is someone who is
    A. friendly with the suspect
    B. afraid of the subject
    C. interested in law enforcement
    D. seeking revenge against the suspect

28. During the course of a routine interview, the BEST tone of voice for an interviewer to use is
    A. authoritative   B. uncertain   C. formal   D. conversational

29. It is recommended that interviews which inquire into the personal background of an individual should be held in private.
The BEST reason for this practice is that privacy
    A. allows the individual to talk freely about the details of his background
    B. induces contemplative thought on the part of the interviewed individual
    C. prevents any interruptions by departmental personnel during the interview
    D. most closely resembles the atmosphere of the individual's personal life

30. Of the following, the MOST preferable way for an investigator to make a reference check on a subject's previous employment in the area is to
    A. write to the employer and ask him to fill out a standard employee evaluation form
    B. call the employer and conduct a telephone interview
    C. write to the employer and request a personal interview
    D. telephone the employer and ask him to submit a written evaluation

31. Of the following, the BEST way for an investigator to prepare himself for a court appearance as a witness is generally by
    A. memorizing every detail of the case in order to give an exact recital of the information
    B. reviewing his notes and trying to fix in his mind the highlights of the case

C. consulting with his superiors in order to ascertain which aspects of the case should be emphasized
D. studying all aspects of the case and writing out in detail the testimony he intends to give under oath

32. When an investigator is called as a witness to relate a series of incidents, his testimony should GENERALLY consist of
    A. a background narrative, followed by important facts and a concluding statement
    B. important facts, followed by a background narrative and a concluding statement
    C. details personally observed followed by any undeveloped leads
    D. a simple chronological account of the events he has observed

33. Of the following, an individual who smokes heavily during interrogation or an interview is LEAST likely to experience a(n)
    A. decrease in mental efficiency
    B. decrease in physical efficiency
    C. state of high emotion during questioning
    D. emotional release during questioning

34. The BEST way for an investigator to handle a situation in which the person interviewed asks a few slightly personal questions is generally to
    A. give quick, evasive answers and continue with the interview
    B. tell the person such questions are irrelevant and objectionable
    C. inquire fully into the person's reasons for wanting such information
    D. answer the questions briefly and truthfully

35. The CHIEF purpose of using surveillance in an investigation is to
    A. obtain information about persons and activities
    B. cause suspected persons to feel continuously uneasy
    C. maintain a close watch over hostile witnesses
    D. induce subjects to volunteer information

36. A *surreptitious* recording of an interview is one which is made
    A. whenever the information is highly technical
    B. to conceal the identity of the interviewee
    C. without the knowledge of the subject
    D. to encourage a subject to be more informative

37. All the means by which any alleged matter of fact, the truth of which is submitted to investigation, is established or disproved is the legal definition of
    A. proof   B. burden of proof
    C. evidence   D. admissibility of evidence

38. That section of an affidavit in which an officer empowered to administer an oath certifies that this document was sworn to before him is called a(n)
    A. affirmation   B. jurat
    C. acknowledgement   D. verification

39. In legal terminology, a *bailee* is a person who
    A. lawfully holds property belonging to another
    B. deposits cash or property for the release of an arrested person
    C. has been released from arrest on a bond that guarantees his court appearance
    D. deposits personal property as collateral for a debt

40. A specimen of handwriting of known authorship which can be used by an investigator for making a comparison with a questioned or suspected writing is called a(n)
    A. inscription   B. precis   C. coordinate   D. exemplar

41. The attorney felt that his client would be *exonerated*.
    In this sentence, *exonerated* means MOST NEARLY
    A. unwilling to testify   B. declared blameless
    C. severely punished   D. placed on probation

42. The two witnesses were suspected of *collusion*.
    In this sentence, the word *collusion* means MOST NEARLY
    A. a conflict of interest   B. an unintentional error
    C. an illegal secret agreement   D. financial irregularities

43. Many of the subject's answers during the interview were *redundant*.
    In this sentence, *redundant* means MOST NEARLY
    A. uninformative   B. thoughtful   C. repetitious   D. argumentative

44. He was assigned to investigate an individual who was *insolvent*.
    In this sentence, *insolvent* means MOST NEARLY
    A. unable to pay debts   B. extremely disrespectful
    C. difficult to understand   D. frequently out of work

45. In his report, the investigator described several *covert* business transactions.
    In this sentence, *covert* means MOST NEARLY
    A. unauthorized   B. joint   C. complicated   D. secret

KEY (CORRECT ANSWERS)

1.	C	11.	C	21.	B	31.	B	41.	B
2.	A	12.	B	22.	D	32.	D	42.	C
3.	C	13.	A	23.	C	33.	C	43.	C
4.	C	14.	B	24.	D	34.	D	44.	A
5.	B	15.	C	25.	A	35.	A	45.	D
6.	A	16.	C	26.	C	36.	C		
7.	C	17.	C	27.	D	37.	C		
8.	C	18.	D	28.	D	38.	B		
9.	D	19.	B	29.	A	39.	A		
10.	C	20.	A	30.	A	40.	D		

TEST 2

DIRECTIONS: Each question or incomplete statement is followed by several suggested answers or completions. Select the one that BEST answers the question or completes the statement. *PRINT THE LETTER OF THE CORRECT ANSWER IN THE SPACE AT THE RIGHT.*

Questions 1-5.

DIRECTIONS: Questions 1 through 5 consist of two sentences which may or may not contain errors in word usage or sentence structure, punctuation, or capitalization. Consider a sentence correct although there may be other correct ways of expressing the same thought.
Mark your answer:
A. If only Sentence I is correct;
B. If only sentence II is correct;
C. If Sentences I and II are both correct;
D. If Sentences I and II are both incorrect.

1. I. Being locked in his desk, the investigator felt sure that the records would be safe.
    II. The reason why the witness changed his statement was because he had been threatened.

2. I. The investigation had just began then an important witness disappeared.
    II. The check that had been missing was located and returned to its owner, Harry Morgan, a resident of Suffolk County, New York.

3. I. A supervisor will find that the establishment of standard procedures enables his staff to work more efficiently.
    II. An investigator hadn't ought to give any recommendations in his report if he is in doubt.

4. I. Neither the investigator nor his supervisor is ready to interview the witnesses.
    II. Interviewing has been and always will be an important asset in investigation.

5. I. One of the investigator's reports has been forwarded to the wrong person.
    II. The investigator stated that he was not familiar with those kind of cases.

Questions 6-8.

DIRECTIONS: Questions 6 through 8 are to be answered SOLELY on the basis of the following passage.

As investigators, we are more concerned with the utilitarian than the philosophical aspects of ethics and ethical standards, procedures, and conduct. As a working consideration, we might view ethics as the science of doing the right thing at the right time in the right manner in conformity with the normal, everyday standards imposed by society; and in conformity with the judgment society would be expected to make concerning the rightness or wrongness of what we have done.

An ethical code might be considered a basic set of rules and regulations to which we must conform in the performance of investigative duties. Ethical standards, procedures, and conduct might be considered the logical workings of our ethical code in its everyday application to our work. Ethics also necessarily involves morals and morality. We must eventually answer the self-imposed question of whether or not we have acted in the right way in conducting our investigative activities in their individual and total aspects.

6. Of the following, the MOST suitable title for the above passage is
   A. The Importance of Rules for Investigators
   B. The Basic Philosophy of a Lawful Society
   C. Scientific Aspects of Investigations
   D. Ethical Guidelines For the Conduct of Investigations

7. According to the above passage, ethical considerations for investigators involve
   A. special standards that are different from those which apply to the rest of society
   B. practices and procedures which cannot be evaluated by others
   C. individual judgments by investigators of the appropriateness of their own actions
   D. regulations which are based primarily upon a philosophical approach

8. Of the following, the author's PRINCIPAL purpose in writing the above passage seems to have been to
   A. emphasize the importance of self-criticism in investigative activities
   B. explain the relationship that exists between ethics and investigative conduct
   C. reduce the amount of unethical conduct in the area of investigations
   D. seek recognition by his fellow investigators for his academic treatment of the subject matter

Questions 9-11.

DIRECTIONS: Questions 9 through 11 are to be answered SOLELY on the basis of the following passage.

The investigator must remember that acts of omission can be as effective as acts of commission in affecting the determination of disputed issues. Acts of omission, such as failure to obtain available information or failure to verify dubious information, manifest themselves in miscarriages of justice and erroneous adjudications. An incomplete investigation is an erroneous investigation because a conclusion predicated upon inadequate facts is based on quicksand.

When an investigator throws up his hands and admits defeat, the reason for this action does not necessarily lie in his possible laziness and ineptitude. It is more likely that the investigator has made his conclusions after exhausting only those avenues of investigation of which he is aware. He has exercised good faith in his belief that nothing else can be done.

This tendency must be overcome by all investigators if they are to operate at top efficiency. If no suggestion for new or additional action can be found in any authority, an investigator should use his own initiative to cope with a given situation. No investigator should ever hesitate to set precedents. It is far better in the final analysis to attempt difficult solutions, even if the chances of error are obviously present, than it is to take refuge in the spinless adage: If you don't do anything, you don't do it wrong.

9. Of the following, the MOST suitable title for the above passage is 9.____
   A. The Need For resourcefulness in Investigations
   B. Procedures For Completing an Investigation
   C. The Development of Standards For Investigators
   D. The Causes of Incomplete Investigations

10. Of the following, the author of this passage considers that the LEAST important consideration in developing new investigative methods is 10.____
    A. efficiency
    B. caution
    C. imagination
    D. thoroughness

11. According to this passage, which of the following statements is INCORRECT? 11.____
    A. Lack of creativity may lead to erroneous investigations.
    B. Acts of omission are sometimes as harmful as acts of commission.
    C. Some investigators who give up on a case are lazy or inept.
    D. An investigator who gives up on a case is usually not acting in good faith.

Questions 12-15.

DIRECTIONS: Questions 12 through 15 are to be answered SOLELY on the basis of the following passage.

Perpetrators of crimes are often described by witnesses or victims in terms of salient facial features. The Bertillon System of Identification, which preceded the widespread use of fingerprints, was based on body measurements. Recently, there have been developments in the quantification of procedures used in the classification and comparison of facial characteristics. Devices are now available which enable a trained operator, with the aid of a witness, to form a composite picture of a suspect's face and to translate that composite into a numerical code. Further developments in this area are possible, using computers to develop efficient sequences of questions so that witnesses may quickly arrive at the proper description.

Recent studies of voice analysis and synthesis, originally motivated by problems of efficient telephone transmission, have led to the development of the audio-frequency profile or "voice print." Each voice print may be sufficiently unique to permit development of a classification system that will make possible positive identification of the source of a voice print. This method of identification, using an expert to identify the voice patterns, has been introduced in more than 40 cases by 15 different police departments. As with all identification systems that rely on experts to perform the identification, controlled laboratory tests are needed to establish with care the relative frequency of errors of omission and commission made by experts.

4 (#2)

12. The MOST appropriate title for the above passage is 12.____
    A. Technology in Modern Investigative Detection
    B. Identification By Physical Features
    C. Verification of Identifications By Experts
    D. The Use of Electronic Identification Techniques

13. According to the above passage, computers may be used in conjunction with 13.____
    which of the following identification techniques?
    A. Fingerprints   B. Bertillon System
    C. Voice prints   D. Composite facial pictures

14. According to the above passage, the ability to identify individuals based on 14.____
    facial characteristics has improved as a result of
    A. an increase in the number of facial types which can be shown to witnesses
    B. information which is derived from other body measurements
    C. coded classification and comparison techniques
    D. greater reliance upon experts to make the identifications

15. According to the above passage, it is CORRECT to state that audio-frequency 15.____
    profiles or voice prints
    A. have been decisive in many prosecutions
    B. reduce the number of errors made by experts
    C. developed as a result of problems in telephonic communications
    D. are unlikely to result in positive identifications

Questions 16-20.

DIRECTIONS: Questions 16 through 20 are to be answered SOLELY on the basis of the following graph.

EMPLOYMENT APPLICATION INFORMATION
CHECKED BY INVESTIGATORS IN DEPARTMENT Z
CENTRAL CITY

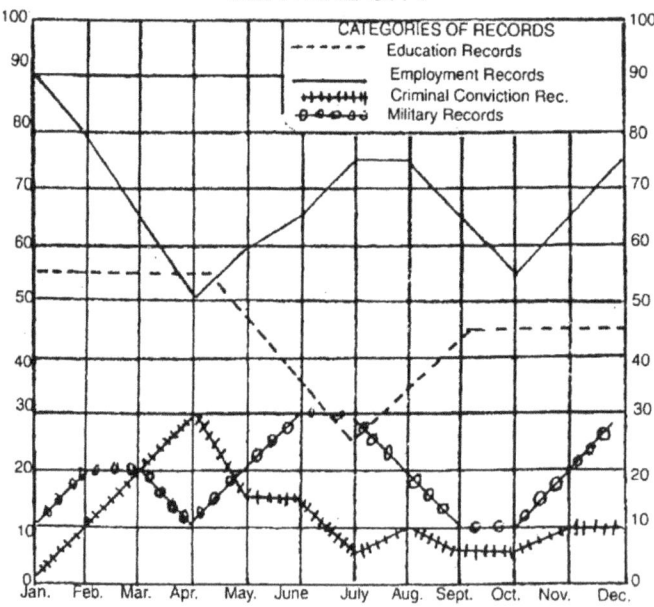

16. The category for which the SMALLEST number of record checks was made in _____ records.
    A. education   B. employment
    C. criminal conviction   D. military

17. In which of the following months did the combined number of criminal conviction record checks and military record checks EXCEED the number of education record checks?
    A. March   B. April   C. May   D. June

18. During which of the following months was the total number of records checked LARGEST?
    A. March   B. April   C. September   D. November

19. Which of the following statements is INCORRECT according to the graph?
    A. Employment records checked each month always exceeded 45.
    B. Education records checked in February did not equal the number of education records checked in November.
    C. Military records checked per month increased from October to December.
    D. Criminal conviction records checked in any given month never exceeded the number of military records checked.

20. Of the total number of records checked in March, the percentage that were education records was MOST NEARLY
    A. 13%   B. 25%   C. 34%   D. 41%

Questions 21-25.

DIRECTIONS: Questions 21 through 25 are to be answered SOLELY on the basis of the information contained in the following tables.

STATUS OF TAX CASES ASSIGNED TO INVESTIGATORS, FISCAL YEAR, CENTRAL CIT, DEPARTMENT Y

Investigator	Cases Assigned	Cases Completed	Cases Pending at End of Fiscal Year
Albert	70	50	20
Bennett	90	60	30
Gordon	82	50	32
Nolton	70	40	30
Paxton	75	50	25
Rich	80	60	20

STATUS OF MISCELLANEOUS CASES ASSIGNED TO INVESTIGATORS
FISCAL YEAR, CENTRAL CITY, DEPARTMENT Y

Investigator	Cases Assigned	Cases Completed	Cases Pending at End of Fiscal Year
Albert	25	20	5
Bennett	20	15	5
Gordon	18	13	5
Nolton	30	23	7
Paxton	17	17	0
Rich	32	24	6

21. Of the following, the investigator who completed the GREATEST percentage of his assigned tax cases in the fiscal year was
    A. Albert   B. Gordon   C. Paxton   D. Rich

22. The total number of the tax cases assigned in the fiscal year EXCEEDED the total number of miscellaneous cases assigned by
    A. 142   B. 325   C. 400   D. 467

23. Of the following, the two investigators who completed the SAME percentage of the miscellaneous cases assigned to them were
    A. Albert and Gordon
    B. Gordon and Nolton
    C. Nolton and Paxton
    D. Bennett and Rich

24. The average number of cases (both tax and miscellaneous) pending per investigator at the end of the fiscal year was MOST NEARLY
    A. 31   B. 28   C. 26   D. 5

25. Assume that the total number of miscellaneous cases pending at the end of the fiscal year is equal to 25% of the number of cases pending at the end of the previous fiscal year.
    What was the TOTAL number of miscellaneous cases pending at the end of the previous fiscal year?
    A. 28   B. 56   C. 74   D. 112

26. The head of an agency, in addressing a group of investigators, stated, *Whenever possible, do all you can to satisfy the needs of members of the public.*
    Which of the following is the LEAST acceptable procedure for investigators to use in implementing this policy?
    A. Handle public grievances and frustrations before they can accumulate.
    B. Satisfy public demands even though organizational goals may be compromised.
    C. Interpret rules and regulations reasonably.
    D. Use mass media to enlist support of programs to win public cooperation.

27. Of the following, the MOST important purpose of having a citizen advisory committee in a public agency is to
    A. make both the citizen groups and the public agency more responsive to the total public interest
    B. prevent fraud and mismanagement within the administration of the agency
    C. improve efficiency and encourage greater diligence on the part of agency personnel
    D. prevent the spread of unfavorable publicity about the agency's activities

28. Of the following, the term *public relations* in its application to any public agency is BEST defined as
    A. all the publicity received by the agency
    B. all the direct and indirect contacts between the agency itself and the clientele it deals with
    C. the sum total of efforts which the agency directs toward performing its functions
    D. de-emphasis of the agency's basic obligations which are not popular with its clientele

29. Assume that you receive a phone call from a man who refuses to identify himself and insists that he *knows for a fact* that an investigator on the staff of your agency has destroyed incriminating records upon receipt of a bribe. The MOST appropriate action for you to take would be to
    A. refuse to discuss the matter unless the caller gives you his name and additional identification
    B. ask the caller for the facts and the name of the suspected investigator
    C. advise the caller that such a serious charge should be reported immediately to the police department
    D. politely advise the caller to report the facts in a letter to your agency head

30. In a public agency, the FIRST step in adopting a system which will give citizens an opportunity to make complaints against the agency's staff members is to
    A. establish an adequate complaint procedure
    B. design a citizen complaint report form
    C. establish physical facilities where complaints to the agency may be received
    D. initiate a public relations campaign informing the public that they may file complaints

31. Which of the following kinds of information is NOT found in the Official Directory of the City (Green Book)?
    A. The number of persons employed in each city agency
    B. A listing of police station houses and fire engine companies in each borough
    C. The names and addresses of all public high schools and city hospitals in each borough
    D. The names and addresses of federal, state, and city courts located within the city

32. An investigator should contact the State Department of Health to obtain information about persons who are licensed or qualified to practice as
    A. x-ray technicians
    B. physiotherapists
    C. chiropractors
    D. pharmacists

33. An employee complains that the city has refused to pay him some back salary for services he performed last year.
    This employee may bring legal action in the Small Claims Part if the amount of his claim does NOT exceed
    A. $1,000   B. $1,500   C. $300   D. $100

34. Experienced investigators have found that using the question-and-answer method in interviewing a witness, instead of allowing the witness to tell his own story freely and without interruption, MOST often tends to _____ the accuracy of the information given by the witness.
    A. *increase* both the scope and
    B. *increase* the scope but *decrease*
    C. *decrease* both the scope and
    D. *decrease* the scope but *increase*

35. Of the following, the STRONGEST indication that the signature on an important document is a forgery is that the suspected signature
    A. is partly illegible
    B. shows a noticeable trembling in certain letters
    C. shows that the writer retouched several letters
    D. is identical in all respects with a signature known to be genuine

36. Prior to writing the complete and final report at the conclusion of an important case, some investigators prepare an outline or blueprint of the investigative data compiled.
    All of the following are important advantages of preparing such an outline or blueprint EXCEPT that it
    A. results in the omission of less important or minor facts
    B. helps in achieving logical arrangement of the materials
    C. lessens chances of omitting essential details
    D. aids in recognizing irrelevant details

37. In determining the validity of a document, the use of oblique lighting renders certain kinds of alterations visible.
    Which of the following alterations would NOT be exposed by use of the oblique lighting technique?
    A. Abrasions and erasures made in order to change some significant part of a document
    B. Rubber-stamp impressions intended to violate a document but made from a non-genuine stamp
    C. Tears, mutilations, or excessive foldings made deliberately in order to conceal or obscure some damaging feature of the document
    D. Traced writing or writing taken from some pattern or model of genuine writing

38. When an investigator takes the witness stand for the prosecution, he must realize that the opposing counsel will GENERALLY endeavor to portray him as a(n)
    A. individual whose moral character is questionable and whose veracity therefore should be doubted
    B. disinterested collector and retailer of facts
    C. interested party who is trying to convict his client on the basis of insufficient evidence
    D. unprejudiced official with competent professional experience

39. Assume that on a certain day, an investigator finds that he has an excessive number of appointments for interviews and believes that he will be unable to keep them all during the course of the day.
    Of the following, the BEST action he could take is to
    A. ask a fellow investigator to help him conduct a group interview
    B. interview the maximum number that can be interviewed properly and reschedule the others for a future date
    C. proceed according to the established schedule
    D. shorten the length of time spent interviewing each person in order to insure that everyone is interviewed

40. There has been a tendency in recent times to publicize the use of instrumentation such as lie detectors, electronic eavesdropping devices, special cameras, and other technical devices in civil and criminal investigations.
    Of the following statements, the one which expresses a MAJOR weakness which results from relying too much on instrumentation as an investigative aid is:
    A. The use of these technical devices invariably violates the constitutional rights of persons subject to investigations
    B. Excessive publicity in the mass media about the success of these mechanical devices in solving difficult cases destroys their value as investigative aids
    C. These technical devices have a very limited value in cases where abundant physical evidence is available
    D. Inexperienced investigators are prone to place their faith in technical methods to the neglect of the more basic investigative procedures

KEY (CORRECT ANSWERS)

1.	D	11.	D	21.	D	31.	A
2.	B	12.	B	22.	B	32.	A
3.	A	13.	D	23.	D	33.	B
4.	C	14.	C	24.	A	34.	B
5.	A	15.	C	25.	D	35.	D
6.	D	16.	C	26.	B	36.	A
7.	C	17.	D	27.	A	37.	B
8.	B	18.	A	28.	B	38.	C
9.	A	19.	D	29.	B	39.	B
10.	B	20.	C	30.	A	40.	D

EXAMINATION SECTION
TEST 1

DIRECTIONS: Each question or incomplete statement is followed by several suggested answers or completions. Select the one that BEST answers the question or completes the statement. *PRINT THE LETTER OF THE CORRECT ANSWER IN THE SPACE AT THE RIGHT.*

1. The one of the following which is the BEST description of a properly objective investigator is one who
   A. is friendly and sensitive to the client's feelings, without becoming emotionally involved
   B. is distant and impersonal, remaining unaffected by what the client says
   C. lets personal emotions enter as far as the client's situation calls for them
   D. becomes emotionally involved with the client's situation but without showing involvement

1.____

2. The one of the following which is MOST necessary for successfully interviewing a person who belongs to a culture different from that of the investigator is for the investigator to
   A. have some appreciation of the other culture
   B. ignore those cultural differences which lead to bias
   C. stay away from sensitive, touchy issues
   D. assume the mannerisms of people in the other culture

2.____

3. In fact-finding interviews, it is generally assumed that the smaller the number of interviewees, the greater the increase of reliability with the addition of others. The PROPER number of interviewees need to insure the accuracy of information obtain generally depends upon the
   A. educational level of those interviewed
   B. number of people who have the required information
   C. directness of the questions asked
   D. variability of the information received

3.____

4. The one of the following which is generally MOST likely to be accurately described in an interview by an interviewee is
   A. the presence of a large painting in the investigator's office
   B. the number of people in the investigator's waiting room
   C. space relations
   D. duration of time

4.____

5. The one of the following which is generally the BEST course of action for an investigator to take when interviewing a person who is reluctant to tell what he knows about a matter under investigation is to
   A. be curt and abrupt, and threaten the person with the consequences of his withholding information

5.____

B. be firm and severe, and pressure the person into telling the needed information
C. be patient and candid with the person being questioned about the investigation since doing otherwise is not ethical
D. give the person false information about the investigation so he will give the needed information without realizing its importance

6. It is often recommended that an investigator prepare in advance a list of questions or topics to be covered in an interview.
The MAIN reason for such a checklist is to
   A. allow investigations to be assigned to less efficient investigators
   B. eliminate a large amount of follow-up paperwork
   C. aid the investigator in remembering to cover all important documents
   D. aid the investigator in maintaining an objective distance from the person interviewed

7. Usually, the CHIEF advantage of a directive approach in an interview is that the
   A. investigator maintains control over the course of the interview
   B. person interviewed is more likely to be put at ease
   C. person interviewed is generally left free to direct the interview
   D. investigator will not suggest answers to the person interviewed

8. Usually, the CHIEF advantage of a non-directive approach by an investigator in conducting an interview is that the
   A. investigator generally conceals what he is looking for in the interview
   B. person interviewed is more likely to express his true feelings about the topic under discussion
   C. person interviewed is more likely to follow an idea introduced by the investigator
   D. investigator can keep the discussion limited to topics he believes to be relevant

9. The one of the following which is generally the LEAST likely to be accurate in a description of an event given to an investigator is a statement about
   A. the presence of an object
   B. the number of people, when their number is small
   C. locations of people
   D. duration of time

10. Assume that you, an investigator, are conducting a character investigation. In an interview, the one of the following character traits of the person being interviewed which can USUALLY be determined with a good degree of reliability is
    A. honesty
    B. dependability
    C. forcefulness
    D. perseverance

11. As an investigator, you have been assigned the task of obtaining a family's social history.
    The BEST place for you to interview members of the family while obtaining this social history would generally be in
    A. the family's home
    B. your agency's general offices
    C. the home of a friend of the family
    D. your own private office

12. You, an investigator, are checking someone's work history.
    The way for you to get the MOST reliable information from a previous employer is to
    A. send personal letters; the employer will respond to the personal attention
    B. send form letters; the employer will cooperate readily since little time or effort is asked of him
    C. arrange a personal interview; the employer may offer information he would not care to put in a letter or speak over the phone
    D. telephone; this method is as effective as a personal interview and is much more convenient

13. The effect that attestation, or the formal taking of an oath, has on witness testimony is to
    A. decrease accuracy, since a witness under oath is more nervous about what is said
    B. makes little difference, since the witness is not too swayed by an oath
    C. increase accuracy, since a witness under oath feels more responsibility for what is said
    D. eliminate inaccuracy unless there is deliberate perjury on the part of the witness

14. If an investigator obtains testimony from persons in interviews by means of interrogation or asking questions rather than by letting the person freely relate the testimony, what is said will GENERALLY be
    A. greater in range and less accurate
    B. greater in range and more accurate
    C. about the same in range and less accurate
    D. about the same in range and more accurate

15. Experienced investigators have learned to phrase their questions carefully in order to obtain the desired response.
    Of the following, the question which would usually elicit the MOST accurate answer is:
    A. "How old are you?"
    B. "What is your income?"
    C. "How are you today?"
    D. "What is your date of birth?"

16. The one of the following questions which would generally lead to the LEAST reliable answer is:
    A. "Did you see a wallet?"
    B. "Was the German Shepherd gray?"
    C. "Didn't you see the stop sign?"
    D. "Did you see the guard on duty?"

17. Some investigators may make a practice of observing details of the surroundings when interviewing in someone's home or office.
Such a practice is GENERALLY considered
    A. *undesirable*, mainly because such snooping is unwarranted, unethical invasion of privacy
    B. *undesirable*, mainly because useful information is rarely, if ever, gained this way
    C. *desirable*, mainly because useful insights into the character of the person interviewed may be gained
    D. *desirable*, mainly because it is impossible to evaluate a person adequately without such observation of his environment

17.____

18. The one of the following questions which MOST often lead to a reliable answer is:
    A. "Was his hair very dark?"
    B. "Wasn't there a clock on the wall?"
    C. "Was the automobile white or gray?"
    D. "Did you see a motorcycle?"

18.____

19. The one of the following which can MOST accurately be determined by an investigator by means of interviewing is
    A. a person's intelligence
    B. factual information about an event
    C. a person's aptitude for a specific task
    D. a person's perceptions of his own abilities

19.____

20. The one of the following which is MOST likely to help a person being interviewed feel at ease is for the investigator to
    A. let him start the conversation
    B. give him an abundance of time
    C. be relaxed himself
    D. open the interview by telling a joke

20.____

21. If the interviewee is to perceive some goal for himself in the interview and thus be motivated to participate in it, it is important that he clearly understands some of the aspects of the interview.
Of the following aspects, the one the interviewee needs LEAST to understand is
    A. the purpose of the interview
    B. the mechanics of interviewing
    C. the use made of the information he contributes
    D. what will be expected of him in the interview

21.____

22. As an investigator working on a project requiring inter-agency cooperation, you find that employees of an agency involved in the project are constantly making it difficult for you to obtain necessary information.
Of the following, the BEST action for you to take FIRST is to
    A. discuss the problem with your supervisor
    B. speak with your counterpart in the other agency

22.____

C. discuss the problem with the head of the uncooperative agency
D. contact the head of your agency

23. The investigator is justified in misleading the interviewee only when, in the investigator's judgment, this is clearly required by the problem being investigated.
Such a practice is
    A. *necessary*; there are times when complete honesty will impede a successful investigation
    B. *unnecessary*; such a tactic is unethical and should never be employed
    C. *necessary*; an investigator must be guided by success rather than ethical considerations in an investigation
    D. *unnecessary*; it is clearly doubtful whether such a practice will help the investigator conclude the investigation successfully

23.____

24. Assume that, in investigating a case of possible welfare fraud, it becomes necessary to hold an interview in the client's home in order to observe family interaction and conditions. Upon arriving, the investigator finds that the client's living room is noisy and crowded, with neighbors present and children running in and out.
Of the following, the BEST course of action for the investigator to take is to
    A. conduct the interview in the living room after telling the children to behave and asking the neighbors to leave
    B. tell the client that it is impossible to conduct the interview in the apartment and make an appointment for the next day in the investigators office
    C. suggest that they move from the living room into the kitchen where there is a table on which he can write
    D. try his best to conduct the interview in the noisy and crowded living room

24.____

25. You, an investigator, are giving testimony in court about a matter you have investigated. An attorney is questioning you in an abrasive, badgering way and, in an insulting manner, calls into doubt your ability as an investigator. You lose your temper and respond angrily, telling the attorney to stop harassing and insulting you.
Of the following, the BEST description of such a response is that it is generally
    A. *appropriate*; as a witness in court, you do not have to take insults from anybody, including an attorney
    B. *inappropriate*; losing your temper will show that you are weak and cannot be trusted as an investigator
    C. *appropriate*; a judge and jury will usually respect someone who responds strongly to unjust provocation
    D. *inappropriate*; such conduct is unprofessional and may unfavorably impress a judge and jury

25.____

KEY (CORRECT ANSWERS)

1.	A	11.	A
2.	A	12.	C
3.	D	13.	C
4.	A	14.	A
5.	C	15.	D
6.	C	16.	B
7.	A	17.	C
8.	B	18.	D
9.	D	19.	D
10.	C	20.	C

21. B
22. A
23. A
24. C
25. D

TEST 2

DIRECTIONS: Each question or incomplete statement is followed by several suggested answers or completions. Select the one that BEST answers the question or completes the statement. *PRINT THE LETTER OF THE CORRECT ANSWER IN THE SPACE AT THE RIGHT.*

1. An investigator may have problems in obtaining information from persons who have a history of mental disturbance CHIEFLY because such persons are
    A. usually highly unstable so that they cannot give a coherent account of anything they have experienced
    B. usually very withdrawn so that they generally are unwilling to talk to anyone they do not know well
    C. often normal in manner so that an investigator may be unaware that their condition may bias information they provide
    D. often violent and may try to attack an investigator who questions them intensively about a topic which is sensitive

1.____

2. Empathy can be defined as the ability of one individual to respond sensitively and imaginatively to another's feelings.
    For an investigator to be empathetic during an interview is USUALLY
    A. *undesirable*, mainly because an investigator should never be influenced by the feelings of the one being interviewed
    B. *desirable*, mainly because an interview will not be productive unless the investigator takes the side of the person interviewed
    C. *undesirable*, mainly because empathy usually leads an investigator to be biased in favor of the person being interviewed
    D. *desirable*, mainly because this ability allows the investigator to direct his questions more effectively to the person interviewed

2.____

3. Assume that an investigator must, in the course of an investigation, question several people who know each other.
    To gather them all in one group and question them together is GENERALLY
    A. *good practice*, since any inaccurate information offered by one person would be corrected by others in the group
    B. *poor practice*, since people in a group rarely pay adequate attention to questions
    C. *good practice*, since the investigator will save much time and effort in this way
    D. *poor practice*, since the presence of several people can inhibit an individual from speaking

3.____

4. While conducting a character investigation of a potential employee, you, as an investigator, notice that most community members interviewed have negative opinions of the candidate.
    Of the following statements about the usefulness of community opinions in such a matter, the one which is LEAST accurate is that

4.____

A. prudence should be exercised in evaluating information received in a community contact
B. a community investigation sometimes elicits gossip which may present an exaggerated picture
C. community opinion is reliable when used to assess an individual's character
D. opinions which cannot be supported by facts must be considered as such

5. An effective investigator should know that the one of the following which LEAST describes why there is a wide range of individual behavior in human relations is that
    A. socio-economic status influences human behavior
    B. physical characteristics do not influence human behavior
    C. education influences human behavior
    D. childhood experience influences human behavior

6. In your investigative unit, you discern a growing friction between two co-workers which is beginning to impede the work of the unit.
Of the following, the approach you should FIRST adopt is to
    A. mediate the friction yourself; if unsuccessful, then inform your supervisor
    B. ignore the friction; although detrimental, it is beyond your authority to settle
    C. promptly discuss the friction and possible course of action with other members of your unit
    D. promptly inform your supervisor of the friction and let him handle the matter

7. In certain cases, in order that an investigation be conducted successfully, an investigator must have the cooperation of people in the community.
The one of the following which BEST describes how an investigator may gain community cooperation in an investigation is by
    A. using persuasion
    B. using authority
    C. spending many hours in the community
    D. being friendly with community leaders

8. During a field investigation, an investigator encounters an uncooperative interviewee.
Of the following, the FIRST thing the investigator should do in such a situation is to
    A. try various appeals to win the interviewee over to a cooperative attitude
    B. try to ascertain the reason for non-cooperation
    C. promise the interviewee that all data will be kept confidential
    D. alter his interviewing technique with the uncooperative interviewee

9. You, as an investigator, discover that an interviewee who was requested to bring with him specific documents for his initial employment interview has forgotten the documents.

Of the following, the BEST course of action to take is to
- A. give the person a reasonable amount of time to furnish the document
- B. tell the person you will let him know how much additional time he could receive
- C. mark the person disqualified for employment; he has failed to provide reasonably requested data on time
- D. mark the person provisionally qualified for employment; upon receipt of the documents, he will be permanently qualified

10. As an investigator checking interviewees' work experience, you realize that the person whom you are to interview is only marginally fluent in English and has, therefore, requested permission to bring a translator with him.
Of the following, the BEST course of action is to inform the interviewee that
    - A. outside translators may not be used
    - B. only city translators may be used
    - C. state law requires fluency in English of all civil servants
    - D. he may be assisted in the interview by his translator

11. Assume that during the course of an interview, an investigator is verbally attacked by the person being interview.
Of the following, it would be MOST advisable for the investigator to
    - A. answer back in a matter-of-fact manner
    - B. ask the person to apologize and discontinue the interview
    - C. ignore the attack but adjourn the interview to another day
    - D. use restraint and continue the interview

12. Assume that an investigator finds that the person he is interviewing has difficulty finishing his sentences and seems to be groping for words.
In such a case, the BEST approach for the investigator to take is to
    - A. say what he thinks the person has in mind
    - B. proceed patiently without calling attention to the problem
    - C. ask the person why he finds it difficult to finish his sentence
    - D. interrupt the interview until the person feels more relaxed

13. The one of the following which BEST describes the effect of the sympathetic approach in interviewing on the interviewee is that it will
    - A. have no discernible effect on the interviewee
    - B. calm the interviewee
    - C. lead the interviewee to understate his problems
    - D. mislead the interviewee

14. The one of the following characteristics which is a PRIMARY requisite for a successful investigative interview is
    - A. total curiosity
    - B. total sympathy
    - C. complete attention
    - D. complete dedication

15. Assume that you, an investigator, become aware that one of your colleagues has a drinking problem which is affecting the operations of your unit.
Of the following, the action which you should take FIRST is to
   A. give your colleague time to resolve the problem himself
   B. discuss the problem with your colleague
   C. inform your supervisor of the problem
   D. not involve yourself in your colleague's problem

15.____

16. Assume that an Assistant District Attorney has asked you, the investigator of an alleged welfare fraud, to conduct a follow-up interview with a primary state witness.
The one of the following which is MOST important in arranging such an interview is to
   A. keep the witness cooperative
   B. conduct the matter in secret
   C. allow the witness to determine where and when the interview takes place
   D. conduct the interview as soon as possible to insure a strong case

16.____

17. Assume that an investigative unit has received a complex task requiring team work.
Of the following, the one which is LEAST essential to the operations of a team effort is
   A. a small group
   B. a leader
   C. regular interaction between team members
   D. separate office space for each team member

17.____

18. By examining a candidate's employment record, an investigator can determine many things about the candidate.
Of the following, the one which is LEAST apparent from an employment record is the candidate's
   A. character
   B. willingness to work
   C. capacity to get along with co-workers
   D. potential for advancing in civil service

18.____

19. Assume that you, an investigator, are conducting an investigative interview in which the person being interviewed is using the interview as a forum for venting his anti-civil service feelings.
Of the following, the FIRST thing that you should do is to
   A. agree with the person; perhaps that will shorten the outburst
   B. respectfully disagree with the person; the decorum of the interview has already been disrupted
   C. courteously and objectively direct the interview to the relevant issue
   D. reschedule the interview to another mutually agreeable time

19.____

5 (#2)

20. The pattern of an investigative interview is LARGELY set by the 20.____
    A. person being interviewed
    B. person conducting the interview
    C. nature of the investigation
    D. policy of the agency employing the interviewer

21. Assume that a person being interviewed, who had been talking freely, suddenly 21.____
    tries to change the subject.
    To a trained interviewer, this behavior would mean that the person PROBABLY
    A. knew very little about the subject
    B. realized that he was telling too much
    C. decided that his privacy was being violated
    D. realized that he was becoming confused

22. Assume that you, an investigator, receive a telephone call from an unknown 22.____
    individual requesting information about a case you are currently investigating.
    In such a situation, the BEST course of action for you to take is to
    A. give him the information over the telephone
    B. tell him to write to your department for the information
    C. send him the information, retaining a copy for your files
    D. tell him to call back, giving you additional time to check into the matter

23. Assume that you, an investigator, are responding to a written query from a 23.____
    member of the public protesting a certain procedure employed by your agency.
    In such a case, your response should stress MOST the
    A. difficulty that a large agency encounters in trying to treat all members of
       the public fairly
    B. idea that the procedure in question will be discontinued if enough
       complaints are received
    C. necessity for the procedure
    D. origin of the procedure

Questions 24-25.

DIRECTIONS: Questions 24 and 25 are to be answered in the light of the information given in
              the following passage.

Assume that a certain agency is having a problem at one of its work locations because a sizable portion of the staff at that location is regularly tardy in reporting to work. The management of the agency is primarily concerned about eliminating the problem and is not yet too concerned about taking any disciplinary action. You are an investigator working for this agency, and though you have never had any contact with this location, you are assigned to investigate to determine, if possible, what might be causing this problem.

After several interviews, you see that low morale created by poor supervision at this location is at least part of the problem. Then, the last person you will interview before submitting your report tells you, when asked the reason for his tardiness, *"Well, I don't know; I just can't get up in the morning. So when I do get going, I've got to rush to get here. And just between you and me, I've lost interest in the job. Working conditions are bad, and it's hard for me to be enthusiastic about working here."*

24. Given the goals of the investigation and assuming that the investor was using a non-directive approach in this interview, of the following, the investigator's MOST effective response should be: 24.____
    A. "You know, you are building a bad record of tardiness."
    B. "Can you tell me more about this situation?"
    C. "What kind of person is your superior?"
    D. "Do you think you are acting fairly towards the agency by being late so often?"

25. Given the goals of the investigation and assuming the investigator was using a directed approach in this interview, of the following, the investigator's response should be 25.____
    A. "That doesn't seem like much of an excuse to me."
    B. "What do you mean by saying that you've lost interest?"
    C. What problems are there with the supervision you are getting?"
    D. "How do you think your tardiness looks in your personnel record?"

KEY (CORRECT ANSWERS)

1.	C		11.	D
2.	D		12.	B
3.	D		13.	B
4.	C		14.	C
5.	B		15.	C
6.	D		16.	A
7.	A		17.	D
8.	B		18.	D
9.	A		19.	C
10.	D		20.	B

21. B
22. B
23. C
24. B
25. C

EXAMINATION SECTION
TEST 1

DIRECTIONS: Each question or incomplete statement is followed by several suggested answers or completions. Select the one that BEST answers the question or completes the statement. *PRINT THE LETTER OF THE CORRECT ANSWER IN THE SPACE AT THE RIGHT.*

1. When a supervisor requests a subordinate to prepare a report, he should not only indicate the areas to be covered in the report but should also indicate to the subordinate

    A. for whom it is intended and its purpose
    B. the conclusions he expects to reach
    C. the decision that he will make based on the facts presented
    D. why that subordinate was chosen to prepare it

1.____

2. The MOST accurate of the following principles of education and learning for a supervisor to keep in mind when planning a training program for the assistant supervisors under her supervision is that

    A. assistant supervisors, like all other individuals, vary in the rate at which they learn new material and in the degree to which they can retain what they do learn
    B. experienced assistant supervisors who have the same basic college education and agency experience will be able to learn new material at approximately the same rate of speed
    C. the speed with which assistant supervisors can learn new material after the age of forty is half as rapid as at ages twenty to thirty
    D. with regard to any specific task, it is easier and takes less time to break an experienced assistant supervisor of old, unsatisfactory work habits than it is to teach him new, acceptable ones

2.____

3. Assume that you are a supervisor and that you are planning to train a group of experienced investigators in certain specific skills which they need in their daily work.
The one of the following methods which may *generally* be expected to be MOST valuable in ascertaining the effectiveness of the training program is to

    A. administer an objective examination to these investigators prior to conducting the training program and an equivalent form of the examination after the program and compare the results
    B. evaluate and compare the work records of these investigators with regard to these skills prior to and after completion of the training program
    C. hold a staff meeting with the investigators after the training program is completed and allow them to discuss frankly their opinions of the values they derived from the various parts of the training
    D. prepare an objective and detailed questionnaire covering the program, have the investigators answer without identifying themselves, and analyze the answers given

3.____

4. A supervisor has received orders for a work assignment to be carried out by his unit. He has firmly decided on methods for carrying out this assignment which he believes will lead to its completion both properly and expeditiously. He has no intention whatsoever of changing his mind. After he has reached his decision, he calls a staff conference to discuss various alternative methods of carrying out the assignments without making clear that he has already decided upon the method to be used.
To hold a conference of this type would GENERALLY be a

   A. *good* idea, ecause his subordinates are likely to carry the assignment through better if they believe that they devised the methods used
   B. *good* idea, because the staff will have the opportunity and be properly motivated to gain knowledge and experience in methodology without endangering staff performance
   C. *poor* idea, because it would be a failure on the part of the supervisor to show the firm leadership which his unit has a right to expect
   D. *poor* idea, because the discovery by the staff that they had not actually participated in deciding upon methods to be used would have an adverse effect upon their morale

5. Supervisors are frequently faced with the necessity of training old employees in new tasks. An employee inexperienced in a task is much more likely to make a mistake than one who is experienced in it.
In delegating authority to an old employee to perform a new task, a supervisor should GENERALLY

   A. delegate the authority as soon as the subordinate gains minimum competence, allowing him to make mistakes which will not do major damage to the client or to the agency program
   B. delegate the authority as soon as the subordinate gains minimum competence but supervise him closely, enough so that he will not have the opportunity to make even minor mistakes
   C. make the delegation of authority dependent upon the importance which the client places upon the problems involved
   D. withhold the authority until the employee has become experienced in performing the task

6. A supervisor has been transferred from supervision of one group of units to another group of units. She spends the first three weeks in her new assignment in getting acquainted with her new subordinates, their problems, and their work. In this process, she notices that some of the records and forms which are submitted to her by two of the assistant supervisors are carelessly or improperly prepared.
The BEST of the following actions for the supervisor to take in this situation is to

   A. carefully check the work submitted by these assistant supervisors during an additional three weeks before taking any more positive action
   B. confer with these offending workers and show each one where her work needs improvement and how to go about achieving it
   C. institute an in-service training program specifically designed to solve such a problem and instruct the entire subordinate staff in proper work methods
   D. make a note of these errors for documentary use in preparing the annual service rating reports and advise the workers involved to prepare their work more carefully

7. A supervisor, who was promoted to this position a year ago, has supervised a certain assistant supervisor for this one year. The work of the assistant supervisor has been very poor because he has done a minimum of work, refused to take sufficient responsibility, been difficult to handle, and required very close supervision. Apparently due to the increasing insistence by his supervisor that he improve the caliber of his work, the assistant supervisor tenders his resignation, stating that the demands of the job are too much for him. The opinion of the previous supervisor, who had supervised this assistant supervisor for two years, agrees substantially with that of the new supervisor. Under such circumstances, the BEST of the following actions the supervisor can take in general is to

   A. recommend that the resignation be accepted and that he be rehired should he later apply when he feels able to do the job
   B. recommend that the resignation be accepted and that he not be rehired should he later so apply
   C. refuse to accept the resignation but try to persuade the assistant supervisor to accept psychiatric help
   D. refuse to accept the resignation, promising the assistant supervisor that he will be less closely supervised in the future since he is now so experienced

8. After completing a conference with a supervisor concerning the ramifications of a complex problem, an employee informs the supervisor that she feels that her assistant supervisor is too strict in her handling of all the workers under her supervision, especially in comparison with the other assistant supervisors.
   The one of the following actions which is *generally* BEST for the supervisor to take is to

   A. advise the worker in a friendly fashion to apply for a transfer to a unit which has a more lenient supervisor
   B. caution the employee that complaining about a fellow employee behind her back is frowned upon by higher authority as it is a sign of disloyalty
   C. inform the employee that she, the supervisor, will investigate the complaint to determine whether or not it has any validity
   D. tell the worker that the closer and stricter a supervisor is, the better and more completely trained will be her subordinate staff

9. Rumors have arisen to the effect that one of the investigators under your supervision has been attending classes at a local university during afternoon hours when he is supposed to be making field visits.
   The BEST of the following ways for you to approach this problem is to

   A. disregard the rumors since, like most rumors, they probably have no actual foundation in fact
   B. have a discreet investigation made in order to determine the actual facts prior to taking any other action
   C. inform the investigator that you know what he has been doing and that such behavior is overt dereliction of duty and is punishable by dismissal
   D. review the investigator's work record, spot check his performance, and take no further action unless the quality of his work is below average for the unit

10. A supervisor must consider many factors in evaluating a worker whom he has supervised for a considerable time. In evaluating the capacity of such a worker to use independent judgment, the one of the following to which the supervisor should *generally* give MOST consideration is the worker's

A. capacity to establish good relationships with people (clients, colleagues)
B. educational background
C. emotional stability
D. the quality and judgment shown by the worker in previous work situations known to the supervisor

11. A supervisor is conducting a special meeting with the assistant supervisors under her supervision to read and discuss some major complex changes in the rules and procedures. She notices that one of the assistant supervisors who is normally attentive at meetings seems to be paying no attention to what is being said. The supervisor stops reading the rules and asks the assistant supervisor a couple of questions about the changed procedure, to which she gets satisfactory answers.
The BEST action of the following for the supervisor to take at the meeting is to

   A. advise the assistant supervisor gently but firmly that these changes are complex and that her undivided attention is required in order to fully comprehend them
   B. avoid further embarrassment to the assistant supervisor by asking the group as a whole to pay more attention to what is being read
   C. discontinue the questioning and resume reading the procedure
   D. politely request the assistant supervisor to stop giving those present the impression that she is uninterested in what goes on about her

12. A supervisor becomes aware that one of her very competent experienced workers never takes notes during an interview with a client except to note an occasional name, address, or date. When asked about this practice by the supervisor, the worker states that she has a good memory for important details and has always been able to satisfactorily record an interview after the client has left.
It would *generally* be BEST for the supervisor to handle this situation by

   A. discussing with her that more extensive note-taking may sometimes be desirable with a client who believes note-taking to be evidence that his problem will receive serious consideration
   B. agreeing with this practice since note-taking interferes with the establishment of a proper worker-client relationship
   C. explaining that, since interviewing is an art form rather than an exact science, a good worker must devise her own personal rules for interviewing and not be bound by general principles
   D. warning the worker that memory is too uncertain a thing to be relied upon and, therefore, notes should be taken during an interview of all matters

13. When an experienced subordinate who has the authority and information necessary to make a decision on a certain difficult matter brings the matter to his supervisor without having made the decision, it would *generally* be BEST for the supervisor to

   A. agree to make the decision for the subordinate after the subordinate has explained why he finds it difficult to make the decision and after he has made a recommendation
   B. make the decision for the subordinate, explaining to him the reasons for arriving at the decision
   C. refuse to make the decision, but discuss the various alternatives with the subordinate in order to clarify the issues involved
   D. refuse to make the decision, explaining to the subordinate that he is deemed to be fully qualified and competent to make the decision

14. The one of the following instances when it is MOST important for an upper-level supervisor to follow the chain of command is when he is

    A. communicating decisions
    B. communicating information
    C. receiving suggestions
    D. seeking information

15. Experts in the field of personnel relations feel that it is generally a bad practice for subordinate employees to become aware of pending or contemplated changes in policy or organizational set-up via the *grapevine* CHIEFLY because

    A. evidence that one or more responsible officials have proved untrustworthy will undermine confidence in the agency
    B. the information disseminated by this method is seldom entirely accurate and generally spreads needless unrest among the subordinate staff
    C. the subordinate staff may conclude that the administration feels the staff cannot be trusted with the true information
    D. the subordinate staff may conclude that the administration lacks the courage to make an unpopular announcement through official channels

16. In order to maintain a proper relationship with a worker who is assigned to staff rather than line functions, a line supervisor should

    A. accept all recommendations of the staff worker
    B. include the staff worker in the conferences called by the supervisor for his subordinates
    C. keep the staff worker informed of developments in the area of his staff assignment
    D. require that the staff worker's recommendations be communicated to the supervisor through the supervisor's own superior

17. Of the following, the GREATEST disadvantage of placing a worker in a staff position under the direct supervision of the supervisor whom he advises is the possibility that the

    A. staff worker will tend to be insubordinate because of a feeling of superiority over the supervisor
    B. staff worker will tend to give advice of the type which the supervisor wants to hear or finds acceptable
    C. supervisor will tend to be mistrustful of the advice of a worker of subordinate rank
    D. supervisor will tend to derive little benefit from the advice because to supervise properly he should know at least as much as his subordinate

18. One factor which might be given consideration in deciding upon the optimum span of control of a supervisor over his immediate subordinates is the position of the supervisor in the hierarchy of the organization.
    It is GENERALLY considered proper that the number of subordinates immediately supervised by a higher, upper echelon supervisor

    A. is unrelated to and tends to form no pattern with the number supervised by lower-level supervisors
    B. should be about the same as the number supervised by a lower-level supervisor
    C. should be larger than the number supervised by a lower-level supervisor
    D. should be smaller than the number supervised by a lower-level supervisor

19. An important administrative problem is how precisely to define the limits on authority that is delegated to subordinate supervisors.
Such definition of limits of authority should be

    A. as precise as possible and practicable in all areas
    B. as precise as possible and practicable in areas of function, but should allow considerable flexibility in the area of personnel management
    C. as precise as possible and practicable in the area of personnel management, but should allow considerable flexibility in the areas of function
    D. in general terms so as to allow considerable flexibility both in the areas of function and in the areas of personnel management

20. The LEAST important of the following reasons why a particular activity should be assigned to a unit which performs activities dissimilar to it is that

    A. close coordination is needed between the particular activity and other activities performed by the unit
    B. it will enhance the reputation and prestige of the unit supervisor
    C. the unit makes frequent use of the results of this particular activity
    D. the unit supervisor has a sound knowledge and understanding of the particular activity

21. In a conference on difficult cases between a recently appointed supervisor and an experienced, above-average employee, the MOST valuable of the following services that the supervisor can offer the employee is a

    A. detached point of view
    B. knowledge of human needs
    C. knowledge of the agency's basic rules and regulations
    D. willingness to make decisions

22. A supervisor is put in charge of a special unit. She is exceptionally well qualified for this assignment by her training and experience. One of her very close personal friends has been working for some time in this unit. Both the supervisor and worker are certain that the rest of the employees in the unit, many of whom have been in the bureau for a long time, know of this close relationship.
Under these circumstances, the MOST advisable action for the supervisor to take is to

    A. ask that either she be allowed to return to her old assignment or, if that cannot be arranged, that her friend be transferred to another unit in the center
    B. avoid any overt sign of favoritism by acting impartiall and with greater reserve when dealing with this employee than with the rest of the staff
    C. discontinue any socializing with this employee either inside or outside the office so as to eliminate any gossip or dissatisfaction
    D. talk the situation over with the employee and arrive at a mutually acceptable plan of proper office decorum

23. A supervisor who wishes to attain established objectives should concentrate on

    A. determining whether management is operating at maximum effectiveness
    B. making suggestions for improving the organization
    C. planning work assignments
    D. securing salary increases for needy employees

24. A usually competent employee complains that he does not understand the procedures to be followed in performing a certain task although the supervisor has explained them twice and has demonstrated them.
Of the following, the BEST course of action for the supervisor to take is to

   A. ask the employee whether he has any problems which are bothering him
   B. assign someone else to the job
   C. explain the procedures again and demonstrate at the same time
   D. have the employee perform the job while he watches and gives additional instructions

24.____

25. GENERALLY, in order to be completely qualified as a supervisor, a person

   A. should be able to perform exceptionally well at least one of the jobs he supervises and have some knowledge of the others
   B. must have an intimate working knowledge of all facets of the jobs which he supervises
   C. should know the basic principles and procedures of the jobs he supervises
   D. need know little or nothing of the jobs which he supervises as long as he knows the principles of supervision

25.____

KEY (CORRECT ANSWERS)

1. A   11. C
2. A   12. A
3. B   13. C
4. D   14. A
5. A   15. B

6. B   16. C
7. B   17. B
8. C   18. D
9. B   19. A
10. D   20. B

21. A
22. A
23. C
24. D
25. C

TEST 2

DIRECTIONS: Each question or incomplete statement is followed by several suggested answers or completions. Select the one that BEST answers the question or completes the statement. *PRINT THE LETTER OF THE CORRECT ANSWER IN THE SPACE AT THE RIGHT.*

1. Your superior has asked you to notify employees of an important change in one of the operating procedures described in the manual. Every employee presently has a copy of this manual.
Which of the following is *normally* the MOST practical way to get the employees to understand such a change?

    A. Notify each employee individually of the change and answer any questions he might have
    B. Send a written notice to key personnel, directing them to inform the people under them
    C. Call a general meeting, distribute a corrected page for the manual, and discuss the change
    D. Send a memo to employees describing the change in general terms and asking them to make the necessary corrections in their copies of the manual

2. A supervisor was directed by the head of his division to report figures for overtime wages. The supervisor asked a clerk under his supervision to give him the figures, and he passed the clerk's figures along to his superior without questioning them. It was then discovered that the clerk had carelessly supplied the wrong information. Who can PROPERLY be held responsible for the mistake, the supervisor or the payroll clerk?

    A. Only the supervisor because he should have known that the clerk would be careless
    B. Only the clerk because it should be unnecessary for supervisors to check the work of their subordinates except for work which is unusually complex or important
    C. Neither of them because it is perfectly understandable that such mistakes will occur from time to time
    D. Both of them because the person to whom a task is delegated is responsible to the supervisor who delegated the task, and the supervisor is responsible to his superior

3. As a supervisor, it is necessary for you to show a new employee how to enter information on standard forms that he will have to prepare. These forms have a number of blanks to be filled in, but the job is fairly simple once a person becomes familiar with it.
The BEST way to show the new employee how to do the job is to

    A. explain how to do it and have him fill out a few forms, helping him with any difficulties
    B. give him a completed form to use as a model and tell him to do all the others exactly the same way
    C. put him on his own immediately and assume that he will learn for himself through trial and error
    D. give him several dozen completed forms to read and ask him to check back with you in a few hours when he feels ready to start work

4. Suppose that a usually competent employee whom you supervise has suddenly begun having difficulty completing his assignments. You ask the employee to speak to you privately about this situation, and he agrees that he would appreciate this opportunity because of a problem he is having.
Of the following, which one would be the BEST technique for you to use in speaking with him?

4.____

   A. Criticize the employee's performance as soon as he mentions his difficulty in completing his assignments
   B. Listen patiently to what the employee has to say before making any comments on your own
   C. Refuse to discuss any personal factors which the employee mentions when he tries to explain his recent work difficulty
   D. Allow the employee to argue with you but plan your attack and defense carefully

5. A certain supervisor does not compliment members of his staff when they come up with good ideas. He feels that coming up with good ideas is part of the job and does not merit special attention.
This supervisor's practice is

5.____

   A. *poor,* because recognition for good ideas is a good motivator
   B. *poor,* because the staff will suspect that the supervisor has no good ideas of his own
   C. *good,* because it is reasonable to assume that employees will tell their supervisor of ways to improve office practice
   D. *good,* because the other members of the staff are not made to seem inferior by comparison

6. An employee under your supervision complains about a decision you have made in assigning work in the office. You consider the matter to be unimportant, but it seems to be very important to him. He is excited and very angry. Of the following, the MOST appropriate action for you to take FIRST is to

6.____

   A. listen to the details of his complaint
   B. refer him to your superior
   C. tell him to *cool off* before discussing the matter
   D. tell him to settle it with the other employees

7. An experienced employee complains to his unit supervisor that the latter's continual, very close supervision of his work is unnecessary and annoying. The unit supervisor has been recently appointed.
Of the following, it would *generally* be BEST for the unit supervisor to

7.____

   A. agree to discontinue all supervision if the employee will agree, if he has any problems, to consult the supervisor
   B. assure the employee that close supervision is necessary but should not be taken personally
   C. consider with the employee what aspects of the supervision could be reduced
   D. explain that he is supervising closely only until he learns what the job is all about

8. A supervisor had a clerk assigned to help him review records. One day the supervisor asked the clerk to continue checking the records, and the clerk said, *No, I'm not doing any more of that today.*
   In this instance, the supervisor should IMMEDIATELY

   A. ask the clerk why he will not check the records
   B. ask another clerk to do the job
   C. tell the clerk he must do it or be transferred
   D. contact his own supervisor

9. Assume that you have been assigned to supervise other employees. You find that one of your subordinates makes many mistakes whenever he prepares a particular report. Of the following, the MOST desirable course of action for you to follow FIRST in such a situation is to

   A. retrain the subordinate in the preparation of the report
   B. transfer the subordinate to another unit
   C. tell the subordinate to improve or resign
   D. give the employee different duties

10. Some employees of a department have sent an anonymous letter containing many complaints to the department head. Of the following, what is this MOST likely to show about the department?

    A. It is probably a good place to work.
    B. Communications are probably poor.
    C. The complaints are probably unjustified.
    D. These employees are probably untrustworthy.

11. Of the following, the BEST reason for rotating employee work assignments is that such rotation

    A. challenges the ingenuity of supervisors in making assignments
    B. gives each employee a chance at both desirable and undesirable assignments
    C. creates specialists among all employees
    D. increases the competitive spirit among employees

12. Although an employee under your supervision frequently protests when receiving a monotonous assignment, he nevertheless performs the assigned task efficiently. His protests, however, disturb the other employees and interfere with their work.
    Of the following actions you may take in handling this employee, the MOST desirable one is for you to

    A. point out to him the effect of his conduct on the staff's work and request his cooperation in accepting such assignments
    B. arrange to issue such assignments to him when the other members of the staff are not present
    C. inform him that you will request his transfer to another unit unless he puts a halt to his unjustifiable protests
    D. ask other members of the staff to tell him that he is disturbing them by his protests

13. A supervisor has had several problems with a clerk who assists him. He calls the clerk in for a discussion of the matters.
    Which of the following should comprise the MAJOR part of the discussion?

    A. All the things the clerk has done wrong
    B. The most recent things the clerk has done wrong
    C. The things the clerk has done well in addition to the things he has done wrong
    D. The clerk's previous experience and personal problems

14. Assume that certain work processed in your office is then sent to another office for further processing. One of the employees in your office tells you that the supervisor in the other office has been complaining about your office's method of handling the work.
    Of the following, the MOST appropriate action for you to take is to

    A. get all the details from the employee and then speak to the other supervisor
    B. ignore the situation and continue to do the best you can
    C. remind the supervisor that it is not his function to evaluate your work
    D. refrain from reporting the matter to your superior

15. It is the practice in your department to make objective evaluations of the performance of different units. This requires looking at the results achieved by a particular unit during a specified period of time; for instance, the number of applications processed, the number of inquiries answered, the number of inspections made, and so forth.
    Of the following, the BEST method of evaluating the performance of each unit is to compare its results with the

    A. results achieved by all units of the same size that are performing other kinds of work
    B. goals that the unit was reasonably expected to meet during the specified period
    C. performance of the same unit during a similar period of time four or five years earlier
    D. amount of money spent to achieve these results

16. It is possible that you may be asked to submit a brief written evaluation of the work of several employees under your supervision.
    Such an evaluation should *normally* give LEAST emphasis to an employee's

    A. attendance record, including tardiness and absence
    B. ability to grasp new assignments and carry them out effectively
    C. educational background and previous employment experience
    D. ability to get along with co-workers

17. Of the following leadership characteristics, the one that is *generally* considered PRIMARY for a supervisor is the ability to

    A. achieve good working relations with fellow supervisors
    B. get subordinates to air their personal problems
    C. take action to get the job done
    D. plan his work efficiently

18. A recently appointed supervisor is placed in charge of a district which includes several senior employees. He finds that while these subordinates are able to learn new tasks and methods, some of them tend to take longer to learn procedural changes than newer, younger workers.
Of the following, the MAIN reason for this is that senior workers

    A. are embarrassed by younger workers' intelligence
    B. have to *unlearn* what was taught them in the past
    C. form learning blocks when they are supervised by a younger person
    D. are more interested in doing the work than in academic discussions

18.____

19. Which of the following is *generally* considered to be the MOST desirable way for a supervisor to begin a discussion of an employee's performance with the employee?

    A. Accentuate the positive by giving credit where credit is due
    B. Encourage the employee to suggest ways in which he can improve
    C. Point out specific instances of poor performance
    D. Suggest training programs that the employee may be interested in

19.____

20. For a supervisor to use consultative supervision with his subordinates effectively, it is ESSENTIAL that he

    A. accept the fact that his formal authority will be weakened by the procedure
    B. admit that he does not know more than all his men together and that his ideas are not always best
    C. utilize a committee system so that the procedure is orderly
    D. make sure that all subordinates are consulted so that no one feels left out

20.____

21. During a conversation with his supervisor, a subordinate begins to discuss what appears to the supervisor to be a deep-seated personality problem that has been bothering the subordinate.
For the supervisor to suggest to the subordinate the possibility of professional help would NORMALLY be

    A. *undesirable;* the necessity of requiring professional help would automatically disqualify the subordinate from being promoted in the future
    B. *desirable;* generally a supervisor can be of limited assistance in personally solving deep-seated personality problems
    C. *undesirable;* since the supervisor was approached by the employee, it is his responsibility as a supervisor to help the employee solve his problem
    D. *desirable;* in accordance with the Civil Service Commission regulations, a supervisor is not allowed to get involved in subordinates' personal problems

21.____

22. When a new method of performing a job operation is to be instituted, the one of the following approaches which will MOST generally gain acceptance of the change by subordinates is to

    A. hold a friendly, informal meeting after the change has been implemented to explain the advantages of the new method
    B. consult the subordinates involved in the change as early as possible in the planning stage
    C. work closely with just one of the subordinates who will be affected by the change so that others need not be taken off the job

22.____

D. implement the change, instruct employees fully in the new method, and then follow up on results

23. Of the following, the supervisory practice which is LEAST likely to produce a favorable work environment is that the supervisor

    A. takes an active interest in subordinates
    B. does not tolerate mistakes, regardless of who has made the mistake
    C. gives praise when justified
    D. disciplines individuals in accordance with their violation of the rules

24. When a supervisor finds it necessary to let a subordinate know that he is dissatisfied with the subordinate's level of performance, which of the following tactics would *usually* prove MOST effective in improving the subordinate's performance?

    A. The supervisor should be angry when criticizing in order to prevent the mistakes from recurring.
    B. Once criticism has been made, the supervisor should be sure to continuously impress the seriousness of the mistakes upon the subordinate.
    C. When making his criticism, the supervisor should guard against referring to any work that was well done since this would reduce the effect of his criticism.
    D. The supervisor should focus his criticism on the mistakes being made and should avoid downgrading the subordinate personally.

25. Of the following, the BEST descriptive statement of an effective supervisor is *generally* that he

    A. works alongside his subordinates on the same type of work
    B. catches all errors when they are made
    C. gives many specific work orders and few general work orders
    D. devotes much of his time to long-range activities, such as planning and improving human relations

KEY (CORRECT ANSWERS)

1. C
2. D
3. A
4. B
5. A

6. A
7. C
8. A
9. A
10. B

11. B
12. A
13. C
14. A
15. B

16. C
17. C
18. B
19. A
20. D

21. B
22. B
23. B
24. D
25. D

EXAMINATION SECTION
TEST 1

DIRECTIONS: Each question or incomplete statement is followed by several suggested answers or completions. Select the one that BEST answers the question or completes the statement. *PRINT THE LETTER OF THE CORRECT ANSWER IN THE SPACE AT THE RIGHT.*

1. Assume that you are a supervisor recently assigned to a new unit. You notice that, for the past few days, one of the employees in your unit whose work is about average has been stopping work at about four o'clock and has been spending the rest of the afternoon relaxing at his desk.
   The BEST of the following actions for you to take in this situation is to
   A. assign more work to this employee since it is apparent that he does not have enough work to keep him busy
   B. observe the employee's conduct more closely for about ten days before taking any more positive action
   C. discuss the matter with the employee, pointing out to him how he can use the extra hour daily to raise the level of his job performance
   D. question the previous supervisor in charge of the unit in order to determine whether he had sanctioned such conduct when he supervised that unit

1.____

2. A supervisor, newly assigned in charge of a small project, discovers that the previous supervisor and one of the employees supervised by him put all their business communications with each other in written form. The newly assigned supervisor finds that the employee is continuing to put his communications in writing and has requested that the supervisor do the same in order to prevent misunderstandings.
   It would generally be BEST for the supervisor to
   A. accede to the request since the likelihood of misunderstandings will be reduced and since, as a newly assigned supervisor, he should not make changes until he is well established and accepted
   B. allow the employee to communicate with him in the way in which he chooses but refuse to communicate with the employee in writing except in cases where he would generally consider written communications to be desirable, on the grounds that too much of the supervisor's time would be wasted thereby
   C. inform the employee that neither one of them is to use written communications excessively in order to reduce the time consumed by communication but with the understanding that the employee may resort to writing in cases where he has serious reason to fear a misunderstanding
   D. instruct the employee to cease the use of written communications in excess of the use of them by the other employees and refuses to accede to his request since the result would be an excessive waste of time

2.____

3. A policy of direct crosswise communication on a project between a member of the management staff and a member of the maintenance staff of equal or superior status rather than following the chain of command upward through the manager and down through the top maintenance supervisor is a policy to be
    A. *discouraged*, primarily because it places responsibility where it does not belong and makes the quality of communication erratic and undependable
    B. *discouraged*, primarily because the manager and upper level supervisors will fail to receive the full information they need to make policy and administrative decisions
    C. *encouraged*, primarily because it results in decision making at the lowest practical level
    D. *encouraged*, primarily because it shortens the communication time and improves the quality of communication

2.____

4. A supervisor in a large department should be thoroughly familiar with modern methods of personnel administration. This statement is
    A. *true*, because this familiarity will help him in performing the normal functions of his office
    B. *false*, because in a large city personnel administration is not a departmental matter, but is centralized in a civil service commission
    C. *true*, because this knowledge will insure the elimination of personnel problems in a department
    D. *false*, because the departmental problems of a minor character are handled by the personnel representative, while major problems are the responsibility of the commissioner

4.____

5. The LEAST true of the following is that a supervisor in a large department
    A. executes the policy laid down by the commissioner or his deputies
    B. in the main, carries out the policies of the commissioner but with some leeway where his own frame of reference is determinative
    C. is never required to formulate policy
    D. is responsible for the successful accomplishment of a section of the department's program

5.____

6. In the supervision of young inexperienced investigators, the MOST important training task for the supervisor is to
    A. encourage investigators to make their own decisions about case problems
    B. give experience-based answers to various problems that arise in cases
    C. teach investigators how to analyze and assess important facts in order to make decisions about case problems
    D. teach investigators how to recognize evidence of mental breakdown

6.____

7. The supervisor is responsible for the accuracy of the work performed by his subordinates. Of the following procedures which he might adopt to insure the accurate copying of long reports from rough draft originals, the MOST effective one is to
    A. examine the rough draft for errors in grammar, punctuation, and spelling before assigning it to a typist to copy

7.____

B. glance through each typed report before it leaves his bureau to detect any obvious errors made by the typist
C. have another employee read the rough draft original to the typist who typed the report, and have the typist make whatever corrections are necessary
D. rotate assignments involving the typing of long reports equally among all the typists in the unit

8. In the course of your duties, you receive a letter which, you believe, should be called to the attention of your superior.
Of the following, the BEST reason for attaching previous correspondence to this letter before giving it to your superior is that
    A. there is less danger, if such a procedure is followed, of misplacing important letters
    B. this letter can probably be better understood in the light of previous correspondence
    C. your supervisor is probably in a better position to understand the letter than you
    D. this letter will have to be filed eventually so there is no additional work involved

8.____

9. The most successful supervisor wins his victories through preventive rather than through curative action.
The one of the following which is the MOST accurate statement on the basis of this counsel is that
    A. success in supervision may be measured more accurately in terms of errors corrected than in terms of errors prevented
    B. anticipating problems makes for better supervision than waiting until problems arise
    C. difficulties that cannot be prevented by the supervisor cannot be overcome
    D. the solution of problems in supervision is best achieved by scientific methods

9.____

10. Suppose that a stenographer recently appointed to your bureau submits a memorandum suggesting a change in office procedure that has been tried before and has been found unsuccessful.
Of the following, the BEST action for you to take is to
    A. send the stenographer a note acknowledging receipt of the suggestion, but do not attempt to carry out the suggestion
    B. point out that suggestions should come from her supervisor, who has a better knowledge of the problems of the office
    C. try out the suggested change a second time, lest the stenographer lose interest in her work
    D. call the stenographer in, explain the change is not practicable, and compliment her for her interest and alertness

10.____

11. Suppose that you are an assistant to one of the important administrators in your department. You receive a note from the head of the department asking your superior to assist with a pressing problem that has arisen by making an immediate recommendation. Your superior is out of town on official business for a few days and cannot be reached. The head of the department, evidently, is not aware of his absence.
Of the following, the BEST action for you to take is
    A. send the note back to the head of the department without comment so as not to incriminate your supervisor
    B. forward the note to one of the administrators in another division of the department
    C. wait until your supervisor returns and bring the note to his attention immediately
    D. get in touch with the head of the department immediately and inform him that your superior is out of town

11.____

12. One of your duties may be to estimate the budget of your unit for the next fiscal year. Suppose that you expect no important changes in the work of your unit during the next year.
Of the following, the MOST appropriate basis for estimating next year's budget is the
    A. average budget of your unit for the last five years
    B. budget of your unit for the current year plus fifty percent to allow for possible expansion
    C. average current budget of units in your department
    D. budget of your unit for the current fiscal year

12.____

13. Suppose that you are acting as supervisor to an important administrator in your department. Of the following, the BEST reason for keeping a separate *pending* file of letters to which answers are expected very soon is that
    A. important correspondence should be placed in a separate, readily accessible file
    B. a periodic check of the *pending* file will indicate the possible need for follow-up letters
    C. correspondence is never final, so provision should be made for keeping files open
    D. there is seldom sufficient room in the permanent files to permit filing all letters

13.____

14. In order to BEST able to teach a newly appointed employee who must learn to do a type of work which is unfamiliar to him, his supervisor should realize that during the first stage in the learning process the subordinate is generally characterized by
    A. acute consciousness of self
    B. acute consciousness of subject matter, with little interest in persons or personalities
    C. inertness or passive acceptance of assigned role
    D. understanding of problems without understanding of the means of solving them

14.____

15. The MOST accurate of the following principles of education and learning for a supervisor to keep in mind when planning a training program for the employees under his supervision is that

    A. his employees, like all other individuals, vary in the rate at which they learn new material and in the degree to which they can retain what they do learn
    B. experienced employees who have the same basic college education and agency experience will be able to learn new material at approximately the same rate of speed
    C. the speed with which employees can learn new material after the age of forty is half as rapid as at ages twenty to thirty
    D. with regard to any specific task, it is easier and takes less time to break an experienced employee of old, unsatisfactory work habits than it is to teach him new, acceptable ones

15.____

16. A supervisor has been transferred from supervision of one group of units to another group of units in the same center. He spends the first three weeks in his new assignment in getting acquainted with his new subordinates, their caseload problems, and their work. In this process, he notices that some of the case records and forms which are submitted to him by two of the assistant supervisors are carelessly or improperly prepared.
The BEST of the following actions for the supervisor to take in this situation is to

    A. carefully check the work submitted by these assistant supervisors during an additional three weeks before taking any more positive action
    B. confer with these offending workers and show each one where his work needs improvement and how to go about achieving it
    C. institute an in-service training program specifically designed to solve such a problem and instruct the entire subordinate staff in proper work methods
    D. make a note of these errors for documentary use in preparing the annual service rating reports and advise the workers involved to prepare their work more carefully

16.____

17. A supervisor, who was promoted to his position a year ago, has supervised a certain assistant supervisor for this one year. The work of the assistant supervisor has been very poor because he has done a minimum of work, refused to take sufficient responsibility, been difficult to handle, and required very close supervision. Apparently, due to the increasing insistency by his supervisor that he improve the caliber of his work, he assistant supervisor tenders his resignation, stating that the demands of the job are too much for him. The opinion of the previous supervisor, who had supervised this assistant supervisor for two years, agrees substantially with that of the new supervisor. Under such circumstances, the BEST of the following actions the supervisor can take in general is to

    A. recommend that the resignation be accepted and that he be rehired should he later apply when he feels able to do the job
    B. recommend that the resignation be accepted and that he not be rehired should he later so apply

17.____

C. refuse to accept the resignation but try to persuade the assistant supervisor to accept psychiatric help
D. refuse to accept the resignation, promising the assistant supervisor that he will be less closely supervised in the future since he is now so experienced

18. Rumors have arisen to the effect that one of the social investigators under your supervision has been attending classes at a local university during afternoon hours when he is supposed to be making field visits.
The BEST of the following ways for you to approach this problem is to
   A. disregard the rumors since, like most rumors, they probably have no actual foundation in fact
   B. have a discreet investigation made in order to determine the actual facts prior to taking any other action
   C. inform the investigator that you know what he has been doing and that such behavior is overt dereliction of duty and is punishable by dismissal
   D. review the investigator's work record, spot check his cases and take no further action unless the quality of his work is below average for the unit

18.____

19. The one of the following instances when it is MOST important for an upper level supervisor to follow the chain of command is when he is
   A. communicating decisions   B. communicating information
   C. receiving suggestions   D. seeking information

19.____

20. In order to maintain a proper relationship with a worker who is assigned to staff rather than line functions, a line supervisor should
   A. accept all recommendations of the staff worker
   B. include the staff worker in the conferences called by the supervisor for his subordinates
   C. keep the staff worker informed of developments in the area of his staff assignment
   D. require that the staff worker's recommendations be communicated to the supervisor through the supervisor's own superior

20.____

21. Of the following, the GREATEST disadvantage of placing a worker in a staff position under the direct supervision of the supervisor whom he advises is the possibility that the
   A. staff worker will tend to be insubordinate because of a feeling of superiority over the supervisor
   B. staff worker will tend to give advice of the type which the supervisor wants to hear or finds acceptable
   C. supervisor will tend to be mistrustful of the advice of a worker of subordinate rank
   D. supervisor will tend to derive little benefit from the advice because to supervise properly he should know at least as much as his subordinate

21.____

22. One factor which might be given consideration in deciding upon the optimum span of control of a supervisor over his immediate subordinates is the position of the supervisor in the hierarchy of the organization. It is generally considered PROPER that the number of subordinates immediately supervised by a higher, upper echelon supervisor
    A. is unrelated to and tends to form no pattern with the number supervised by lower level supervisors
    B. should be about the same as the number supervised by a lower level supervisor
    C. should be larger than the number supervised by a lower level supervisor
    D. should be smaller than the number supervised by a lower level supervisor

22.____

23. An important administrative problem is how precisely to define the limits on authority that are delegated to subordinate supervisors. Such definition of limits of authority should be
    A. as precise as possible and practicable in all areas
    B. as precise as possible and practicable in areas of function, but should allow considerable flexibility in the area of personnel management
    C. as precise as possible and practicable in the area of personnel management, but should allow considerable flexibility both in the areas of function and in the areas of personnel management
    D. in general terms so as to allow considerable flexibility both in the areas of function and in the areas of personnel management

23.____

24. The one of the following causes of clerical error which is usually considered to be LEAST attributable to faulty supervision or inefficient management is
    A. inability to carry out instructions
    B. too much work to do
    C. an inappropriate record-keeping system
    D. continual interruptions

24.____

25. Assume that you are the supervisor of a clerical unit in a large agency. One of your subordinates violates a rule of the agency, a violation which requires that the employee be suspended from his work for one day. The violated rule is one that you have found to be unduly strict and you have recommended to the management of the agency that the rule be changed or abolished. The management has been considering your recommendation but has not yet reached a decision on the matter.
In these circumstances, you should
    A. not initiate disciplinary action, but, instead, explain to the employee that the rule may be changed shortly
    B. delay disciplinary action on the violation until the management has reached a decision on changing the rule
    C. modify the disciplinary action by reprimanding the employee and informing him that further action may be taken when the management has reached a decision on changing the rule
    D. initiate the prescribed disciplinary action without commenting on the strictness of the rule or on your recommendation

25.____

KEY (CORRECT ANSWERS)

1.	C	11.	D
2.	C	12.	D
3.	D	13.	B
4.	A	14.	A
5.	C	15.	A
6.	C	16.	B
7.	C	17.	B
8.	B	18.	B
9.	B	19.	A
10.	D	20.	C

21.	B
22.	D
23.	A
24.	A
25.	D

TEST 2

DIRECTIONS: Each question or incomplete statement is followed by several suggested answers or completions. Select the one that BEST answers the question or completes the statement. *PRINT THE LETTER OF THE CORRECT ANSWER IN THE SPACE AT THE RIGHT.*

1. As a supervisor, assume that a newly appointed employee is assigned to your unit.
   The one of the following which is likely to have the LEAST value in motivating the new employee when he first reports to you is
   A. an explanation of disciplinary measures which may be taken against employees
   B. indication by you that he can always come to you for help
   C. the first impression he gets of you and his fellow employees
   D. your emphasis on the importance of the work when interviewing him

1.____

2. Assume that you are in charge of a unit of employees. A new appointee reports to you for the first time.
   Of the following, the MOST advisable action for you to take first is to
   A. attempt to evaluate his attitude towards the work he will be required to perform
   B. discuss with him the general nature of the duties he is to perform
   C. explain the opportunities he will have for promotion within the department
   D. have him read over any available material pertaining to departmental rules and regulations for employees

2.____

3. Your department conducts a formal training course for new appointees.
   Under these circumstances, a supervisor should assume that
   A. he can safely delegate all responsibility for any additional training required to one of his experienced men who will work with the new appointee in the field
   B. he is thus relieved of the effort required to train new appointees who may be assigned to his unit
   C. he will still be responsible for supplementary training of new appointees assigned to his unit
   D. his responsibility for training should be limited to making suggestions for improving the formal training program based on his observation of the work of new appointees

3.____

4. In the development of an on-the-job training program, the FIRST step should be
   A. consideration of the cost of such a program
   B. consideration of the problem of interesting the workers in such a program
   C. determination of the training facilities which may be available
   D. determination of those areas in which training is required

4.____

2 (#2)

5. Assume that a recent appointee has completed whatever basic training was provided for him. It becomes necessary to give him a special assignment for which he has not been specifically trained. He is given this assignment without any instructions as to how it should be carried out. This should be considered as
   A. *advisable*, because a worker has to feel his own way on special assignments
   B. *advisable*, because there comes a time when a worker should be encouraged to exercise his own initiative
   C. *inadvisable*, because a worker needs guidance on any aspect of the job with which he is unfamiliar
   D. *inadvisable*, because various superior officials of the department may have different ideas concerning the methods to be used in special assignments

5.____

6. Assume that you are holding a conference with the works in your unit. During the conference, one of the employees, in an offensive manner, challenges a statement you make. You are reasonably sure but not certain that what you have said is correct.
   The MOST advisable action for you to take at the conference is to
   A. admit that you may be in error but reprimand the man for his manner of speaking
   B. avail yourself of the opportunity to point out to the group what constitutes bad manners
   C. ignore the man's manner but make sure that the group feels your statement is correct
   D. say that you will determine the correct facts as soon as possible and inform the staff

6.____

7. Suppose that a new inspectional procedure has been ordered by the chief of your bureau. You think that it may meet with some objection by your staff. As a unit supervisor, the MOST advisable action for you to take in order to minimize such resistance is to
   A. appoint a committee from your staff to study the procedure and report on its advantages and disadvantages
   B. discuss, at a staff conference, the intent of the new procedure and the means of carrying it out
   C. inform the staff that this is an order coming from a higher authority and it must be carried out regardless of personal feelings
   D. issue detailed instructions concerning the new procedure to each member of your staff

7.____

8. Suppose that at conferences with your staff, you find that, usually, only one of the men participates in the discussion.
   Under these circumstances, the MOST advisable action for you to take is to
   A. speak to him privately and ask him to refrain from speaking so much at staff conferences
   B. stimulate the other men by asking them direct questions at staff conferences

8.____

C. tell him directly, at conferences, that you would prefer to hear from the other men for a change
D. use the technique of not looking at this man when asking questions in order to prevent him from getting the floor

9. Which of the following do you consider to be the MOST important factor to be considered in evaluating the work of an employee. His
    A. ability to maintain good personal relationships with his supervisor, his fellow workers, and the community
    B. effectiveness in helping to carry out the objectives of the program
    C. observance of departmental rules and regulations governing employees
    D. personal awareness of the significance of his work to the welfare of the community

9.____

10. Of the following, the MOST valid statement concerning the supervisor and the probationary period is:
    A. Proper personnel selection methods should make it unnecessary for supervisory personnel to be concerned with evaluation of probationers
    B. Requiring an immediate supervisor to report on the capability of a candidate at the end of his probationary period is inadvisable since he usually has had no part in the initial selection of personnel
    C. The probationary period should be considered as an integral part of the personnel selection process and, thus, should be an active concern of immediate supervisors
    D. The value of a probationary period is likely to be greater when the supervisor is required to report only when he considers a candidate not suitable for permanent appointment rather when he is required to certify that a candidate is suitable

10.____

11. An employee under your supervision complains to you about the fact that you recommended him for a performance rating indicating merely satisfactory work. He feels that he deserves a higher rating, while you are convinced that your recommendation was justified.
    Of the following, the MOST advisable action for you to take is to
    A. advise him of his right to appeal the rating given and the required procedure for making such an appeal
    B. explain to him that, as a supervisor, your experience and your opportunity to evaluate his work against that of other employees enable you to give him a fair and just rating
    C. give him your specific reasons for considering his performance average or satisfactory and not qualifying for a higher rating
    D. point out to him that relatively few persons receive an above-average rating and that there is always opportunity for a higher rating in the future

11.____

12. Assume that your superior has assigned to your unit a special investigation which is to be completed by a certain date. Considering the regular work load, you feel that the investigation cannot be completed in the allotted time. You point this out to him but he insists that you handle the assignment without any increase in staff.
Of the following, the MOST advisable course of action for you to take is to
    A. agree to undertake the assignment but insist upon some assurance that this situation will not be repeated
    B. be as noncommittal as possible with the determination to secure evidence to show that you should not be given the assignment
    C. take the matter up with higher authority but inform him that you have done so
    D. undertake the assignment with the intention to keep him closely informed concerning the progress of the work

13. Assume that, as a supervisor, you have received somewhat conflicting orders from two superiors not of equal rank.
Of the following, the MOST advisable course of action for you to follow is to
    A. attempt to carry out the orders of each superior as far as you can
    B. carry out the orders of the person higher in rank
    C. consult your immediate superior concerning the situation
    D. use your own judgment and follow those orders which seem more reasonable

14. Assume that you are a supervisor. Your immediate superior frequently gives assignments to your subordinates without your knowledge.
Of the following, the MOST advisable way for you to handle this situation is to
    A. discuss it with your immediate supervisor
    B. instruct your staff that they are to accept assignments only from you
    C. keep a record of such instances and forward a memorandum concerning them to higher authority in the department
    D. realize and accept the fact that, as your superior, he has authority over you

15. Of the following, the one which would LEAST likely aid a supervisor in long-range planning is
    A. a practical attitude of not worrying about possible problems until they arise
    B. estimating future needs on the basis of past experience
    C. obtaining early knowledge of contemplated changes
    D. staff conferences with the employees under his supervision

16. Of the following, the one that is likely to be of LEAST value as a direct source of help for a supervisor is
    A. a compilation of departmental rules and regulations
    B. a manual of standard operating procedures
    C. civil service rules and regulations
    D. the personnel officer of the department

17. Assume that you suspect that a field worker under your supervision goes home early in the afternoon. In spotchecking one of his daily reports, you find that he has indicated that his last inspection was made at a certain establishment at 4 P.M. The owner of the establishment states that the inspection was made at 1 P.M.
Of the following, the MOST advisable course of action for you to take FIRST is to
   A. attempt to determine whether any animosity exists between the owner of this establishment and the employee
   B. check with owners of establishments listed on the report as having been visited before the establishment in question was visited
   C. confront the employee with the information you have obtained from the owner of the establishment
   D. send a report of these circumstances to your immediate supervisor

17.____

18. Assume that one of the employees under your supervision is frequently absent. Although you have discussed the matter with him several times, his attendance record remains unsatisfactory.
The MOST advisable course of action for you to take NEXT is to
   A. discuss the problem again with the employee to see if any new factors have arisen which cause his continued absence
   B. give him another chance
   C. recommend that appropriate penalties be applied since the problem has already been discussed with him
   D. advise him to seek expert counsel concerning his personal problems

18.____

19. Assume that you are a supervisor. One of the men you supervise angrily demands an interview with you to discuss his dissatisfaction with his work assignment.
Of the following, the course of action you should take FIRST in this situation is to
   A. advise him to take the matter up with your superior
   B. arrange for a private interview as soon as possible to discuss his grievance
   C. explain to the employee that all assignments are made by you only after consideration of what is best for satisfactory accomplishment of the work of the unit
   D. promise the employee that you will review the work assignments in your unit to determine whether any changes are warranted

19.____

20. Of the following, the one which would likely aid a supervisor MOST in maintaining morale among his staff is
   A. ignoring any rumors that are transmitted through the organization's grapevine
   B. maintenance of an aloof attitude in his contacts with the group under his supervision

20.____

C. scrupulous care in not revealing any information which the administration requests him to treat as confidential
D. seeking, through consultation with his own superior, to find a remedy if situations outside of his division threaten to upset his own group

21. Of the following, the one which a supervisor should try to avoid MOST is
    A. consideration that rumors in the organization may contain some elements of truth
    B. handling of grievances which are voiced by his entire staff, as opposed to individual grievances
    C. offering personal counsel when it is requested of him by subordinates
    D. use of disciplinary measures to secure proper conduct of subordinates

    21._____

22. Suppose that you are a supervisor. At a social function which you attend, unfavorable remarks concerning certain activities of our department are made in the course of conversation. You happen to be in agreement with what is being said.
    Under these circumstances, you should consider that
    A. it is best to be noncommittal in such situations
    B. it is necessary for you to convince the others of the value of these activities
    C. it would be advisable for you to suggest that those interested write a group letter of complaint to the department
    D. you are a private citizen as well as a public employee and, therefore, are free to express your personal opinion at a social function

    22._____

23. Assume that you are a supervisor in charge of an inspectional unit. A merchant whose weighing and measuring devices were tested by one of the inspectors under your supervision takes the trouble to write a letter of complaint to the Commissioner of the department. In this letter he states that the manner in which the inspection was conducted gave customers in the store the impression that improper devices were being used although no violations were found. The letter is referred to you for appropriate action.
    Of the following, the MOST advisable action for you to take FIRST is to
    A. arrange for an inspector not known by the accused inspector to observe him in the field and report his findings to you
    B. call a staff meeting at which you will discuss proper procedures to be used when making inspections
    C. interview the inspector involved to get his version of the incident
    D. make personal observations, in the field, of the manner in which inspections are being conducted

    23._____

24. In attempting to protect consumers against various types of fraud, the law states that, in certain instances, possession of a certain substance by a dealer is presumptive evidence of his intent to use it to defraud.
    From the point of view of the enforcing agency, the PRINCIPAL value of such legislation is that
    A. it offers more protection of the rights of the consumer than it does of the rights of the dealer

    24._____

B. such evidence, by its very nature, is superior to direct evidence
C. the agency is relieved of the difficulties involved in attempting to obtain direct evidence
D. this constitutes a more comprehensive definition of the offense involved

25. Departments of municipal government frequently suggest the enactment of legislation in fields in which they are interested.
Such suggestions are
   A. *advisable*, because basic legislation is already available
   B. *advisable*, because the departments have the best knowledge of their problems and needs
   C. *inadvisable*, because the city already has a Law Department
   D. *inadvisable*, because departments have biased viewpoints

KEY (CORRECT ANSWERS)

1.	A		11.	C
2.	B		12.	D
3.	C		13.	C
4.	D		14.	A
5.	C		15.	A
6.	D		16.	C
7.	B		17.	B
8.	B		18.	C
9.	B		19.	B
10.	C		20.	D

21.	D
22.	A
23.	C
24.	C
25.	B

EXAMINATION SECTION
TEST 1

DIRECTIONS: Each question or incomplete statement is followed by several suggested answers or completions. Select the one that BEST answers the question or completes the statement. *PRINT THE LETTER OF THE CORRECT ANSWER IN THE SPACE AT THE RIGHT.*

Questions 1 and 2 are to be answered in accordance with the following statement.

The process of validating a factual proposition is quite distinct from the process of validating a value judgment. The former is validated by its agreement with the facts, the latter by human authority.

1. According to the above statement, the one of the following methods which is MOST acceptable for determining whether or not a proposition is factually correct is to

    A. prove that a related proposition is factually correct
    B. derive it logically from accepted assumptions
    C. show that it will lead to desired results
    D. compare it with experience

1.____

2. Assuming that the above statement is correct, the theory that the correctness of all ethical propositions can be tested empirically is

    A. *correct,* testing empirically is validating by agreement with facts
    B. *incorrect,* ethical propositions are value judgments
    C. *correct,* ethical propositions are based on rational hypotheses
    D. *incorrect,* a factual proposition is validated by its agreement with facts

2.____

Questions 3 and 4 are to be answered on the basis of the following passage.

Ideally, then, the process of budget formulation would consist of a flow of directives down the organization, and a reverse flow of recommendations in terms of alternatives among which selection would be made at every level. Ideally, also, a change in the recommendations at any level would require reconsideration and revision at all lower levels. By a process of successive approximation, everything would be taken into account and all points of view harmonized. Such a process, however, would be ideal only if the future could be foreseen clearly and time did not matter. As it is, in a complicated organization like the Federal government, the initial policy objectives established for the budget become out-of-date, before such a procedure could be carried through. While this difficulty does not in any way impugn the principle that the budget should be considered in terms of alternatives, it may call for short-cut methods of estimation rather than long drawn-out ones.

3. According to the above passage,

    A. the ideal method for estimating purposes is a short one
    B. the ideal method is not ideal for use in the Federal government
    C. directives should flow up and down via short methods
    D. the Federal government needs to speed up its reverse flow of recommendations for greater budgetary estimates

3.____

4. A suitable title for the above passage would be

   A. FORMULATING THE FEDERAL GOVERNMENT'S BUDGETARY PRINCIPLES
   B. DIRECTIVES AND RECOMMENDATIONS: BUDGETARY FLOW
   C. THE PROCESS OF BUDGET FORMULATION
   D. THE APPLICATION OF THE IDEAL ESTIMATE TO THE FEDERAL GOVERNMENT

Questions 5 and 6 are to be answered in accordance with the following passage.

For purposes of budget formulation, the association of budgeting with accounting is less fortunate. Preparing for the future and recording the past do not necessarily require the same aptitudes or attitudes. The task of the accountant is to record past transactions in meticulous detail. Budgeting involves estimates of an uncertain future. But, because of the influence of accounts, government's budgets are prepared in a degree of detail that is quite unwarranted by the uncertain assumptions on which the estimates are based. A major source of government waste could be eliminated if estimates were prepared in no greater detail than was justified by their accuracy.

5. The author of the above paragraph

   A. is undermining the accounting profession
   B. believes accountants dwell solely in the past and cannot deal with the future efficiently
   C. wants the accountants out of government unless they become more accurate in their findings
   D. wishes to redirect the accountants' handling of budgetary procedures

6. The author's attitude appears to be

   A. tongue-in-cheek   B. morose
   C. strident   D. constructive

Questions 7 through 9 are to be answered SOLELY on the basis of the following situation.

John Foley, a top administrator, is responsible for output in his organization. Because productivity had been lagging for two periods in a row, Foley decided to establish a committee of his subordinate managers to investigate the reasons for the poor performance and to make recommendations for improvements. After two meetings, the committee came to the conclusions and made the recommendations that follow.

Output forecasts had been handed down from the top without prior consultation with middle management and first level supervision. Lines of authority and responsibility had been unclear. The planning and control process should be decentralized.

After receiving the committee's recommendations, Foley proceeded to take the following actions. Foley decided he would retain final authority to establish quotas but would delegate to the middle managers the responsibility for meeting quotas.

After receiving Foley's decision, the middle managers proceeded to delegate to the first-line supervisors the authority to establish their own quotas. The middle managers eventually received and combined the first-line supervisors' quotas so that these conformed to Foley's.

7. Foley's decision to delegate responsibility for meeting quotas to the middle managers is inconsistent with sound management principles because

   A. Foley should not have involved himself in the first place
   B. middle managers do not have the necessary skills
   C. quotas should be established by the chief executive
   D. responsibility should not be delegated

8. The principle of co-extensiveness of responsibility and authority bears on Foley's decision.
   In this case, it implies that

   A. authority should exceed responsibility
   B. authority should be delegated to match the degree of responsibility
   C. both authority and responsibility should be retained and not delegated
   D. responsibility should be delegated, but authority should be retained

9. The middle managers' decision to delegate to the first-line supervisors the authority to establish quotas was INCORRECTLY reasoned because

   A. delegation and control must go together
   B. first-line supervisors are in no position to establish quotas
   C. one cannot delegate authority that one does not possess
   D. the meeting of quotas should not be delegated

Questions 10 through 13 are to be answered SOLELY on the basis of the information contained in the following passage.

The Commissioner and, with the approval of the Commissioner, the Inspectors General and any person under the supervision of the Commissioner or Inspectors General may require any officer or employee of the city to answer questions concerning any matter related to the performance of his or her official duties or any person dealing with the city concerning such dealings with the city, after first being advised that neither their statements nor any information or evidence derived therefrom will be used against them in a subsequent criminal prosecution other than for perjury or contempt arising from such testimony. The refusal of an officer or employee to answer questions on the condition described in this paragraph shall constitute cause for removal from office or employment or other appropriate penalty.

Every officer or employee of the city shall cooperate fully with the Commissioner and the Inspectors General. Interference with or obstruction of an investigation conducted by the Commissioner or an Inspector General shall constitute cause for removal from office or employment or other appropriate penalty.

Every officer and employee of the city shall have the affirmative obligation to report, directly and without undue delay, to the Commissioner or an Inspector General any and all information concerning conduct which they know or should reasonably know to involve corrupt or other criminal activity or conflict of interest, (1) by another city officer or employee, which concerns his or her office or employment, or (2) by persons dealing with the city, which concerns their dealings with the city. The knowing failure of any officer or employee to report as required above shall constitute cause for removal from office or employment or other appropriate penalty.

10. According to the above passage, if a city employee has information concerning criminal wrongdoing by her supervisor in his work with a private agency, she should FIRST

   A. speak with her supervisor about the matter
   B. inform the Inspector General of the information she has
   C. explore the matter further to try to uncover more evidence
   D. speak to her co-workers to determine whether her suspicions are valid

11. Of the following, the passage is MOST concerned with

   A. preventing corrupt or other criminal activity or conflicts of interest in city dealings
   B. establishing what constitutes corrupt or criminal activities by city employees
   C. establishing guidelines for removing city employees from office who do not assist the Inspector General
   D. city employees' responsibilities regarding investigations conducted by the Office of the Inspector General

12. Based on the above passage, it is NOT always necessary to report which one of the following to the Inspector General?

   A. a city employee who accepts a gift from a private business
   B. a private agency whose work for the city presents a conflict of interest
   C. a private vendor who offers a city employee special favors if awarded a city contract
   D. a city employee who conducts private business during his city working hours Of the following, the above passage does NOT discuss the type of penalty a city employee might receive for

13. Of the following, the above passage does NOT discuss the type of penalty a city employee might receive for

   A. intentionally giving misleading answers to questions asked by the Inspector General
   B. criminal actions he committed and which subsequently are uncovered by an investigation of the Inspector General
   C. interfering with an investigation being conducted by the Inspector General
   D. delaying to report corrupt activity to the Inspector General

Questions 14 through 16 are to be answered SOLELY on the basis of the information contained in the following passage.

In 2003, funding for the Older Americans Act programs will be cut by 10% from the 2002 funding levels. There will be 4.6 million dollars less in funds available for congregate and home-delivered meals, employment, and social services for the city's 1.2 million elderly residents. Funding for the Title V Senior Community Services Employment program would be effectively discontinued, resulting in the loss of jobs for 684 elderly persons working in nutrition sites for the elderly, senior centers, day care centers, and hospitals. This job loss would add to the almost 800 jobs in N.Y.C. defunded by the elimination of the Job Opportunity Program Reductions in the Title IIIC Nutrition and Commodity Foods/cash in lieu programs will jeopardize the delivery of over 500,000 congregate and home-delivered meals annually, and the operation of seven senior citizens centers. Title IIIB services, which include home care, escort, shopping, and transportation services, will be spared in 2003 because of the availability of prior year funds, but will be reduced by nearly one million dollars in 2004, causing the interruption of these supportive services for thousands of elderly persons in the city.

14. According to the information in the above passage, funding cuts for the Title V Senior Community Services Employment program would

    A. not affect the availability of home-delivered meals for the elderly
    B. be greater in 2003 because of an overall decline in the city's population
    C. result in the loss of 1,484 jobs for the elderly
    D. impact mostly on the staff assigned to senior centers

15. Based on the information in the above passage, which of the following statements is MOST correct?

    A. Funding cuts will affect only a small portion of the city's elderly population
    B. The largest funding cuts will take place in Title IIIC programs.
    C. The Job Opportunity Program will not be affected by cuts in Title IIIB programs.
    D. Funding for Older Americans Act programs will be cut by an additional 10% in 2004.

16. Based on the information in the above passage, it can be inferred that escort services for the elderly will

    A. continue in 2003 but be eliminated in 2004
    B. not be affected in 2004 due to prior year funding
    C. be reduced in 2003 and eliminated in 2004
    D. not be affected in 2003 but reduced in 2004

KEY (CORRECT ANSWERS)

1.	D	9.	C
2.	B	10.	B
3.	B	11.	D
4.	C	12.	A
5.	D	13.	B
6.	D	14.	A
7.	D	15.	C
8.	B	16.	D

READING COMPREHENSION
UNDERSTANDING AND INTERPRETING WRITTEN MATERIAL
EXAMINATION SECTION
TEST 1

DIRECTIONS: Each question or incomplete statement is followed by several suggested answers or completions. Select the one that BEST answers the question or completes the statement. *PRINT THE LETTER OF THE CORRECT ANSWER IN THE SPACE AT THE RIGHT.*

Questions 1-2.

DIRECTIONS: Questions 1 and 2 are to be answered SOLELY on the basis of the information given in the following paragraph.

It is argued by some that the locale of the trial should be given little or no consideration. Facts are facts, they say, and if presented properly to a jury panel they will be productive of the same results regardless of where the trial is held. However, experience shows great differences in the methods of handling claims by juries. In some counties, large demands in personal injury suits are viewed with suspicion by the jury. In others, the jurors are liberal in dealing with someone else's funds.

1. According to the above paragraph, it would be ADVISABLE for an examiner on a personal injury case to

    A. get information as to the kind of verdicts that are usually awarded by juries in the county of trial
    B. give little or no consideration to the locale of the trial
    C. look for incomplete and improper presentation of facts to the jury if the verdict was not justified by the facts
    D. offer a high but realistic initial settlement figure so that no temptation is left to the claimant to gamble on the jury's verdict

1.____

2. According to the above statement, the argument that the location of a trial in a personal injury suit CANNOT counteract the weight of the evidence is

    A. basically sound
    B. disproven by the differences in awards for similar claims
    C. substantiated in those cases where the facts are properly and carefully presented to the injury
    D. supported by experience which shows great differences in the methods of handling claims by juries

2.____

Questions 3-6.

DIRECTIONS: Questions 3 through 6 are to be answered SOLELY on the basis of the following excerpt from a recorded annual report of the police department. This material should be read first and then referred to in answering these questions.

LEGAL BUREAU

One of the more important functions of this bureau is to analyze and furnish the department with pertinent information concerning Federal and State statutes and local laws which affect the department, law enforcement or crime prevention. In addition, all measure introduced in the State Legislature and the City Council which may affect this department are carefully reviewed by members of the Legal Bureau and, where necessary, opinions and recommendations thereon are prepared.

Another important function of this office is the prosecution of cases in the Criminal Courts. This is accomplished by assignment of attorneys who are members of the Legal Bureau to appear in those cases which are deemed to raise issues of importance to the department or questions of law which require technical presentation to facilitate proper determination; and also in those cases where request is made for such appearances by a judge or magistrate, some other official of the city, or a member of the force.

Proposed legislation was prepared and sponsored for introduction in the State Legislature and, at this writing, one of these proposals has already been enacted into law and five others are presently on the Governor's desk awaiting executive action. The new law prohibits the sale or possession of a hypodermic syringe or needle by an unauthorized person. The bureau's proposals awaiting executive action pertain to an amendment to the Criminal Procedure Law prohibiting desk officers from taking bail in gambling cases or in cases mentioned in the Criminal Procedure Law, including confidence men and swindlers as jostlers in the Penal Law; prohibiting the sale of switchblade knives of any size to children under 16 and bills extending the licensing period of gunsmiths.

The Legal Bureau has regularly cooperated with the Corporation Counsel and the District Attorneys in respect to matters affecting this department, and has continued to advise and represent the Police Athletic League, the Police Sports Association, the Police Relief Fund, and the Police Pension Fund.

3. Members of the Legal Bureau frequently appear in Criminal Court for the purpose of

   A. defending members of the Police Force
   B. raising issues of important to the Police Department
   C. prosecuting all offenders arrested by members of the Force
   D. facilitating proper determination of questions of law requiring technical presentation

4. The Legal Bureau sponsored a bill that would

   A. extend the licenses of gunsmiths
   B. prohibit the sale of switchblade knives to children of any size
   C. place confidence men and swindlers in the same category as jostlers in the Penal Law
   D. prohibit desk officers from admitting gamblers, confidence men, and swindlers to bail

5. One of the functions of the Legal Bureau is to

   A. review and make recommendations on proposed Federal laws affecting law enforcement
   B. prepare opinions on all measures introduced in the State Legislature and the City Council
   C. furnish the Police Department with pertinent information concerning all new Federal and State laws
   D. analyze all laws affecting the work of the Police Department

6. The one of the following that is NOT a function of the Legal Bureau is

   A. law enforcement and crime prevention
   B. prosecution of all cases in Women's Court
   C. advise and represent the Police Sports Association
   D. lecturing at the Police Academy

7. It is usual in public service for recruits to serve a probationary period before they receive tenured positions. The objective of this is to observe them in actual service, to teach them the duties of their position, and to provide a means for eliminating those who prove they are not suited for this kind of work. During this period, firings may be made at the discretion of the chief.
   Which one of the following is BEST supported by the above selection?

   A. Demonstrated fitness for the job is the basis for retention of probationary employees.
   B. Trial appointments protect the appointee from unfair dismissal practices.
   C. Public service employees need experience and instruction before permanent appointment.
   D. Exams must be given to determine the ability of probationary employees.

8. As the fundamental changes sought to be brought about in the inmates of a correctional institution can be accomplished only under good leadership, it follows that the quality of the staff whose duty it is to influence and guide the inmates in the right direction is more important than the physical facilities of the institution.
   Of the following, the MOST accurate conclusion based on the preceding statement is that

   A. the development of leadership is the fundamental change brought about in inmates by good quality staff
   B. the physical facilities of an institution are not very important in bringing about fundamental changes in the inmates
   C. with proper training the entire staff of a correctional institution can be developed into good leaders
   D. without good leadership the basic changes desired in the inmates of a correctional institution cannot be brought about

Questions 9-11.

DIRECTIONS: Questions 9 through 11 are to be answered SOLELY on the basis of the following paragraph.

The law enforcement agency is one of the most important agencies in the field of juvenile delinquency prevention. This is so not because of the social work connected with this problem, however, for this is not a police matter, but because the officers are usually the first to come in contact with the delinquent. The manner of arrest and detention makes a deep impression upon him and affects his life-long attitude toward society and the law. The juvenile court is perhaps the most important agency in this work. Contrary to the general opinion, however, it is not primarily concerned with putting children into correctional schools. The main purpose of the juvenile court is to save the child and to develop his emotional make-up in order that he can grow up to be a decent and well-balanced citizen. The system of probation is the means whereby the court seeks to accomplish these goals.

9. According to this paragraph, police work is an important part of a program to prevent juvenile delinquency because

   A. social work is no longer considered important in juvenile delinquency prevention
   B. police officers are the first to have contact with the delinquent
   C. police officers jail the offender in order to be able to change his attitude toward society and the law
   D. it is the first step in placing the delinquent in jail

10. According to this paragraph, the CHIEF purpose of the juvenile court is to

    A. punish the child for his offense
    B. select a suitable correctional school for the delinquent
    C. use available means to help the delinquent become a better person
    D. provide psychiatric care for the delinquent

11. According to this paragraph, the juvenile court directs the development of delinquents under its care CHIEFLY by

    A. placing the child under probation
    B. sending the child to a correctional school
    C. keeping the delinquent in prison
    D. returning the child to his home

Questions 12-14.

DIRECTIONS: Questions 12 through 14 are to be answered on the basis of the following paragraph.

An assassination is an act that consists of a plotted, attempted or actual murder of a prominent political figure by an individual who performs this act in other than a governmental role. This definition draws a distinction between political execution and assassination. An execution may be regarded as a political killing, but it is initiated by the organs of the state, while an assassination can always be characterized as an illegal act. A prominent figure must be the target of the killing, since the killing of lesser members of the political community is included within a wider category of internal political turmoil, namely, terrorism. Assassination is also to be distinguished from homicide. The target of the aggressive act must be a political figure rather than a private person. The killing of a prime minister by a member of an insurrectionist or underground group clearly qualifies as an assassination. So does an act by a deranged individual who tries to kill not just any individual, but the individual in his political role - as President, for example.

12. Assume that a nationally prominent political figure is charged with treason by the state, tried in a court of law, found guilty, and hanged by the state. According to the above passage, it would be MOST appropriate to regard his death as a(n)

    A. assassination
    B. execution
    C. aggressive act
    D. homicide

13. According to the above passage, which of the following statements is CORRECT?

    A. The assassination of a political figure is an illegal act.
    B. A private person may be the target of an assassination attempt.
    C. The killing of an obscure member of a political community is considered an assassination event.
    D. An execution may not be regarded as a political killing.

14. Of the following, the MOST appropriate title for this passage would be

    A. ASSASSINATION - LEGAL ASPECTS
    B. POLITICAL CAUSES OF ASSASSINATION
    C. ASSASSINATION - A DEFINITION
    D. CATEGORIES OF ASSASSINATION

Questions 15-17.

DIRECTIONS: Questions 15 through 17 are to be answered SOLELY on the basis of the following paragraph.

All applicants for an original license to operate a catering establishment shall be fingerprinted. This shall include the officers, employees, and stockholders of the company and the members of a partnership. In case of a change, by addition or substitution, occurring during the existence of a license, the person added or substituted shall be fingerprinted. However, in the case of a hotel containing more than 200 rooms, only the officer or manager filing the application is required to be fingerprinted. The police commissioner may also, at his discretion, exempt the employees and stockholders of any company. The fingerprints shall be taken on one copy of Form C.E. 20 and on two copies of C.E. 21. One copy of Form C.E. 21 shall accompany the application. Fingerprints are not required with a renewal application.

15. According to the above paragraph, an employee added to the payroll of a licensed catering establishment which is not in a hotel must be fingerprinted

    A. always
    B. unless he has been previously fingerprinted for another license
    C. unless exempted by the police commissioner
    D. only if he is the manager or an officer of the company

16. According to the above paragraph, it would be MOST accurate to state that

    A. Form C.E. 20 must accompany a renewal application
    B. Form C.E. 21 must accompany all applications
    C. Form C.E. 21 must accompany an original application
    D. both Forms C.E. 20 and C.E. 21 must accompany all applications

17. A hotel of 270 rooms has applied for a license to operate a catering establishment on the premises.
   According to the instructions for fingerprinting given in the above paragraph, the _____ shall be fingerprinted.

   A. officers, employees, and stockholders
   B. officers and the manager
   C. employees
   D. officer filing the application

17._____

Questions 18-24.

DIRECTIONS: Read the following two paragraphs. Then answer the questions by selecting the answer
   A - if the paragraphs indicate it is TRUE
   B - if the paragraphs indicate it is PROBABLY true
   C - if the paragraphs indicate it is PROBABLY false
   D - if the paragraphs indicate it is FALSE

The fallacy underlying what some might call the eighteenth and nineteenth century misconceptions of the nature of scientific investigations seems to lie in a mistaken analogy. Those who said they were investigating the structure of the universe imagined themselves as the equivalent of the early explorers and map makers. The explorers of the fifteenth and sixteenth centuries had opened up new worlds with the aid of imperfect maps; in their accounts of distant lands, there had been some false and many ambiguous statements. But by the time everyone came to believe the world was round, the maps of distant continents were beginning to assume a fairly consistent pattern. By the seventeenth century, methods of measuring space and time had laid the foundations for an accurate geography.

On this basic issue there is far from complete agreement among philosophers *of* science today. You can, each of you, choose your side and find highly distinguished advocates for the point of view you have selected. However, in view of the revolution in physics, anyone who now asserts that science is an exploration of the universe must be prepared to shoulder a heavy burden of proof. To my mind, the analogy between the map maker and the scientist is false. A scientific theory is not even the first approximation to a map; it is not a need; it is a policy -- an economical and fruitful guide to action, by scientific investigators.

18. The author thinks that 18th and 19th century science followed the same technique as the 15th century geographers.

18._____

19. The author disagrees with the philosophers who are labelled realists.

19._____

20. The author believes there is a permanent structure to the universe.

20._____

21. A scientific theory is an economical guide to exploring what cannot be known absolutely.

21._____

22. Philosophers of science accept the relativity implications of recent research in physics.

22._____

23. It is a matter of time and effort before modern scientists will be as successful as the geographers.

23._____

24. The author believes in an indeterminate universe.

24._____

25. Borough X reports that its police force makes fewer arrests per thousand persons than any of the other boroughs.
From this statement, it is MOST probable that

   A. sufficient information has not been given to warrant any conclusion
   B. the police force of Borough X is less efficient
   C. fewer crimes are being committed in Borough X
   D. fewer crimes are being reported in Borough X

KEY (CORRECT ANSWERS)

1. A
2. B
3. D
4. C
5. D

6. A
7. A
8. D
9. B
10. C

11. A
12. B
13. A
14. C
15. C

16. C
17. D
18. D
19. B
20. D

21. A
22. D
23. D
24. B
25. A

TEST 2

DIRECTIONS: Each question or incomplete statement is followed by several suggested answers or completions. Select the one that BEST answers the question or completes the statement. *PRINT THE LETTER OF THE CORRECT ANSWER IN THE SPACE AT THE RIGHT.*

Questions 1-2.

DIRECTIONS: Questions 1 and 2 are to be answered on the basis of the information given in the following passage.

Assume that a certain agency is having a problem at one of its work locations because a sizable portion of the staff at that location is regularly tardy in reporting to work. The management of the agency is primarily concerned about eliminating the problem and is not yet too concerned about taking any disciplinary action. An investigator is assigned to investigate to determine, if possible, what might be causing this problem.

After several interviews, the investigator sees that low morale created by poor supervision at this location is at least part of the problem. In addition, there is a problem of tardiness and lack of interest.

1. Given the goals of the investigation and assuming that the investigator was using a non-directive approach in this interview, of the following, the investigator's MOST effective response should be:

    A. You know, you are building a bad record of tardiness
    B. Can you tell me more about this situation?
    C. What kind of person is your superior?
    D. Do you think you are acting fairly towards the agency by being late so often?

2. Given the goals of the investigation and assuming the investigator was using a directed approach in this interview, of the following, the investigator's response should be:

    A. That doesn't seem like much of an excuse to me
    B. What do you mean by saying that you've lost interest?
    C. What problems are there with the supervision you are getting?
    D. How do you think your tardiness looks in your personnel record?

Questions 3-5.

DIRECTIONS: Questions 3 through 5 are to be answered SOLELY on the basis of the following passage.

As investigators, we are more concerned with the utilitarian than the philosophical aspects of ethics and ethical standards, procedures, and conduct. As a working consideration, we might view ethics as the science of doing the right thing at the right time in the right manner in conformity with the normal, everyday standards imposed by society; and in conformity with the judgment society would be expected to make concerning the rightness or wrongness of what we have done.

An ethical code might be considered a basic set of rules and regulations to which we must conform in the performance of investigative duties. Ethical standards, procedures, and conduct might be considered the logical workings of our ethical code in its everyday application to our work. Ethics also necessarily involves morals and morality. We must eventually answer the self-imposed question of whether or not we have acted in the right way in conducting our investigative activities in their individual and total aspects.

3. Of the following, the MOST suitable title for the above passage is

   A. THE IMPORTANCE OF RULES FOR INVESTIGATORS
   B. THE BASIC PHILOSOPHY OF A LAWFUL SOCIETY
   C. SCIENTIFIC ASPECTS OF INVESTIGATIONS
   D. ETHICAL GUIDELINES FOR THE CONDUCT OF INVESTIGATIONS

4. According to the above passage, ethical considerations for investigators involve

   A. special standards that are different from those which apply to the rest of society
   B. practices and procedures which cannot be evaluated by others
   C. individual judgments by investigators of the appropriateness of their own actions
   D. regulations which are based primarily upon a philosophical approach

5. Of the following, the author's PRINCIPAL purpose in writing the above passage seems to have been to

   A. emphasize the importance of self-criticism in investigative activities
   B. explain the relationship that exists between ethics and investigative conduct
   C. reduce the amount of unethical conduct in the area of investigations
   D. seek recognition by his fellow investigators for his academic treatment of the subject matter

Questions 6-8.

DIRECTIONS: Questions 6 through 8 are to be answered SOLELY on the basis of the following passage.

The investigator must remember that acts of omission can be as effective as acts of commission in affecting the determination of disputed issues. Acts of omission, such as failure to obtain available information or failure to verify dubious information, manifest themselves in miscarriages of justice and erroneous adjudications. An incomplete investigation is an erroneous investigation because a conclusion predicated upon inadequate facts is based on quicksand.

When an investigator throws up his hands and admits defeat, the reason for this action does not necessarily lie in his possible laziness and ineptitude. It is more likely that the investigator has made his conclusions after exhausting only those avenues of investigation of which he is aware. He has exercised good faith in his belief that nothing else can be done.

This tendency must be overcome by all investigators if they are to operate at top efficiency. If no suggestion for new or additional action can be found in any authority, an investigator should use his own initiative to cope with a given situation. No investigator should ever hesitate to set precedents. It is far better in the final analysis to attempt difficult solutions, even if the chances of error are obviously present, than it is to take refuge in the spineless adage: If you don't do anything, you don't do it wrong.

6. Of the following, the MOST suitable title for the above passage is
   A. THE NEED FOR RESOURCEFULNESS IN INVESTIGATIONS
   B. PROCEDURES FOR COMPLETING AN INVESTIGATION
   C. THE DEVELOPMENT OF STANDARDS FOR INVESTIGATORS
   D. THE CAUSES OF INCOMPLETE INVESTIGATIONS

7. Of the following, the author of this passage considers that the LEAST important consideration in developing new investigative methods is
   A. efficiency
   B. caution
   C. imagination
   D. thoroughness

8. According to this passage, which of the following statements is INCORRECT?
   A. Lack of creativity may lead to erroneous investigations.
   B. Acts of omission are sometimes as harmful as acts of commission.
   C. Some investigators who give up on a case are lazy or inept.
   D. An investigator who gives up on a case is usually not acting in good faith.

Questions 9-12.

DIRECTIONS: Questions 9 through 12 are to be answered on the basis of the following paragraph.

A report of investigation should not be weighed down by a mass of information which is hardly material or only remotely relevant, or which fails to prove a point, clarify an issue, or aid the inquiry even by indirection. Some investigative agencies, however, value the report for its own sake, considering it primarily as a justification of the investigative activity contained therein. Every step is listed to show that no logical measure has been overlooked and to demonstrate that the reporting agent is beyond criticism. This system serves to provide reviewing authorities with a ready means of checking subordinates and provides order, method, and routine to investigative activity. In addition, it may offer supervisors and investigators a sense of security; the investigator would know within fairly exact limits what is expected of him and the supervisor may be comforted by the knowledge that his organization may not be reasonably criticized in a particular case on the grounds of obvious omissions or inertia. To the state's attorney and others, however, who must take administrative action on the basis of the report, the irrelevant and immaterial information thwarts the purpose of the investigation by dimming the issues and obscuring the facts that are truly contributory to the proof.

9. From the point of view of the supervising investigator, a drawback of having the investigator prepare the type of report which the state's attorney would like is that it
   A. gives a biased and one-sided view of what should have been an impartial investigation
   B. has only limited usefulness as an indication that all proper investigative methods were used by the investigator
   C. overlooks logical measures, removing the responsibility for taking those measures which the investigator should otherwise have been expected to take
   D. sets fairly exact limits to what the supervisor can expect of the investigator

10. District attorneys do not like reports of investigations in which every step is listed because

   A. their administrative action is then based on irrelevant and immaterial information
   B. it places the investigator beyond criticism, making the responsibility of the district attorney that much greater
   C. of the difficulty of finding among the mass of information the portion which is meaningful and useful
   D. the inclusion of indirect or hardly material information is not in accord with the order in which the steps were taken

11. As expressed in the above paragraph, the type of report which MOST investigators prefer to prepare is

   A. a step-by-step account of their activities, including both fruitful and unfruitful steps, since to do so provides order and method and gives them a sense of security
   B. not made clear, even though current practice in some agencies is to include every step taken in the investigation
   C. one from which useless and confusing information has been excluded because it is not helpful and is poor practice
   D. one not weighed down by a mass of irrelevant information but one which shows within fairly exact limits what was expected of them

12. With regard to the type of information which an investigator should include in his report, the above paragraph expresses the opinion that

   A. it is best to include in the report only that information which supports the conclusions of the investigator
   B. reports should include all relevant and clarifying information and exclude information on inquiries which had no productive result
   C. reports should include sufficient information to demonstrate that the investigator has been properly attending to his duties and all the information which contributes toward proof of what occurred in the case
   D. the most logical thing to do is to list every step in the investigation and its result

Questions 13-17.

DIRECTIONS: Questions 13 through 17 are to be answered SOLELY on the basis of the following paragraph.

Those statutes of limitations which are of interest to a claim examiner are the ones affecting third party actions brought against an insured covered by a liability policy of insurance. Such statutes of limitations are legislative enactments limiting the time within which such actions at law may be brought. Research shows that such periods differ from state to state and vary within the states with the type of action brought. The laws of the jurisdiction in which the action is brought govern and determine the period within which the action may be instituted, regardless of the place of the cause of action or the residence of the parties at the time of cause of action. The period of time set by a statute of limitations for a tort action starts from the moment the alleged tort is committed. The period usually extends continuously until its expiration, upon which legal action may no longer be brought. However, there is a suspension of the running of the period when a defendant has concealed himself in order to avoid service of legal process. The suspension continues until the defendant discontinues his concealment and then the period starts running again. A defendant may, by his agreement or conduct, be legally barred from asserting the statute of limitations as a defense to an action. The insurance carrier for the defendant may, by the misrepresentation of the claims man, cause such a bar against use of the statute of limitations by the defendant. If the claim examiner of the insurance carrier has by his conduct or assertion lulled the plaintiff into a false sense of security by false representations, the defendant may be barred from setting up the statute of limitations as a defense.

13. Of the following, the MOST suitable title for the above paragraph is

    A. FRAUDULENT USE OF THE STATUTE OF LIMITATIONS
    B. PARTIES AT INTEREST IN A LAWSUIT
    C. THE CLAIM EXAMINER AND THE LAW
    D. THE STATUTE OF LIMITATIONS IN CLAIMS WORK

14. The period of time during which a third party action may be brought against an insured covered by a liability policy depends on

    A. the laws of the jurisdiction in which the action is brought
    B. where the cause of action which is the subject of the suit took place
    C. where the claimant lived at the time of the cause of action
    D. where the insured lived at the time of the cause of action

15. Time limits in third party actions which are set by the statutes of limitations described above are

    A. determined by claimant's place of residence at start of action
    B. different in a state for different actions
    C. the same from state to state for the same type of action
    D. the same within a state regardless of type of action

16. According to the above paragraph, grounds which may be legally used to prevent a defendant from using the statute of limitations as a defense in the action described are

    A. defendant's agreement or concealment; a charge of liability for death and injury
    B. defendant's agreement or conduct; misrepresentation by the claims man
    C. fraudulent concealment by claim examiner; a charge of liability for death or injury; defendant's agreement
    D. misrepresentation by claim examiner of carrier; defendant's agreement; plaintiff's concealment

17. Suppose an alleged tort was commited on January 1, 2008 and that the period in which action may be taken is set at three years by the statute of limitations. Suppose further that the defendant, in order to avoid service of legal process, had concealed himself from July 1, 2010 through December 31, 2010.
    In this case, the defendant may not use the statute of limitations as a defense unless action is brought by the plaintiff after _____, 2011.

    A. January 1   B. February 28
    C. June 30   D. August 1

Questions 18-20.

DIRECTIONS: Questions 18 through 20 are to be answered SOLELY on the basis of information contained in the following passage.

No matter how well the interrogator adjusts himself to the witness and how precisely he induces the witness to describe his observations, mistakes still can be made. The mistakes made by an experienced interrogator may be comparatively few, but as far as the witness is concerned, his path is full of pitfalls. Modern *witness psychology* has shown that even the most honest and trustworthy witnesses are apt to make grave mistakes in good faith. It is, therefore, necessary that the interrogator get an idea of the weak links in the testimony in order to check up on them in the event that something appears to be strange or not quite satisfactory.

Unfortunately, modern witness psychology does not yet offer any means of directly testing the credibility of testimony. It lacks precision and method, in spite of worthwhile attempts on the part of learned men. At the same time, witness psychology, through the gathering of many experiences concerning the weaknesses of human testimony, has been of invaluable service. It shows clearly that only evidence of a technical nature has absolute value as proof.

Testimony may be separated into the following stages: (1) perception, (2) observation, (3) mind fixation of the observed occurrences, in which fantasy, association of ideas, and personal judgment participate, and (4) expression in oral or written form, where the testimony is transferred from one witness to another or to the interrogator.

Each of these stages offers innumerable possibilities for the distortion of testimony.

18. The above passage indicates that having witnesses talk to each other before testifying is a practice which is GENERALLY   18._____

    A. *desirable,* since the witnesses will be able to correct each other's errors in observation before testimony
    B. *undesirable,* since the witnesses will collaborate on one story to tell the investigator
    C. *undesirable,* since one witness may distort his testimony because of what another witness may erroneously say
    D. *desirable,* since witnesses will become aware of discrepancies in their own testimony and can point out the discrepancies to the investigator

19. According to the above passage, the one of the following which would be the MOST reliable for use as evidence would be the testimony of a   19._____

    A. handwriting expert about a signature on a forged check
    B. trained police officer about the identity of a criminal
    C. laboratory technician about an accident he has observed
    D. psychologist who has interviewed any witnesses who relate conflicting stories

20. Concerning the validity of evidence, it is CLEAR from the above passage that   20._____

    A. only evidence of a technical nature is at all valuable
    B. the testimony of witnesses is so flawed that it is usually valueless

C. an investigator, by knowing modern witness psychology, will usually be able to perceive mistaken testimony
D. an investigator ought to expect mistakes in even the most reliable witness testimony

Questions 21-22.

DIRECTIONS: Questions 21 and 22 are to be answered SOLELY on the basis of the information contained in the passage below. This passage represents a report prepared by a subordinate superior concerning a school demonstration.

On April 1, a group of students, each holding an anti-apartheid sign, was involved in a demonstration on the grounds of Columbia University. The students began by locking the main entrance doors to the Administration Building and preventing faculty and students from entering or leaving the building.

The C.O. of the police detail at the scene requested additional assistance of four female detectives, an Emergency Service van, and a police photographer equipped with a Polaroid instamatic camera.

When the additional assistance arrived, the Commanding Officer directed the students to disperse. His justification for the order was that the demonstrators were violating the rights of other students and certain faculty members by denying them access to the Administration Building. The students ignored the order to disperse and the Commanding Officer of the police detail ordered them to be removed.

Another group of students who had been standing in front of the library were sympathetic toward the demonstrators and charged the police. Several police officers were injured during the ensuing hostilities.

Eventually, order was restored. That evening, the television coverage presented a neutral and fairly accurate account of the incident.

21. Which of the following statements MOST clearly and accurately reflects the contents of the report? 21.___

　　A. A large group of students, all of whom were holding anti-apartheid signs, was involved in a demonstration on the grounds of Columbia University.
　　B. A large group of students, some of whom were holding anti-apartheid signs, was involved in a demonstration on the grounds of Columbia University.
　　C. Each of a group of Columbia students carrying anti-apartheid signs was involved in a demonstration on the grounds of Columbia University.
　　D. Each of the students involved in the demonstration on the grounds of Columbia University was holding an anti-apartheid sign.

22. Which of the following statements MOST clearly and accurately reflects the contents of the report? 22.___

A. The Commanding Officer of the police detail justified his order that the demonstrators disperse when the additional assistance arrived.
B. When the additional assistance arrived, the Commanding Officer of the police detail justified his order that the demonstrators disperse.
C. The Commanding Officer of the police detail directed the students to disperse when the additional assistance arrived.
D. The Commanding Officer of the police detail requested additional assistance because the student demonstrators were violating the rights of other students and certain faculty members.

23. Which of the following statements MOST clearly and accurately reflects the contents of the report?

    A. Another group of students charged the police because they were sympathetic toward the police.
    B. The evening television coverage of the demonstration was fair and accurate.
    C. The group of students who had been standing in front of the library was sympathetic toward the demonstrators.
    D. Several police officers were injured during the hostilities which took place in front of the library.

Questions 24-25.

DIRECTIONS: Questions 24 and 25 are to be answered SOLELY on the basis of the information given in the following paragraph.

Credibility of a witness is usually governed by his character and is evidenced by his reputation for truthfulness. Personal or financial reasons or a criminal record may cause a witness to give false information to avoid being implicated. Age, sex, physical and mental abnormalities, loyalty, revenge, social and economic status, indulgence in alcohol, and the influence of other persons are some of the many factors which may affect the accuracy, willingness, or ability with which witnesses observe, interpret, and describe occurrences.

24. According to the above paragraph, a witness may, for personal reasons, give wrong information about an occurrence because he

    A. wants to protect his reputation for truthfulness
    B. wants to embarrass the investigator
    C. doesn't want to become involved
    D. doesn't really remember what happened

25. According to the above paragraph, factors which influence the witness of an occurrence may affect

    A. not only what he tells about it but what he was able and wanted to see of it
    B. only what he describes and interprets later but not what he actually sees at the time of the event
    C. what he sees but not what he describes
    D. what he is willing to see but not what he is able to see

KEY (CORRECT ANSWERS)

1.	B	11.	B
2.	C	12.	B
3.	D	13.	D
4.	C	14.	A
5.	B	15.	B
6.	A	16.	B
7.	B	17.	C
8.	D	18.	C
9.	B	19.	A
10.	C	20.	D

21. D
22. C
23. C
24. C
25. A

PREPARING WRITTEN MATERIAL

EXAMINATION SECTION

TEST 1

DIRECTIONS: Each question or incomplete statement is followed by several suggested answers or completions. Select the one that BEST answers the question or completes the statement. *PRINT THE LETTER OF THE CORRECT ANSWER IN THE SPACE AT THE RIGHT.*

1. The one of the following sentences which is LEAST acceptable from the viewpoint of correct usage is:
    A. The police thought the fugitive to be him.
    B. The criminals set a trap for whoever would fall into it.
    C. It is ten years ago since the fugitive fled from the city.
    D. The lecturer argued that criminals are usually cowards.
    E. The police removed four bucketfuls of earth from the scene of the crime.

1.____

2. The one of the following sentences which is LEAST acceptable from the viewpoint of correct usage is:
    A. The patrolman scrutinized the report with great care.
    B. Approaching the victim of the assault, two bruises were noticed by the patrolman.
    C. As soon as I had broken down the door, I stepped into the room.
    D. I observed the accused loitering near the building, which was closed at the time.
    E. The storekeeper complained that his neighbor was guilty of violating a local ordinance.

2.____

3. The one of the following sentences which is LEAST acceptable from the viewpoint of correct usage is:
    A. I realized immediately that he intended to assault the woman, so I disarmed him.
    B. It was apparent that Mr. Smith's explanation contained many inconsistencies.
    C. Despite the slippery condition of the street, he managed to stop the vehicle before injuring the child.
    D. Not a single one of them wish, despite the damage to property, to make a formal complaint.
    E. The body was found lying on the floor.

3.____

4. The one of the following sentences which contains NO error in usage is:
    A. After the robbers left, the proprietor stood tied in his chair for about two hours before help arrived.
    B. In the cellar I found the watchman's hat and coat.
    C. The persons living in adjacent apartments stated that they had heard no unusual noises.

4.____

D. Neither a knife or any firearms were found in the room.
E. Walking down the street, the shouting of the crowd indicated that something was wrong.

5. The one of the following sentences which contains NO error in usage is:
   A. The policeman lay a firm hand on the suspect's shoulder.
   B. It is true that neither strength nor agility are the most important requirement for a good patrolman.
   C. Good citizens constantly strive to do more than merely comply the restraints imposed by society.
   D. No decision was made as to whom the prize should be awarded.
   E. Twenty years is considered a severe sentence for a felony.

6. Which of the following sentences is NOT expressed in standard English usage?
   A. The victim reached a pay-phone booth and manages to call police headquarters.
   B. By the time the call was received, the assailant had left the scene.
   C. The victim has been a respected member of the community for the past eleven years.
   D. Although the lighting was bad and the shadows were deep, the storekeeper caught sight of the attacker.
   E. Additional street lights have since been installed, and the patrols have been strengthened.

7. Which of the following sentences is NOT expressed in standard English usage?
   A. The judge upheld the attorney's right to question the witness about the missing glove.
   B. To be absolutely fair to all parties is the jury's chief responsibility.
   C. Having finished the report, a loud noise in the next room startled the sergeant.
   D. The witness obviously enjoyed having played a part in the proceedings.
   E. The sergeant planned to assign the case to whoever arrived first.

8. In which of the following sentences is a word misused?
   A. As a matter of principle, the captain insisted that the suspect's partner be brought for questioning.
   B. The principle suspect had been detained at the station house for most of the day.
   C. The principal in the crime had no previous criminal record, but his closest associate had been convicted of felonies on two occasions.
   D. The interest payments had been made promptly, but the firm had been drawing upon the principal for these payments.
   E. The accused insisted that his high school principal would furnish him a character reference.

9. Which of the following statements is ambiguous? 9.____
   A. Mr. Sullivan explained why Mr. Johnson had been dismissed from his job.
   B. The storekeeper told the patrolman he had made a mistake.
   C. After waiting three hours, the patients in the doctor's office were sent home.
   D. The janitor's duties were to maintain the building in good shape and to answer tenants' complaints.
   E. The speed limit should, in my opinion, be raised to sixty miles an hour on that stretch of road.

10. In which of the following is the punctuation or capitalization faulty? 10.____
    A. The accident occurred at an intersection in the Kew Gardens section of Queens, near the bus stop.
    B. The sedan, not the convertible, was struck in the side.
    C. Before any of the patrolmen had left the police car received an important message from headquarters.
    D. The dog that had been stolen was returned to his master, John Dempsey, who lived in East Village.
    E. The letter had been sent to 12 Hillside Terrace, Rutland, Vermont 05702.

Questions 11-25.

DIRECTIONS: Questions 11 through 25 are to be answered in accordance with correct English usage; that is, standard English rather than nonstandard or substandard. Nonstandard and substandard English includes words or expressions usually classified as slang, dialect, illiterate, etc., which are not generally accepted as correct in current written communication. Standard English also requires clarity, proper punctuation and capitalization and appropriate use of words. Write the letter of the sentence NOT expressed in standard English usage in the space at the right.

11. A. There were three witnesses to the accident. 11.____
    B. At least three witnesses were found to testify for the plaintiff.
    C. Three of the witnesses who took the stand was uncertain about the defendant's competence to drive.
    D. Only three witnesses came forward to testify for the plaintiff.
    E. The three witnesses to the accident were pedestrians.

12. A. The driver had obviously drunk too many martinis before leaving for home. 12.____
    B. The boy who drowned had swum in these same waters many times before.
    C. The petty thief had stolen a bicycle from a private driveway before he was apprehended.
    D. The detectives had brung in the heroin shipment they intercepted.
    E. The passengers had never ridden in a converted bus before.

13. A. Between you and me, the new platoon plan sounds like a good idea.
    B. Money from an aunt's estate was left to his wife and he.
    C. He and I were assigned to the same patrol for the first time in two months.
    D. Either you or he should check the front door of that store.
    E. The captain himself was not sure of the witness's reliability.

13.____

14. A. The alarm had scarcely begun to ring when the explosion occurred.
    B. Before the firemen arrived at the scene, the second story had been destroyed.
    C. Because of the dense smoke and heat, the firemen could hardly approach the now-blazing structure.
    D. According to the patrolman's report, there wasn't nobody in the store when the explosion occurred.
    E. The sergeant's suggestion was not at all unsound, but no one agreed with him.

14.____

15. A. The driver and the passenger they were both found to be intoxicated.
    B. The driver and the passenger talked slowly and not too clearly.
    C. Neither the driver nor his passengers were able to give a coherent account of the accident.
    D. In a corner of the room sat the passenger, quietly dozing.
    E. the driver finally told a strange and unbelievable story, which the passenger contradicted.

15.____

16. A. Under the circumstances I decided not to continue my examination of the premises.
    B. There are many difficulties now not comparable with those existing in 1960.
    C. Friends of the accused were heard to announce that the witness had better been away on the day of the trial.
    D. The two criminals escaped in the confusion that followed the explosion.
    E. The aged man was struck by the considerateness of the patrolman's offer.

16.____

17. A. An assemblage of miscellaneous weapons lay on the table.
    B. Ample opportunities were given to the defendant to obtain counsel.
    C. The speaker often alluded to his past experience with youthful offenders in the armed forces.
    D. The sudden appearance of the truck aroused my suspicions.
    E. Her studying had a good affect on her grades in high school.

17.____

18. A. He sat down in the theater and began to watch the movie.
    B. The girl had ridden horses since she was four years old.
    C. Application was made on behalf of the prosecutor to cite the witness for contempt.
    D. The bank robber, with his two accomplices, were caught in the act.
    E. His story is simply not credible.

18.____

19. A. The angry boy said that he did not like those kind of friends.
    B. The merchant's financial condition was so precarious that he felt he must avail himself of any offer of assistance.
    C. He is apt to promise more than he can perform.
    D. Looking at the messy kitchen, the housewife felt like crying.
    E. A clerk was left in charge of the stolen property.

19._____

20. A. His wounds were aggravated by prolonged exposure to sub-freezing temperatures.
    B. The prosecutor remarked that the witness was not averse to changing his story each time he was interviewed.
    C. The crime pattern indicated that the burglars were adapt in the handling of explosives.
    D. His rigid adherence to a fixed plan brought him into renewed conflict with his subordinates.
    E. He had anticipated that the sentence would be delivered by noon.

20._____

21. A. The whole arraignment procedure is badly in need of revision.
    B. After his glasses were broken in the fight, he would of gone to the optometrist if he could.
    C. Neither Tom nor Jack brought his lunch to work.
    D. He stood aside until the quarrel was over.
    E. A statement in the psychiatrist's report disclosed that the probationer vowed to have his revenge.

21._____

22. A. His fiery and intemperate speech to the striking employees fatally affected any chance of a future reconciliation.
    B. The wording of the statute has been variously construed.
    C. The defendant's attorney, speaking in the courtroom, called the official a demagogue who contempuously disregarded the judge's orders.
    D. The baseball game is likely to be the most exciting one this year.
    E. The mother divided the cookies among her two children.

22._____

23. A. There was only a bed and a dresser in the dingy room.
    B. John was one of the few students that have protested the new rule.
    C. It cannot be argued that the child's testimony is negligible; it is, on the contrary, of the greatest importance.
    D. The basic criterion for clearance was so general that officials resolved any doubts in favor of dismissal.
    E. Having just returned from a long vacation, the officer found the city unbearably hot.

23._____

24. A. The librarian ought to give more help to small children.
    B. The small boy was criticized by the teacher because he often wrote careless.
    C. It was generally doubted whether the women would permit the use of her apartment for intelligence operations.
    D. The probationer acts differently every time the officer visits him.
    E. Each of the newly appointed officers has 12 years of service.

24._____

25.
- A. The North is the most industrialized region in the country.
- B. L. Patrick Gray 3d, the bureau's acting director, stated that, while "rehabilitation is fine" for some convicted criminals, "it is a useless gesture for those who resist every such effort."
- C. Careless driving, faulty mechanism, narrow or badly kept roads all play their part in causing accidents.
- D. The childrens' books were left in the bus.
- E. It was a matter of internal security; consequently, he felt no inclination to rescind his previous order.

25.____

KEY (CORRECT ANSWERS)

1.	C		11.	C
2.	B		12.	D
3.	D		13.	B
4.	C		14.	D
5.	E		15.	A
6.	A		16.	C
7.	C		17.	E
8.	B		18.	D
9.	B		19.	A
10.	C		20.	C

21. B
22. E
23. B
24. B
25. D

TEST 2

DIRECTIONS: Each question or incomplete statement is followed by several suggested answers or completions. Select the one that BEST answers the question or completes the statement. *PRINT THE LETTER OF THE CORRECT ANSWER IN THE SPACE AT THE RIGHT.*

Questions 1-6.

DIRECTIONS: Each of Questions 1 through 6 consists of a statement which contains a word (one of those underlined) that is either incorrectly used because it is not in keeping with the meaning the quotation is evidently intended to convey, or is misspelled. There is only one INCORRECT word in each quotation. Of the four underlined words, determine if the first one should be replaced by the word lettered A, the second replaced by the word lettered B, the third replaced by the word lettered C, or the fourth replaced by the word lettered D.

1. Whether one depends on fluorescent or artificial light or both, adequate standards should be maintained by means of systematic tests.
   A. natural   B. safeguards   C. established   D. routine

2. A police officer has to be prepared to assume his knowledge as a social scientist in the community.
   A. forced   B. role   C. philosopher   D. street

3. It is practically impossible to indicate whether a sentence is too long simply by measuring its length.
   A. almost   B. tell   C. very   D. guessing

4. Strong leaders are required to organize a community for delinquency prevention and for dissemination of organized crime and drug addiction.
   A. tactics   B. important   C. control   D. meetings

5. The demonstrators who were taken to the Criminal Courts building in Manhattan (because it was large enough to accommodate them), contended that the arrests were unwarranted.
   A. demonstraters   B. Manhatten
   C. accomodate   D. unwarranted

6. They were guaranteed a calm atmosphere, free from harassment, which would be conducive to quiet consideration of the indictments.
   A. guarenteed   B. atmspher
   C. harassment   D. inditements

1.____
2.____
3.____
4.____
5.____
6.____

Questions 7-11.

DIRECTIONS: Each of Questions 7 through 11 consists of a statement containing four words in capital letters. One of these words in capital letters is not in keeping with the meaning which the statement is evidently intended to carry. The four words in capital letters in each statement are reprinted after the statement. Print the capital letter preceding the one of the four words which does MOST to spoil the true meaning of the statement in the space at the right.

7. Retirement and pension systems are essential not only to provide employees with with a means of support in the future, but also to prevent longevity and CHARITABLE considerations from UPSETTING the PROMOTIONAL opportunities RETIRED members of the career service.   7.____
   A. charitable   B. upsetting   C. promotional   D. retired

8. Within each major DIVISION in a properly set up public or private organization, provision is made so that each NECESSARY activity is CARED for and lines of authority and responsibility are clear-cut and INFINITE.   8.____
   A. division   B. necessary   C. cared   D. infinite

9. In public service, the scale of salaries paid must be INCIDENTAL to the services rendered, with due CONSIDERATION for the attraction of the desired MANPOWER and for the maintenance of a standard of living COMMENSURATE with the work to be performed.   9.____
   A. incidental   B. consideration
   C. manpower   D. commensurate

10. An understanding of the AIMS of an organization by the staff will AID greatly in increasing the DEMAND of the correspondence work of the office, and will to a large extent DETERMINE the nature of the correspondence.   10.____
    A. aims   B. aid   C. demand   D. determine

11. BECAUSE the Civil Service Commission strongly feels that the MERIT system is a key factor in the MAINTENANCE of democratic government, it has adopted as one of its major DEFENSES the progressive democratization of its own procedures in dealing with candidates for positions in the public service.   11.____
    A. Because   B. merit   C. maintenance   D. defenses

Questions 12-14.

DIRECTIONS: Questions 12 through 14 consist of one sentence each. Each sentence contains an incorrectly used word. First, decide which is the incorrectly used word. Then, from among the options given, decide which word, when substituted for the incorrectly used word, makes the meaning of the sentence clear.
EXAMPLE:
The U.S. national income exhibits a pattern of long term deflection.
   A. reflection   B. subjection   C. rejoicing   D. growth

The word *deflection* in the sentence does not convey the meaning the sentence evidently intended to convey. The word *growth* (Answer D), when substituted for the word *deflection*, makes the meaning of the sentence clear. Accordingly, the answer to the question is D.

12. The study commissioned by the joint committee fell compassionately short of the mark and would have to be redone.
    A. successfully B. insignificantly
    C. experimentally D. woefully

13. He will not idly exploit any violation of the provisions of the order.
    A. tolerate B. refuse C. construe D. guard

14. The defendant refused to be virile and bitterly protested service.
    A. irked B. feasible C. docile D. credible

Questions 15-25.

DIRECTIONS: Questions 15 through 25 consist of short paragraphs. Each paragraph contains one word which is INCORRECTLY used because it is NOT in keeping with the meaning of the paragraph. Find the word in each paragraph which is INCORRECTLY used and then select as the answer the suggested word which should be substituted for the incorrectly used word.

SAMPLE QUESTION:
In determining who is to do the work in your unit, you will have to decide just who does what from day to day. One of your lowest responsibilities is to assign work so that everybody gets a fair share and that everyone can do his part well.
    A. new B. old C. important D. performance

EXPLANATION:
The word which is NOT in keeping with the meaning of the paragraph is *lowest*. This is the INCORRECTLY used word. The suggested word *important* would be in keeping with the meaning of the paragraph and should be substituted for *lowest*. Therefore, the CORRECT answer is choice C.

15. If really good practice in the elimination of preventable injuries is to be achieved and held in any establishment, top management must refuse full and definite responsibility and must apply a good share of its attention to the task.
    A. accept B. avoidable C. duties D. problem

16. Recording the human face for identification is by no means the only service performed by the camera in the field of investigation. When the trial of any issue takes place, a word picture is sought to be distorted to the court of incidents, occurrences, or events which are in dispute.
    A. appeals B. description C. portrayed D. deranged

17. In the collection of physical evidence, it cannot be emphasized too strongly that a haphazard systematic search at the scene of the crime is vital. Nothing must be overlooked. Often the only leads in a case will come from the results of this search.
    A. important
    B. investigation
    C. proof
    D. thorough

    17.____

18. If an investigator has reason to suspect that the witness is mentally stable, or a habitual drunkard, he should leave no stone unturned in his investigation to determine if the witness was under the influence of liquor or drugs, or was mentally unbalanced either at the time of the occurrence to which he testified or at the time of the trial.
    A. accused
    B. clue
    C. deranged
    D. question

    18.____

19. The use of records is a valuable step in crime investigation and is the main reason every department should maintain accurate reports. Crimes are not committed through the use of departmental records alone but from the use of all records, of almost every type, wherever they may be found and whenever they give any incidental information regarding the criminal.
    A. accidental
    B. necessary
    C. reported
    D. solved

    19.____

20. In the years since passage of the Harrison Narcotic Act of 1914, making the possession of opium amphetamines illegal in most circumstances, drug use has become a subject of considerable scientific interest and investigation. There is at present a voluminous literature on drug use of various kinds.
    A. ingestion
    B. derivatives
    C. addiction
    D. opiates

    20.____

21. Of course, the fact that criminal laws are extremely patterned in definition does not mean that the majority of persons who violate them are dealt with as criminals. Quite the contrary, for a great many forbidden acts are voluntarily engaged in within situations of privacy and go unobserved and unreported.
    A. symbolic
    B. casual
    C. scientific
    D. broad-gauged

    21.____

22. The most punitive way to study punishment is to focus attention on the pattern of punitive action: to study how a penalty is applied, too study what is done to or taken from an offender.
    A. characteristic
    B. degrading
    C. objective
    D. distinguished

    22.____

23. The most common forms of punishment in times past have been death, physical torture, mutilation, branding, public humiliation, fines, forfeits of property, banishment, transportation, and imprisonment. Although this list is by no means differentiated, practically every form of punishment has had several variations and applications.
    A. specific
    B. simple
    C. exhaustive
    D. characteristic

    23.____

24. There is another important line of inference between ordinary and professional criminals, and that is the source from which they are recruited. The professional criminal seems to be drawn from legitimate employment and, in many instances, from parallel vocations or pursuits.
    A. demarcation   B. justification   C. superiority   D. reference

24.____

25. He took the position that the success of the program was insidious on getting additional revenue.
    A. reputed   B. contingent   C. failure   D. indeterminate

25.____

KEY (CORRECT ANSWERS)

1.	A	11.	D
2.	B	12.	D
3.	B	13.	A
4.	C	14.	C
5.	D	15.	A
6.	C	16.	C
7.	D	17.	D
8.	D	18.	C
9.	A	19.	D
10.	C	20.	B

21. D
22. C
23. C
24. A
25. B

TEST 3

DIRECTIONS: Each question or incomplete statement is followed by several suggested answers or completions. Select the one that BEST answers the question or completes the statement. *PRINT THE LETTER OF THE CORRECT ANSWER IN THE SPACE AT THE RIGHT.*

Questions 1-5.

DIRECTIONS: Questions 1 through 5 are to be answered on the basis of the following.

You are a supervising officer in an investigative unit. Earlier in the day, you directed Detectives Tom Dixon and Sal Mayo to investigate a reported assault and robbery in a liquor store within your area of jurisdiction.

Detective Dixon has submitted to you a preliminary investigative report containing the following information:

- At 1630 hours on 2/20, arrived at Joe's Liquor Store at 350 SW Avenue with Detective Mayo to investigate A & R.
- At store interviewed Rob Ladd, store manager, who stated that he and Joe Brown (store owner) had been stuck up about ten minutes prior to our arrival.
- Ladd described the robbers as male whites in their late teens or early twenties. Further stated that one of the robbers displayed what appeared to be an automatic pistol as he entered the store, and said, *Give us the money or we'll kill you*. Ladd stated that Brown then reached under the counter where he kept a loaded .38 caliber pistol. Several shots followed, and Ladd threw himself to the floor.
- The robbers fled, and Ladd didn't know if any money had been taken.
- At this point, Ladd realized that Brown was unconscious on the floor and bleeding from a head wound.
- Ambulance called by Ladd, and Brown was removed by same to General Hospital.
- Personally interviewed John White, 382 Dartmouth Place, who stated he was inside store at the time of occurrence. White states that he hid behind a wine display upon hearing someone say, *Give us the money*. He then heard shots and saw two young men run from the store to a yellow car parked at the curb. White was unable to further describe auto. States the taller of the two men drove the car away while the other sat on passenger side in front.
- Recovered three spent .38 caliber bullets from premises and delivered them to Crime Lab.
- To General Hospital at 1800 hours but unable to interview Brown, who was under sedation and suffering from shock and a laceration of the head.
- Alarm #12487 transmitted for car and occupants.
- Case Active.

Based solely on the contents of the preliminary investigation submitted by Detective Dixon, select one sentence from the following groups of sentences which is MOST accurate and is grammatically correct.

2 (#3)

1. A. Both robbers were armed.
    B. Each of the robbers were described as a male white.
    C. Neither robber was armed.
    D. Mr. Ladd stated that one of the robbers was armed.

    1.____

2. A. Mr. Brown fired three shots from his revolver.
    B. Mr. Brown was shot in the head by one of the robbers.
    C. Mr. Brown suffered a gunshot wound of the head during the course of the robbery.
    D. Mr. Brown was taken to General Hospital by ambulance.

    2.____

3. A. Shots were fired after one of the robbers said, *Give us the money or we'll kill you.*
    B. After one of the robbers demanded the money from Mr. Brown, he fired a shot.
    C. The preliminary investigation indicated that although Mr. Brown did not have a license for the gun, he was justified in using deadly physical force.
    D. Mr. Brown was interviewed at General Hospital.

    3.____

4. A. Each of the witnesses were customers in the store at the time of occurrence.
    B. Neither of the witnesses interviewed was the owner of the liquor store.
    C. Neither of the witnesses interviewed were the owner of the store.
    D. Neither of the witnesses was employed by Mr. Brown.

    4.____

5. A. Mr. Brown arrived at General Hospital at about 5:00 P.M.
    B. Neither of the robbers was injured during the robbery.
    C. The robbery occurred at 3:30 P.M. on February 10.
    D. One of the witnesses called the ambulance.

    5.____

Questions 6-10.

DIRECTIONS: Each of Questions 6 through 10 consists of information given in outline form and four sentences labeled A, B, C, and D. For each question, choose the one sentence which CORRECTLY expresses the information given in outline form and which also displays PROPER English usage.

6. Client's Name: Joanna Jones
    Number of Children: 3
    Client's Income: None
    Client's Marital Status: Single

    6.____

    A. Joanna Jones is an unmarried client with three children who have no income.
    B. Joanna Jones, who is single and has no income, a client she has three children.
    C. Joanna Jones, whose three children are clients, is single and has no income.
    D. Joanna Jones, who has three children, is an unmarried client with no income.

7. Client's Name: Bertha Smith
Number of Children: 2
Client's Rent: $1050 per month
Number of Rooms: 4

   A. Bertha Smith, a client, pays $1050 per month for her four rooms with two children.
   B. Client Bertha Smith has two children and pays $1050 per month for four rooms.
   C. Client Bertha Smith is paying $1050 per month for two children with four rooms.
   D. For four rooms and two children client Bertha Smith pays $1050 per month.

7._____

8. Name of Employee: Cynthia Dawes
Number of Cases Assigned: 9
Date Cases were Assigned: 12/16
Number of Assigned Cases Completed: 8

   A. On December 16, employee Cynthia Dawes was assigned nine cases; she has completed eight of these cases.
   B. Cynthia Dawes, employee on December 16, assigned nine cases, completed eight.
   C. Being employed on December 16, Cynthia Dawes completed eight of nine assigned cases.
   D. Employee Cynthia Dawes, she was assigned nine cases and completed eight, on December 16.

8._____

9. Place of Audit: Broadway Center
Names of Auditors: Paul Cahn, Raymond Perez
Date of Audit: 11/20
Number of Cases Audited: 41

   A. On November 20, at the Broadway Center 41 cases was audited by auditors Paul Cahn and Raymond Perez.
   B. Auditors Raymond Perez and Paul Cahn has audited 41 cases at the Broadway Center on November 20.
   C. At the Broadway Center, on November 20, auditors Paul Cahn and Raymond Perez audited 41 cases.
   D. Auditors Paul Cahn and Raymond Perez at the Broadway Center, on November 20, is auditing 41 cases.

9._____

10. Name of Client: Barbra Levine
Client's Monthly Income: $2100
Client's Monthly Expenses: $4520

    A. Barbra Levine is a client, her monthly income is $2100 and her monthly expenses is $4520.
    B. Barbra Levine's monthly income is $2100 and she is a client, with whose monthly expenses are $4520.

10._____

4 (#3)

C. Barbra Levine is a client whose monthly income is $2100 and whose monthly expenses are $4520.
D. Barbra Levine, a client, is with a monthly income which is $2100 and monthly expenses which are $4520.

Questions 11-13.

DIRECTIONS: Questions 11 through 13 involve several statements of fact presented in a very simple way. These statements of fact are followed by 4 choices which attempt to incorporate all of the facts into one logical statement which is properly constructed and grammatically correct.

11. I. Mr. Brown was sweeping the sidewalk in front of his house.
    II. He was sweeping it because it was dirty.
    III. He swept the refuse into the street.
    IV. Police Officer gave him a ticket.

    Which one of the following BEST presents the information given above?
    A. Because his sidewalk was dirty, Mr. Brown received a ticket from Officer Green when he swept the refuse into the street.
    B. Police Officer Green gave Mr. Brown a ticket because his sidewalk was dirty and he swept the refuse into the street.
    C. Police Officer Green gave Mr. Brown a ticket for sweeping refuse into the street because his sidewalk was dirty.
    D. Mr. Brown, who was sweeping refuse from his dirty sidewalk into the street, was given a ticket by Police Officer Green.

11._____

12. I. Sergeant Smith radioed for help.
    II. The sergeant did so because the crowd was getting larger.
    III. It was 10:00 A.M. when he made his call.
    IV. Sergeant Smith was not in uniform at the time of occurrence.

    Which one of the following BEST presents the information given above?
    A. Sergeant Smith, although not on duty at the time, radioed for help at 10 o'clock because the crowd was getting uglier.
    B. Although not in uniform, Sergeant Smith called for help at 10:00 A.M. because the crowd was getting uglier.
    C. Sergeant Smith radioed for help at 10:00 A.M. because the crowd was getting larger.
    D. Although he was not in uniform, Sergeant Smith radioed for help at 10:00 A.M. because the crowd was getting larger.

12._____

13. I. The payroll office is open on Fridays.
    II. Paychecks are distributed from 9:00 A.M. to 12 Noon.
    III. The office is open on Fridays because that's the only day the payroll staff is available.
    IV. It is open for the specified hours in order to permit employees to cash checks at the bank during lunch hour.

13._____

The choice below which MOST clearly and accurately presents the above idea is:
  A. Because the payroll office is open on Fridays from 9:00 A.M. to 12 Noon, employees can cash their checks when the payroll staff is available.
  B. Because the payroll staff is only available on Fridays until noon, employees can cash their checks during their lunch hour.
  C. Because the payroll staff is available only on Fridays, the office is open from 9:00 A.M. to 12 Noon to allow employees to cash their checks.
  D. Because of payroll staff availability, the payroll office is open on Fridays. It is open from 9:00 A.M. to 12 Noon so that distributed paychecks can be cashed at the bank while employees are on their lunch hour.

Questions 14-16.

DIRECTIONS: In each of Questions 14 through 6, the four sentences are from a paragraph in a report. They are not in the right order. Which of the following arrangements is the BEST one?

14. I. An executive may answer a letter by writing his reply on the face of the letter itself instead of having a return letter typed.
    II. This procedure is efficient because it saves the executive's time, the typist's time, and saves office file space.
    III. Copying machines are used in small offices as well as large offices to save time and money in making brief replies to business letters.
    IV. A copy is made on a copy machine to go into the company files, while the original is mailed back to the sender.

    The CORRECT answer is:
    A. I, II, IV, III   B. I, IV, II, III   C. III, I, IV, II   D. III, IV, II, I

14.____

15. I. Most organizations favor one of the types but always include the others to a lesser degree.
    II. However, we can detect a definite trend toward greater use of symbolic control.
    III. We suggest that our local police agencies are today primarily utilizing material control.
    IV. Control can be classified into three types: physical, material, and symbolic.

    The CORRECT answer is:
    A. IV, II, III, I   B. II, I, IV, III   C. III, IV, II, I   D. IV, I, III, II

15.____

16. I. They can and do take advantage of ancient political and geographical boundaries, which often give them sanctuary from effective policy activity.
    II. This country is essentially a country of small police forces, each operating independently within the limits of its jurisdiction.
    III. The boundaries that define and limit police operations do not hinder the movement of criminals, of course.
    IV. The machinery of law enforcement in America is fragmented, complicated, and frequently overlapping.

16.____

The CORRECT answer is:
A. III, I, IV   B. II, IV, I, III   C. IV, II, III, I   D. IV, III, II, I

17. Examine the following sentence, and then choose from below the words which should be inserted in the blank spaces to produce the best sentence.
The unit has exceeded _____ goals and the employees are satisfied with _____ accomplishments.
A. their, it's   B. it's; it's   C. its, there   D. its, their

18. Examine the following sentence, and then choose from below the words which should be inserted in the blank spaces to produce the best sentence.
Research indicates that employees who _____ no opportunity for close social relationships often find their work unsatisfying, and this _____ of satisfaction often reflects itself in low production.
A. have; lack   B. have; excess   C. has; lack   D. has; excess

19. Words in a sentence must be arranged properly to make sure that the intended meaning of the sentence is clear.
The sentence below that does NOT make sense because a clause has been separated from the word on which its meaning depends is:
A. To be a good writer, clarity is necessary.
B. To be a good writer, you must write clearly.
C. You must write clearly to be a good writer.
D. Clarity is necessary to good writing.

Questions 20-21.

DIRECTIONS: Each of Questions 20 and 21 consists of a statement which contains a word (one of those underlined) that is either incorrectly used because it is not in keeping with the meaning the quotation is evidently intended to convey, or is misspelled. There is only one INCORRECT word in each quotation. Of the four underlined words, determine if the first one should be replaced by the word lettered A, the second one replaced by the word lettered B, the third one replaced by the word lettered C, or the fourth one replaced by the word lettered D.

20. The alleged killer was occasionally permitted to excercise in the corridor.
A. alledged   B. ocasionally   C. permited   D. exercise

21. Defense counsel stated, in affect, that their conduct was permissible under the First Amendment.
A. council   B. effect   C. there   D. permissable

Question 22.

DIRECTIONS: Question 22 consists of one sentence. This sentence contains an incorrectly used word. First, decide which is the incorrectly used word. Then, from among the options given, decide which word, when substituted for the incorrectly used word, makes the meaning of the sentence clear.

22. As today's violence has no single cause, so its causes have no single scheme. 22.____
    A. deference   B. cure   C. flaw   D. relevance

23. In the sentence, *A man in a light-grey suit waited thirty-five minutes in the ante-room for the all-important document*, the word IMPROPERLY hyphenated is 23.____
    A. light-grey   B. thirty-five
    C. ante-room   D. all-important

24. In the sentence, *The candidate wants to file his application for preference before it is too late*, the word *before* is used as a(n) 24.____
    A. preposition   B. subordinating conjunction
    C. pronoun   D. adverb

25. In the sentence, *The perpetrators ran from the scene*, the word *from* is a 25.____
    A. preposition   B. pronoun   C. verb   D. conjunction

KEY (CORRECT ANSWERS)

1.	D	11.	D
2.	D	12.	D
3.	A	13.	D
4.	B	14.	C
5.	D	15.	D
6.	D	16.	C
7.	B	17.	D
8.	A	18.	A
9.	C	19.	A
10.	C	20.	D

21. B
22. B
23. C
24. B
25. A

PHILOSOPHY, PRINCIPLES, PRACTICES, AND TECHNICS
OF
SUPERVISION, ADMINISTRATION, MANAGEMENT, AND ORGANIZATION

TABLE OF CONTENTS

	Page
MEANING OF SUPERVISION	1
THE OLD AND THE NEW SUPERVISION	1
THE EIGHT (8) BASIC PRINCIPLES OF THE NEW SUPERVISION	1
I. Principle of Responsibility	1
II. Principle of Authority	2
III. Principle of Self-Growth	2
IV. Principle of Individual Worth	2
V. Principle of Creative Leadership	2
VI. Principle of Success and Failure	2
VII. Principle of Science	3
VIII. Principle of Cooperation	3
WHAT IS ADMINISTRATION?	3
I. Practices Commonly Classed as "Supervisory"	3
II. Practices Commonly Classed as "Administrative"	3
III. Practices Commonly Classed as Both "Supervisory" and "Administrative"	4
RESPONSIBILITIES OF THE SUPERVISOR	4
COMPETENCIES OF THE SUPERVISOR	4
THE PROFESSIONAL SUPERVISOR-EMPLOYEE RELATIONSHIP	4
MINI-TEXT IN SUPERVISION, ADMINISTRATION, MANAGEMENT, AND ORGANIZATION	5
I. Brief Highlights	5
A. Levels of Management	6
B. What the Supervisor Must Learn	6
C. A Definition of Supervision	6
D. Elements of the Team Concept	6
E. Principles of Organization	6
F. The Four Important Parts of Every Job	7
G. Principles of Delegation	7
H. Principles of Effective Communications	7
I. Principles of Work Improvement	7
J. Areas of Job Improvement	7
K. Seven Key Points in Making Improvements	8

	L.	Corrective Techniques for Job Improvement	8
	M.	A Planning Checklist	8
	N.	Five Characteristics of Good Directions	9
	O.	Types of Directions	9
	P.	Controls	9
	Q.	Orienting the New Employee	9
	R.	Checklist for Orienting New Employees	9
	S.	Principles of Learning	10
	T.	Causes of Poor Performance	10
	U.	Four Major Steps in On-the-Job Instructions	10
	V.	Employees Want Five Things	10
	W.	Some Don'ts in Regard to Praise	11
	X.	How to Gain Your Workers' Confidence	11
	Y.	Sources of Employee Problems	11
	Z.	The Supervisor's Key to Discipline	11
	AA.	Five Important Processes of Management	12
	BB.	When the Supervisor Fails to Plan	12
	CC.	Fourteen General Principles of Management	12
	DD.	Change	12
II.	Brief Topical Summaries		13
	A.	Who/What is the Supervisor?	13
	B.	The Sociology of Work	13
	C.	Principles and Practices of Supervision	14
	D.	Dynamic Leadership	14
	E.	Processes for Solving Problems	15
	F.	Training for Results	15
	G.	Health, Safety, and Accident Prevention	16
	H.	Equal Employment Opportunity	16
	I.	Improving Communications	16
	J.	Self-Development	17
	K.	Teaching and Training	17
		1. The Teaching Process	17
		a. Preparation	17
		b. Presentation	18
		c. Summary	18
		d. Application	18
		e. Evaluation	18
		2. Teaching Methods	18
		a. Lecture	18
		b. Discussion	18
		c. Demonstration	19
		d. Performance	19
		e. Which Method to Use	19

PHILOSOPHY, PRINCIPLES, PRACTICES, AND TECHNICS
OF
SUPERVISION, ADMINISTRATION, MANAGEMENT, AND ORGANIZATION

MEANING OF SUPERVISION

The extension of the democratic philosophy has been accompanied by an extension in the scope of supervision. Modern leaders and supervisors no longer think of supervision in the narrow sense of being confined chiefly to visiting employees, supplying materials, or rating the staff. They regard supervision as being intimately related to all the concerned agencies of society, they speak of the supervisor's function in terms of "growth," rather than the "improvement" of employees.

This modern concept of supervision may be defined as follows: Supervision is leadership and the development of leadership within groups which are cooperatively engaged in inspection, research, training, guidance, and evaluation.

THE OLD AND THE NEW SUPERVISION

TRADITIONAL
1. Inspection
2. Focused on the employee
3. Visitation
4. Random and haphazard
5. Imposed and authoritarian
6. One person usually

MODERN
1. Study and analysis
2. Focused on aims, materials, methods, supervisors, employees, environment
3. Demonstrations, intervisitation, workshops, directed reading, bulletins, etc.
4. Definitely organized and planned (scientific)
5. Cooperative and democratic
6. Many persons involved (creative)

THE EIGHT (8) BASIC PRINCIPLES OF THE NEW SUPERVISION

I. Principle of Responsibility
Authority to act and responsibility for acting must be joined.
   A. If you give responsibility, give authority.
   B. Define employee duties clearly.
   C. Protect employees from criticism by others.
   D. Recognize the rights as well as obligations of employees.
   E. Achieve the aims of a democratic society insofar as it is possible within the area of your work.
   F. Establish a situation favorable to training and learning.
   G. Accept ultimate responsibility for everything done in your section, unit, office, division, department.
   H. Good administration and good supervision are inseparable.

II. Principle of Authority
The success of the supervisor is measured by the extent to which the power of authority is not used.
   A. Exercise simplicity and informality in supervision
   B. Use the simplest machinery of supervision
   C. If it is good for the organization as a whole, it is probably justified.
   D. Seldom be arbitrary or authoritative.
   E. Do not base your work on the power of position or of personality.
   F. Permit and encourage the free expression of opinions.

III. Principle of Self-Growth
The success of the supervisor is measured by the extent to which, and the speed with which, he is no longer needed.
   A. Base criticism on principles, not on specifics.
   B. Point out higher activities to employees.
   C. Train for self-thinking by employees to meet new situations.
   D. Stimulate initiative, self-reliance, and individual responsibility
   E. Concentrate on stimulating the growth of employees rather than on removing defects.

IV. Principle of Individual Worth
Respect for the individual is a paramount consideration in supervision.
   A. Be human and sympathetic in dealing with employees.
   B. Don't nag about things to be done.
   C. Recognize the individual differences among employees and seek opportunities to permit best expression of each personality.

V. Principle of Creative Leadership
The best supervision is that which is not apparent to the employee.
   A. Stimulate, don't drive employees to creative action.
   B. Emphasize doing good things.
   C. Encourage employees to do what they do best.
   D. Do not be too greatly concerned with details of subject or method.
   E. Do not be concerned exclusively with immediate problems and activities.
   F. Reveal higher activities and make them both desired and maximally possible.
   G. Determine procedures in the light of each situation but see that these are derived from a sound basic philosophy.
   H. Aid, inspire, and lead so as to liberate the creative spirit latent in all good employees.

VI. Principle of Success and Failure
There are no unsuccessful employees, only unsuccessful supervisors who have failed to give proper leadership.
   A. Adapt suggestions to the capacities, attitudes, and prejudices of employees.
   B. Be gradual, be progressive, be persistent.
   C. Help the employee find the general principle; have the employee apply his own problem to the general principle.
   D. Give adequate appreciation for good work and honest effort.
   E. Anticipate employee difficulties and help to prevent them.
   F. Encourage employees to do the desirable things they will do anyway.
   G. Judge your supervision by the results it secures.

VII. Principle of Science
Successful supervision is scientific, objective, and experimental. It is based on facts, not on prejudices.
   A. Be cumulative in results.
   B. Never divorce your suggestions from the goals of training.
   C. Don't be impatient of results.
   D. Keep all matters on a professional, not a personal, level.
   E. Do not be concerned exclusively with immediate problems and activities.
   F. Use objective means of determining achievement and rating where possible.

VIII. Principle of Cooperation
Supervision is a cooperative enterprise between supervisor and employee.
   A. Begin with conditions as they are.
   B. Ask opinions of all involved when formulating policies.
   C. Organization is as good as its weakest link.
   D. Let employees help to determine policies and department programs.
   E. Be approachable and accessible—physically and mentally.
   F. Develop pleasant social relationships.

WHAT IS ADMINISTRATION

Administration is concerned with providing the environment, the material facilities, and the operational procedures that will promote the maximum growth and development of supervisors and employees. (Organization is an aspect and a concomitant of administration.)

There is no sharp line of demarcation between supervision and administration; these functions are intimately interrelated and, often, overlapping. They are complementary activities.

I. Practices Commonly Classed as "Supervisory"
   A. Conducting employees' conferences
   B. Visiting sections, units, offices, divisions, departments
   C. Arranging for demonstrations
   D. Examining plans
   E. Suggesting professional reading
   F. Interpreting bulletins
   G. Recommending in-service training courses
   H. Encouraging experimentation
   I. Appraising employee morale
   J. Providing for intervisitation

II. Practices Commonly Classified as "Administrative"
   A. Management of the office
   B. Arrangement of schedules for extra duties
   C. Assignment of rooms or areas
   D. Distribution of supplies
   E. Keeping records and reports
   F. Care of audio-visual materials
   G. Keeping inventory records
   H. Checking record cards and books

    I. Programming special activities
    J. Checking on the attendance and punctuality of employees

III. Practices Commonly Classified as Both "Supervisory" and "Administrative"
    A. Program construction
    B. Testing or evaluating outcomes
    C. Personnel accounting
    D. Ordering instructional materials

RESPONSIBILITIES OF THE SUPERVISOR

A person employed in a supervisory capacity must constantly be able to improve his own efficiency and ability. He represent the employer to the employees and only continuous self-examination can make him a capable supervisor.

Leadership and training are the supervisor's responsibility. An efficient working unit is one in which the employees work with the supervisor. It is his job to bring out the best in his employees. He must always be relaxed, courteous, and calm in his association with his employees. Their feelings are important, and a harsh attitude does not develop the most efficient employees.

COMPETENCES OF THE SUPERVISOR

   I.   Complete knowledge of the duties and responsibilities of his position.
   II. To be able to organize a job, plan ahead, and carry through.
   III. To have self-confidence and initiative.
   IV. To be able to handle the unexpected situation and make quick decisions.
   V.   To be able to properly train subordinates in the positions they are best suited for.
   VI. To be able to keep good human relations among his subordinates.
   VII. To be able to keep good human relations between his subordinates and himself and to earn their respect and trust.

THE PROFESSIONAL SUPERVISOR-EMPLOYEE RELATIONSHIP

There are two kinds of efficiency: one kind is only apparent and is produced in organizations through the exercise of mere discipline; this is but a simulation of the second, or true, efficiency which springs from spontaneous cooperation. If you are a manager, no matter how great or small your responsibility, it is your job, in the final analysis, to create and develop this involuntary cooperation among the people whom you supervise. For, no matter how powerful a combination of money, machines, and materials a company may have, this is a dead and sterile thing without a team of willing, thinking, and articulate people to guide it.

The following 21 points are presented as indicative of the exemplary basic relationship that should exist between supervisor and employee:

1. Each person wants to be liked and respected by his fellow employee and wants to be treated with consideration and respect by his superior.
2. The most competent employee will make an error. However, in a unit where good relations exist between the supervisor and his employees, tenseness and fear do not exist. Thus, errors are not hidden or covered up, and the efficiency of a unit is not impaired.

3. Subordinates resent rules, regulations, or orders that are unreasonable or unexplained.
4. Subordinates are quick to resent unfairness, harshness, injustices, and favoritism.
5. An employee will accept responsibility if he knows that he will be complimented for a job well done, and not too harshly chastised for failure; that his supervisor will check the cause of the failure, and, if it was the supervisor's fault, he will assume the blame therefore. If it was the employee's fault, his supervisor will explain the correct method or means of handling the responsibility.
6. An employee wants to receive credit for a suggestion he has made, that is used. If a suggestion cannot be used, the employee is entitled to an explanation. The supervisor should not say "no" and close the subject.
7. Fear and worry slow up a worker's ability. Poor working environment can impair his physical and mental health. A good supervisor avoids forceful methods, threats, and arguments to get a job done.
8. A forceful supervisor is able to train his employees individually and as a team, and is able to motivate them in the proper channels.
9. A mature supervisor is able to properly evaluate his subordinates and to keep them happy and satisfied.
10. A sensitive supervisor will never patronize his subordinates.
11. A worthy supervisor will respect his employees' confidences.
12. Definite and clear-cut responsibilities should be assigned to each executive.
13. Responsibility should always be coupled with corresponding authority.
14. No change should be made in the scope or responsibilities of a position without a definite understanding to that effect on the part of all persons concerned.
15. No executive or employee, occupying a single position in the organization, should be subject to definite orders from more than one source.
16. Orders should never be given to subordinates over the head of a responsible executive. Rather than do this, the officer in question should be supplanted.
17. Criticisms of subordinates should, whoever possible, be made privately, and in no case should a subordinate be criticized in the presence of executives or employees of equal or lower rank.
18. No dispute or difference between executives or employees as to authority or responsibilities should be considered too trivial for prompt and careful adjudication.
19. Promotions, wage changes, and disciplinary action should always be approved by the executive immediately superior to the one directly responsible.
20. No executive or employee should ever be required, or expected, to be at the same time an assistant to, and critic of, another.
21. Any executive whose work is subject to regular inspection should, wherever practicable, be given the assistance and facilities necessary to enable him to maintain an independent check of the quality of his work.

MINI-TEXT IN SUPERVISION, ADMINISTRATION, MANAGEMENT, AND ORGANIZATION

I. Brief Highlights

Listed concisely and sequentially are major headings and important data in the field for quick recall and review.

A. Levels of Management
Any organization of some size has several levels of management. In terms of a ladder, the levels are:

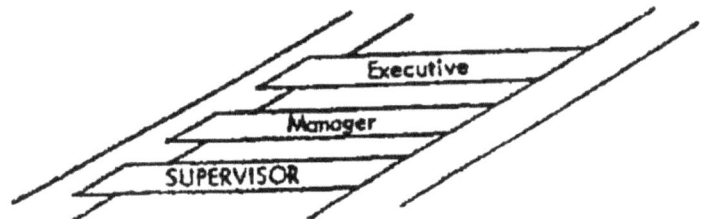

The first level is very important because it is the beginning point of management leadership.

B. What the Supervisor Must Learn
A supervisor must learn to:
1. Deal with people and their differences
2. Get the job done through people
3. Recognize the problems when they exist
4. Overcome obstacles to good performance
5. Evaluate the performance of people
6. Check his own performance in terms of accomplishment

C. A Definition of Supervisor
The term supervisor means any individual having authority, in the interests of the employer, to hire, transfer, suspend, lay-off, recall, promote, discharge, assign, reward, or discipline other employees or responsibility to direct them, or to adjust their grievances, or effectively to recommend such action, if, in connection with the foregoing, exercise of such authority is not of a merely routine or clerical nature but requires the use of independent judgment.

D. Elements of the Team Concept
What is involved in teamwork? The component parts are:
1. Members
2. A leader
3. Goals
4. Plans
5. Cooperation
6. Spirit

E. Principles of Organization
1. A team member must know what his job is.
2. Be sure that the nature and scope of a job are understood.
3. Authority and responsibility should be carefully spelled out.
4. A supervisor should be permitted to make the maximum number of decisions affecting his employees.
5. Employees should report to only one supervisor.
6. A supervisor should direct only as many employees as he can handle effectively.
7. An organization plan should be flexible.

8. Inspection and performance of work should be separate.
9. Organizational problems should receive immediate attention.
10. Assign work in line with ability and experience.

F. The Four Important Parts of Every Job
1. Inherent in every job is the *accountability* for results.
2. A second set of factors in every job is *responsibilities*.
3. Along with duties and responsibilities one must have the *authority* to act within certain limits without obtaining permission to proceed.
4. No job exists in a vacuum. The supervisor is surrounded by key *relationships*.

G. Principles of Delegation
Where work is delegated for the first time, the supervisor should think in terms of these questions:
1. Who is best qualified to do this?
2. Can an employee improve his abilities by doing this?
3. How long should an employee spend on this?
4. Are there any special problems for which he will need guidance?
5. How broad a delegation can I make?

H. Principles of Effective Communications
1. Determine the media.
2. To whom directed?
3. Identification and source authority.
4. Is communication understood?

I. Principles of Work Improvement
1. Most people usually do only the work which is assigned to them.
2. Workers are likely to fit assigned work into the time available to perform it.
3. A good workload usually stimulates output.
4. People usually do their best work when they know that results will be reviewed or inspected.
5. Employees usually feel that someone else is responsible for conditions of work, workplace layout, job methods, type of tools/equipment, and other such factors.
6. Employees are usually defensive about their job security.
7. Employees have natural resistance to change.
8. Employees can support or destroy a supervisor.
9. A supervisor usually earns the respect of his people through his personal example of diligence and efficiency.

J. Areas of Job Improvement
The areas of job improvement are quite numerous, but the most common ones which a supervisor can identify and utilize are:
1. Departmental layout
2. Flow of work
3. Workplace layout
4. Utilization of manpower
5. Work methods
6. Materials handling

7. Utilization
8. Motion economy

K. Seven Key Points in Making Improvements
1. Select the job to be improved
2. Study how it is being done now
3. Question the present method
4. Determine actions to be taken
5. Chart proposed method
6. Get approval and apply
7. Solicit worker participation

l. Corrective Techniques of Job Improvement
Specific Problems
1. Size of workload
2. Inability to meet schedules
3. Strain and fatigue
4. Improper use of men and skills
5. Waste, poor quality, unsafe conditions
6. Bottleneck conditions that hinder output
7. Poor utilization of equipment and machine
8. Efficiency and productivity of labor

General Improvement
1. Departmental layout
2. Flow of work
3. Work plan layout
4. Utilization of manpower
5. Work methods
6. Materials handling
7. Utilization of equipment
8. Motion economy

Corrective Techniques
1. Study with scale model
2. Flow chart study
3. Motion analysis
4. Comparison of units produced to standard allowance
5. Methods analysis
6. Flow chart and equipment study
7. Down time vs. running time
8. Motion analysis

M. A Planning Checklist
1. Objectives
2. Controls
3. Delegations
4. Communications
5. Resources
6. Manpower

7. Equipment
8. Supplies and materials
9. Utilization of time
10. Safety
11. Money
12. Work
13. Timing of improvements

N. Five Characteristics of Good Directions
In order to get results, directions must be:
1. Possible of accomplishment
2. Agreeable with worker interests
3. Related to mission
4. Planned and complete
5. Unmistakably clear

O. Types of Directions
1. Demands or direct orders
2. Requests
3. Suggestion or implication
4. volunteering

P. Controls
A typical listing of the overall areas in which the supervisor should establish controls might be:
1. Manpower
2. Materials
3. Quality of work
4. Quantity of work
5. Time
6. Space
7. Money
8. Methods

Q. Orienting the New Employee
1. Prepare for him
2. Welcome the new employee
3. Orientation for the job
4. Follow-up

R. Checklist for Orienting New Employees   Yes   No
1. Do you appreciate the feelings of new employees
   when they first report for work?   ___   ___
2. Are you aware of the fact that the new employee must
   make a big adjustment to his job?   ___   ___
3. Have you given him good reasons for liking the job and
   the organization?   ___   ___
4. Have you prepared for his first day on the job?   ___   ___
5. Did you welcome him cordially and make him feel needed?   ___   ___

	Yes	No

6. Did you establish rapport with him so that he feels free to talk and discuss matters with you?
7. Did you explain his job to him and his relationship to you?
8. Does he know that his work will be evaluated periodically on a basis that is fair and objective?
9. Did you introduce him to his fellow workers in such a way that they are likely to accept him?
10. Does he know what employee benefits he will receive?
11. Does he understand the importance of being on the job and what to do if he must leave his duty station?
12. Has he been impressed with the importance of accident prevention and safe practice?
13. Does he generally know his way around the department?
14. Is he under the guidance of a sponsor who will teach the right way of doing things?
15. Do you plan to follow-up so that he will continue to adjust successfully to his job?

S. Principles of Learning
1. Motivation
2. Demonstration or explanation
3. Practice

T. Causes of Poor Performance
1. Improper training for job
2. Wrong tools
3. Inadequate directions
4. Lack of supervisory follow-up
5. Poor communications
6. Lack of standards of performance
7. Wrong work habits
8. Low morale
9. Other

U. Four Major Steps in On-The-Job Instruction
1. Prepare the worker
2. Present the operation
3. Tryout performance
4. Follow-up

V. Employees Want Five Things
1. Security
2. Opportunity
3. Recognition
4. Inclusion
5. Expression

W. Some Don'ts in Regard to Praise
1. Don't praise a person for something he hasn't done.
2. Don't praise a person unless you can be sincere.
3. Don't be sparing in praise just because your superior withholds it from you.
4. Don't let too much time elapse between good performance and recognition of it

X. How to Gain Your Workers' Confidence
Methods of developing confidence include such things as:
1. Knowing the interests, habits, hobbies of employees
2. Admitting your own inadequacies
3. Sharing and telling of confidence in others
4. Supporting people when they are in trouble
5. Delegating matters that can be well handled
6. Being frank and straightforward about problems and working conditions
7. Encouraging others to bring their problems to you
8. Taking action on problems which impede worker progress

Y. Sources of Employee Problems
On-the-job causes might be such things as:
1. A feeling that favoritism is exercised in assignments
2. Assignment of overtime
3. An undue amount of supervision
4. Changing methods or systems
5. Stealing of ideas or trade secrets
6. Lack of interest in job
7. Threat of reduction in force
8. Ignorance or lack of communications
9. Poor equipment
10. Lack of knowing how supervisor feels toward employee
11. Shift assignments

Off-the-job problems might have to do with:
1. Health
2. Finances
3. Housing
4. Family

Z. The Supervisor's Key to Discipline
There are several key points about discipline which the supervisor should keep in mind:
1. Job discipline is one of the disciplines of life and is directed by the supervisor.
2. It is more important to correct an employee fault than to fix blame for it.
3. Employee performance is affected by problems both on the job and off.
4. Sudden or abrupt changes in behavior can be indications of important employee problems.
5. Problems should be dealt with as soon as possible after they are identified.
6. The attitude of the supervisor may have more to do with solving problems than the techniques of problem solving.
7. Correction of employee behavior should be resorted to only after the supervisor is sure that training or counseling will not be helpful.

8. Be sure to document your disciplinary actions.
9. Make sure that you are disciplining on the basis of facts rather than personal feelings.
10. Take each disciplinary step in order, being careful not to make snap judgments, or decisions based on impatience.

AA. Five Important Processes of Management
1. Planning
2. Organizing
3. Scheduling
4. Controlling
5. Motivating

BB. When the Supervisor Fails to Plan
1. Supervisor creates impression of not knowing his job
2. May lead to excessive overtime
3. Job runs itself—supervisor lacks control
4. Deadlines and appointments missed
5. Parts of the work go undone
6. Work interrupted by emergencies
7. Sets a bad example
8. Uneven workload creates peaks and valleys
9. Too much time on minor details at expense of more important tasks

CC. Fourteen General Principles of Management
1. Division of work
2. Authority and responsibility
3. Discipline
4. Unity of command
5. Unity of direction
6. Subordination of individual interest to general interest
7. Remuneration of personnel
8. Centralization
9. Scalar chain
10. Order
11. Equity
12. Stability of tenure of personnel
13. Initiative
14. Esprit de corps

DD. Change

Bringing about change is perhaps attempted more often, and yet less well understood, than anything else the supervisor does. How do people generally react to change? (People tend to resist change that is imposed upon them by other individuals or circumstances.

Change is characteristic of every situation. It is a part of every real endeavor where the efforts of people are concerned.

1. Why do people resist change?
   People may resist change because of:
   a. Fear of the unknown
   b. Implied criticism
   c. Unpleasant experiences in the past
   d. Fear of loss of status
   e. Threat to the ego
   f. Fear of loss of economic stability

2. How can we best overcome the resistance to change?
   In initiating change, take these steps:
   a. Get ready to sell
   b. Identify sources of help
   c. Anticipate objections
   d. Sell benefits
   e. Listen in depth
   f. Follow up

II. Brief Topical Summaries

   A. Who/What is the Supervisor?
   1. The supervisor is often called the "highest level employee and the lowest level manager."
   2. A supervisor is a member of both management and the work group. He acts as a bridge between the two.
   3. Most problems in supervision are in the area of human relations, or people problems.
   4. Employees expect: Respect, opportunity to learn and to advance, and a sense of belonging, and so forth.
   5. Supervisors are responsible for directing people and organizing work. Planning is of paramount importance.
   6. A position description is a set of duties and responsibilities inherent to a given position.
   7. It is important to keep the position description up-to-date and to provide each employee with his own copy.

   B. The Sociology of Work
   1. People are alike in many ways; however, each individual is unique.
   2. The supervisor is challenged in getting to know employee differences. Acquiring skills in evaluating individuals is an asset.
   3. Maintaining meaningful working relationships in the organization is of great importance.
   4. The supervisor has an obligation to help individuals to develop to their fullest potential.
   5. Job rotation on a planned basis helps to build versatility and to maintain interest and enthusiasm in work groups.
   6. Cross training (job rotation) provides backup skills.

7. The supervisor can help reduce tension by maintaining a sense of humor, providing guidance to employees, and by making reasonable and timely decisions. Employees respond favorably to working under reasonably predictable circumstances.
8. Change is characteristic of all managerial behavior. The supervisor must adjust to changes in procedures, new methods, technological changes, and to a number of new and sometimes challenging situations.
9. To overcome the natural tendency for people to resist change, the supervisor should become more skillful in initiating change.

C. Principles and Practices of Supervision
1. Employees should be required to answer to only one superior.
2. A supervisor can effectively direct only a limited number of employees, depending upon the complexity, variety, and proximity of the jobs involved.
3. The organizational chart presents the organization in graphic form. It reflects lines of authority and responsibility as well as interrelationships of units within the organization.
4. Distribution of work can be improved through an analysis using the "Work Distribution Chart."
5. The "Work Distribution Chart" reflects the division of work within a unit in understandable form.
6. When related tasks are given to an employee, he has a better chance of increasing his skills through training.
7. The individual who is given the responsibility for tasks must also be given the appropriate authority to insure adequate results.
8. The supervisor should delegate repetitive, routine work. Preparation of recurring reports, maintaining leave and attendance records are some examples.
9. Good discipline is essential to good task performance. Discipline is reflected in the actions of employees on the job in the absence of supervision.
10. Disciplinary action may have to be taken when the positive aspects of discipline have failed. Reprimand, warning, and suspension are examples of disciplinary action.
11. If a situation calls for a reprimand, be sure it is deserved and remember it is to be done in private.

D. Dynamic Leadership
1. A style is a personal method or manner of exerting influence.
2. Authoritarian leaders often see themselves as the source of power and authority.
3. The democratic leader often perceives the group as the source of authority and power.
4. Supervisors tend to do better when using the pattern of leadership that is most natural for them.
5. Social scientists suggest that the effective supervisor use the leadership style that best fits the problem or circumstances involved.
6. All four styles—telling, selling, consulting, joining—have their place. Using one does not preclude using the other at another time.

7. The theory X point of view assumes that the average person dislikes work, will avoid it whenever possible, and must be coerced to achieve organizational objectives.
8. The theory Y point of view assumes that the average person considers work to be a natural as play, and, when the individual is committed, he requires little supervision or direction to accomplish desired objectives.
9. The leader's basic assumptions concerning human behavior and human nature affect his actions, decisions, and other managerial practices.
10. Dissatisfaction among employees is often present, but difficult to isolate. The supervisor should seek to weaken dissatisfaction by keeping promises, being sincere and considerate, keeping employees informed, and so forth.
11. Constructive suggestions should be encouraged during the natural progress of the work.

E. Processes for Solving Problems
1. People find their daily tasks more meaningful and satisfying when they can improve them.
2. The causes of problems, or the key factors, are often hidden in the background. Ability to solve problems often involves the ability to isolate them from their backgrounds. There is some substance to the cliché that some persons "can't see the forest for the trees."
3. New procedures are often developed from old ones. Problems should be broken down into manageable parts. New ideas can be adapted from old one.
4. People think differently in problem-solving situations. Using a logical, patterned approach is often useful. One approach found to be useful includes these steps:
   a. Define the problem
   b. Establish objectives
   c. Get the facts
   d. Weigh and decide
   e. Take action
   f. Evaluate action

F. Training for Results
1. Participants respond best when they feel training is important to them.
2. The supervisor has responsibility for the training and development of those who report to him.
3. When training is delegated to others, great care must be exercised to insure the trainer has knowledge, aptitude, and interest for his work as a trainer.
4. Training (learning) of some type goes on continually. The most successful supervisor makes certain the learning contributes in a productive manner to operational goals.
5. New employees are particularly susceptible to training. Older employees facing new job situations require specific training, as well as having need for development and growth opportunities.
6. Training needs require continuous monitoring.
7. The training officer of an agency is a professional with a responsibility to assist supervisors in solving training problems.

8. Many of the self-development steps important to the supervisor's own growth are equally important to the development of peers and subordinates. Knowledge of these is important when the supervisor consults with others on development and growth opportunities.

G. Health, Safety, and Accident Prevention
1. Management-minded supervisors take appropriate measures to assist employees in maintaining health and in assuring safe practices in the work environment.
2. Effective safety training and practices help to avoid injury and accidents.
3. Safety should be a management goal. All infractions of safety which are observed should be corrected without exception.
4. Employees' safety attitude, training and instruction, provision of safe tools and equipment, supervision, and leadership are considered highly important factors which contribute to safety and which can be influenced directly by supervisors.
5. When accidents do occur, they should be investigated promptly for very important reasons, including the fact that information which is gained can be used to prevent accidents in the future.

H. Equal Employment Opportunity
1. The supervisor should endeavor to treat all employees fairly, without regard to religion, race, sex, or national origin.
2. Groups tend to reflect the attitude of the leader. Prejudice can be detected even in very subtle form. Supervisors must strive to create a feeling of mutual respect and confidence in every employee.
3. Complete utilization of all human resources is a national goal. Equitable consideration should be accorded women in the work force, minority-group members, the physically and mentally handicapped, and the older employee. The important question is: "Who can do the job?"
4. Training opportunities, recognition for performance, overtime assignments, promotional opportunities, and all other personnel actions are to be handled on an equitable basis.

I. Improving Communications
1. Communications is achieving understanding between the sender and the receiver of a message. It also means sharing information—the creation of understanding.
2. Communication is basic to all human activity. Words are means of conveying meanings; however, real meanings are in people.
3. There are very practical differences in the effectiveness of one-way, impersonal, and two-way communications. Words spoken face-to-face are better understood. Telephone conversations are effective, but lack the rapport of person-to-person exchanges. The whole person communicates.
4. Cooperation and communication in an organization go hand in hand. When there is a mutual respect between people, spelling out rules and procedures for communicating is unnecessary.
5. There are several barriers to effective communications. These include failure to listen with respect and understanding, lack of skill in feedback, and misinterpreting the meanings of words used by the speaker. It is also common

practice to listen to what we want to hear, and tune out things we do not want to hear.
6. Communication is management's chief problem. The supervisor should accept the challenge to communicate more effectively and to improve interagency and intra-agency communications.
7. The supervisor may often plan for and conduct meetings. The planning phase is critical and may determine the success or the failure of a meeting.
8. Speaking before groups usually requires extra effort. Stage fright may never disappear completely, but it can be controlled.

J. Self-Development
1. Every employee is responsible for his own self-development.
2. Toastmaster and toastmistress clubs offer opportunities to improve skills in oral communications.
3. Planning for one's own self-development is of vital importance. Supervisors know their own strengths and limitations better than anyone else.
4. Many opportunities are open to aid the supervisor in his developmental efforts, including job assignments; training opportunities, both governmental and non-governmental—to include universities and professional conferences and seminars.
5. Programmed instruction offers a means of studying at one's own rate.
6. Where difficulties may arise from a supervisor's being away from his work for training, he may participate in televised home study or correspondence courses to meet his self-development needs.

K. Teaching and Training
1. The Teaching Process
Teaching is encouraging and guiding the learning activities of students toward established goals. In most cases this process consists of five steps: preparation, presentation, summarization, evaluation, and application.

   a. Preparation
   Preparation is two-fold in nature; that of the supervisor and the employee. Preparation by the supervisor is absolutely essential to success. He must know what, when, where, how, and whom he will teach. Some of the factors that should be considered are:
   1) The objectives
   2) The materials needed
   3) The methods to be used
   4) Employee participation
   5) Employee interest
   6) Training aids
   7) Evaluation
   8) Summarization

   Employee preparation consists in preparing the employee to receive the material. Probably the most important single factor in the preparation of the employee is arousing and maintaining his interest. He must know the objectives of the training, why he is there, how the material can be used, and its importance to him.

b. Presentation
In presentation, have a carefully designed plan and follow it. The plan should be accurate and complete, yet flexible enough to meet situations as they arise. The method of presentation will be determined by the particular situation and objectives.

c. Summary
A summary should be made at the end of every training unit and program. In addition, there may be internal summaries depending on the nature of the material being taught. The important thing is that the trainee must always be able to understand how each part of the new material relates to the whole.

d. Application
The supervisor must arrange work so the employee will be given a chance to apply new knowledge or skills while the material is still clear in his mind and interest is high. The trainee does not really know whether he has learned the material until he has been given a chance to apply it. If the material is not applied, it loses most of its value.

e. Evaluation
The purpose of all training is to promote learning. To determine whether the training has been a success or failure, the supervisor must evaluate this learning.
In the broadest sense, evaluation includes all the devices, methods, skills, and techniques used by the supervisor to keep himself and the employees informed as to their progress toward the objectives they are pursuing. The extent to which the employee has mastered the knowledge, skills, and abilities, or changed his attitudes, as determined by the program objectives, is the extent to which instruction has succeeded or failed.
Evaluation should not be confined to the end of the lesson, day, or program but should be used continuously. We shall note later the way this relates to the rest of the teaching process.

2. Teaching Methods
A teaching method is a pattern of identifiable student and instructor activity used in presenting training material.
All supervisors are faced with the problem of deciding which method should be used at a given time.

a. Lecture
The lecture is direct oral presentation of material by the supervisor. The present trend is to place less emphasis on the trainer's activity and more on that of the trainee.

b. Discussion
Teaching by discussion or conference involves using questions and other techniques to arouse interest and focus attention upon certain areas, and by doing so creating a learning situation. This can be one of the most

valuable methods because it gives the employees an opportunity to express their ideas and pool their knowledge.

c. Demonstration
The demonstration is used to teach how something works or how to do something. It can be used to show a principle or what the results of a series of actions will be. A well-staged demonstration is particularly effective because it shows proper methods of performance in a realistic manner.

d. Performance
Performance is one of the most fundamental of all learning techniques or teaching methods. The trainee may be able to tell how a specific operation should be performed but he cannot be sure he knows how to perform the operation until he has done so.
As with all methods, there are certain advantages and disadvantages to each method.

e. Which Method to Use
Moreover, there are other methods and techniques of teaching. It is difficult to use any method without other methods entering into it. In any learning situation, a combination of methods is usually more effective than any one method alone.

Finally, evaluation must be integrated into the other aspects of the teaching-learning process.

It must be used in the motivation of the trainees; it must be used to assist in developing understanding during the training; and it must be related to employee application of the results of training.

This is distinctly the role of the supervisor.

CRIMINAL INVESTIGATION

TECHNIQUE OF INTERVIEWS AND INTERROGATION

TABLE OF CONTENTS

		Page
1.	General	1
2.	Purpose of Interview	1
3.	Preparation for Interview	1
4.	Time of Interview	2
5.	Place of Interview	2
6.	Introduction of the Investigator	2
7.	Control Over Interviews	2
8.	Rights of Person Interviewed	2
9.	Attitude and Demeanor of Investigator	2
10.	Types of Approaches	3
11.	Interview of Complainants	3
12.	Interview of Victims	3
13.	Interview of Witnesses	3
14.	Types of Witnesses	4
15.	Assistance to Witnesses in Descriptions	4
16.	Credibility of Witnesses	4
17.	Evaluation During Interview	5
18.	Interview Notes	5
19.	Purpose of Interrogation	5
20.	Preparation for Interrogation	6
21.	Classification of Suspects	6
22.	Length of Interrogation	6
23.	Persons at Interrogation	7
24.	Interrogation Checklist	7
25.	Introduction of Investigator	7
26.	Rights of Person Being Interrogated	7
27.	Attitude of Investigator	8
28.	Types of Approach	8
29.	Interrogation Notes	9
30.	Scientific Aids to Interrogation	9
31.	Lie Detecting Set	9
32.	Narco-Analysis	10

CRIMINAL INVESTIGATION

TECHNIQUE OF INTERVIEWS AND INTERROGATION

1. **GENERAL**
   The successful investigation of criminal offenses depends in a great measure upon the effective questioning of complainants, witnesses, informants, suspects, and other persons encountered during the course of an investigation. Questioning is divided into two broad classifications: *interviews*, which are conducted to learn facts from persons who may have knowledge of a wrongful act but who are not themselves implicated; and *interrogations*, which are conducted to learn facts and to obtain admissions or confessions of wrongful acts from persons who are implicated in a wrongful act. Persons who have been interviewed may later be interrogated. An interrogation is not necessarily confined to individuals suspected of criminal acts, but may include persons who may have been accessories, or who may have knowledge of the crime which, for various motives, they are reluctant to admit. It is usually advisable to take statements from persons being interviewed or interrogated. When an interview or interrogation develops information that will have definite value as evidence, that information or evidence must be recorded in a written, signed, and witnessed statement, or preserved through mechanical recording.

2. **PURPOSE OF INTERVIEW**
   An interview is an informal questioning to learn facts. The successful investigation of crime requires that the investigator be able to learn, through personal questioning, what the person interviewed has observed through his five senses: sight, hearing, taste, smell, and touch. Each individual interviewed is presumed to possess certain information that may lead to the solution of a crime. Effective interviewing requires that the interviewer make full use of all the knowledge of human nature he possesses, so that the individual interviewed will disclose all that he knows about the matter in question. If a person does not possess knowledge of the crime, the interview should establish that fact. Pertinent negative evidence is as much a part of a complete investigation as positive information.

3. **PREPARATION FOR INTERVIEW**
   Interviews other than those conducted at the scene of the crime should be planned carefully and thoroughly to prevent repetition of the interview. The investigator must review thoroughly all developments in the investigation prior to the interview. He must also consider the relationship of the person to be interviewed to the investigation; i.e., complainant, victim, witness, or informant. An effective interviewer combines his knowledge of human nature with all available information about the person to be interviewed, such as education, character, reputation, associates, habits, and past criminal record. This background information is used advantageously in the interview. The investigator should estimate the extent and kind of information that he may expect to elicit. He should prepare, by noting pertinent facts to be developed, to detect inconsistencies and discrepancies in the statements of the person being interviewed, to evaluate them, and to require their clarification. The investigator should prepare a plan for the interview

which takes into consideration the information available to him about the person to be interviewed: the time, place, and environment for the interview; as well as the legal proof to be developed in the crime.

4. **TIME OF INTERVIEW**
An interview should be conducted as soon as possible after the discovery of a crime. The investigator should take as much time as is required for a complete and thorough interview.

5. **PLACE OF INTERVIEW**
When possible, the place of the interview should be so selected as to assure a favorable environment. When possible, the interview should be conducted in a comfortable room and in an environment familiar to the person interviewed. The person to be interviewed should never be brought to the investigator.

6. **INTRODUCTION OF THE INVESTIGATR**
Usually the investigator and the person to be interviewed are strangers. The investigator should introduce himself, present his credentials (when appropriate), and begin by making a general statement regarding the purpose of the interview. The introduction should be made in such a manner as to establish a cordial relationship between the investigator and the person being interviewed.

7. **CONTROL OVER INTERVIEWS**
An investigator must maintain absolute control of the interview at all times. He must be careful not to elicit false information through improper questioning. He may permit digression or discussion of matters seemingly unrelated to the crime in order to place the person interviewed at ease but he must not permit the person being interviewed to become evasive. If the person interviewed should become so evasive as to obscure the purpose of the interview, effective results may be obtained by a more formal type of questioning, taking notes, or by the aggressiveness of the investigator.

8. **RIGHTS OF PERSON INTERVIEWED**
Although an investigator has no legal power to compel a person being interviewed to divulge information, he may, if he is clever and alert, induce him to disclose what he knows. When an interview develops into an interrogation, the investigator must warn the person being interviewed of his rights (Par. 26).

9. **ATTITUDE AND DEMEANOR OF INVESTIGATOR**
The attitude and demeanor of an investigator contributes immeasurably to the success or failure of an interview. The investigator should be friendly, yet businesslike. He should endeavor to lead the person being interviewed into talkativeness. He should then direct the conversation toward the investigation. The individual being interviewed should be permitted to give an uninterrupted account while the investigator makes mental notes of omissions, inconsistencies, or discrepancies that require clarification by later questioning. The investigator should strive to turn to advantage the subject's prejudices. He rarely reveals the precise objective of an interview, and usually obtains a more accurate account

from the person interviewed if he claims only to be attempting to establish facts. He should avoid a clash of personalities; acts of undue familiarity; the use of profanity or violent expressions such as "kill," "steal," "confess," "murder"; improbable stories; or distracting mannerisms such as pacing the floor or fumbling with objects.

10. **TYPES OF APPROACHES**

    The *indirect* approach employed in interviewing consists of discussion carried on in a conversational tone that permits the person being interviewed to talk without having to answer direct questions. The *direct* approach consists of direct questioning as in interrogations (Par. 28a). The use of interrogation technique often succeeds when the person interviewed fears or dislikes police officers, fears retribution from a criminal, desires to protect a friend or relative, is impudent, or, for diverse reasons, is unwilling to cooperate with the investigator. Unreliable persons or liars should always be permitted to give their version of an incident. They may, through contradiction or denial, trip themselves into admissions through which the true facts may be obtained. When interviewing shy or nervous persons, the investigator may be obliged to obtain information piecemeal. He should interview in the normal environment of such persons and should be as casual and calm as possible. The talkative person should be allowed to speak freely and to use his own expressions, but should be confined to the subject by appropriate questions. When persons pretend to know nothing about an incident, the investigator should ask many questions, any one which, if answered, will refute their claim that they know nothing at all. Disinterested persons may divulge more information if their personal interest can be aroused by an indirect approach. Investigators should always attempt to put uneducated witnesses at ease and to help them express themselves as best they can, but should not put word into their mouths. Flattery is most often successful when alcoholics or braggarts are interviewed. Information gained from such individuals must be corroborated.

11. **INTERVIEW OF COMPLAINANTS**

    In interviewing complainants, the investigator should be considerate, understanding, tactful, and impartial, regardless of the motive for the complaint, and should inform the complainant that appropriate action will be initiated promptly.

12. **INTERVIEW OF VICTIMS**

    When interviewing victims, the investigator must consider their emotional state, particularly in crimes of violence. Frequently, victims have unsupported beliefs regarding the circumstances connected with the crime. Their observations may be partial and imperfect because of excitement and tension. It is imperative that the investigator obtain from the victim an accurate account of the circumstances that existed immediately before, during, and after the incident. The investigator should consider the reputation of the victim in determining the credibility of his complaint.

13. **INTERVIEW OF WITNESSES**

    The investigator must frequently assist witnesses to recall and relate facts exactly as they observed them. He must know what affect a person's ability to observe and describe acts, articles, or circumstances related to a crime (CH. 3). He should lead witnesses toward accurate statements of fact by assisting them to recall in detail their experiences.

14. **TYPES OF WITNESSSES**

In general, children from 7 to 12 years of age are good observers, although their testimony may be inadmissible in court. Teenage children are also good observers but may exaggerate. Young adults are often poor witnesses; middle-aged and older persons are the best witnesses. Persons differ in their physical and mental characteristics as well as in their experience and training. These differences may cause them to notice only those aspects of a situation in which they may have had a particular experience. As a consequence, they differ in their observations, interpretations, and descriptions. If a witness cannot recall what he has observed, poor memory may be the cause. Preoccupation of a witness may often prevent him from recalling exactly what occurred. Lack of education may make it difficult for a witness to describe what he observed; such a person is sometimes reluctant to divulge information because of embarrassment over his diction. That which has been observed, because of exaggeration, misrepresentation, or inaccurate interpretation, may result in faulty information; i.e., a squeal of joy may be misinterpreted as a scream of terror. The emotions of witnesses before, during, and after an incident, and when interviewed, greatly affect their recall of events as they actually occurred. A frightened witness may recall events differently than a calm, unruffled person. Witnesses may exaggerate more each time their observations are repeated.

15. **ASSISTANCE TO WITNESSES IN DESCRIPTIONS**

The investigator should provide certain indexes to assist witnesses in describing size, height, weight, distance, and colors. The eye-level method of determining height may be used as standard. By asking a witness to tell how far another person's eyes were above or below his own, the investigator may obtain an estimate of height. Speed is difficult to estimate accurately; even opinions based on long experience may be subject to influence by noise, light, weather, and other conditions. Age is difficult for witnesses to judge because of differences among races, nationalities, and individuals; if selected individuals are used for comparison, they must be chosen carefully. In situations which are strange or which involve unusual circumstances, the witness may have no standards or associations on which to base his judgment and may be unable to utilize the standards presented for comparison. A detailed review or reconstruction of events will sometimes help the witness to recall events, but the investigator must be careful to avoid confusing the actual event with the reconstruction.

16. **CREDIBILITY OF WITNESSES**

Credibility of a witness is usually governed by his character and is evidenced by his reputation for veracity. Personal or financial reason or previous criminal activity may cause a witness to give false information to avoid being implicated. Hope of gain by informants or prisoners; political, racial, or religious factors; and hatred for the police or the suspect are some of the reasons why a witness may make a false statement. Age, sex, physical and mental abnormalities, loyalty, revenge, social and economic status, indulgence in alcohol, and the influence of other persons are some of the many factors which may affect the accuracy, willingness, or ability with which witnesses observe, interpret, and describe occurrences.

17. **EVALUATION DURING INTERVIEW**
During an interview, the investigator must evaluate continuously the mannerisms and the emotional state of the person in terms of the information developed. The manner in which a person relates his story or answers questions may indicate that he is not telling the truth or is concealing information. Evasiveness, hesitation, or unwillingness to discuss situations may signify a lack of cooperation. The relation of body movements to the emotional state of persons must be carefully considered by the investigator. A dry mouth indicated by the wetting of the lips, fidgeting, or vague movements of the hands may indicate nervousness or deception. A "cold sweat" or pale face may indicate fear. A slight gasp, holding the breath, or an unsteady voice may indicate that the knowledge of the investigator has shocked the person being interviewed. The pumping of the heart may be observed by the pulse in the neck. A ruddy or flushed face may be an indication of anger or embarrassment, not necessarily guilt, and may also indicate that the matter under discussion is of vital importance, or that some information is being withheld. Although such symptoms are not necessarily valid indications of guilt or innocence and may be a manifestation of the physical condition or health of the individual, they are often related to the emotional state of the person.

18. **INTERVIEW NOTES**
Complete notes are essential to effective investigation and reporting. Normally, most people have no objection to note-taking; however, the investigator should not take notes until he has had an opportunity to gage the person's reactions, since note-taking may create a reluctance to divulge information. If he does not take notes, the investigator should record, at the first opportunity after the interview, all pertinent information while it is fresh in his mind. Notes on interviews should contain the case number; hour, date, and place of interview; complete identification of the person interviewed; names of other persons present; and a resume of the interview.

19. **PURPOSE OF INTERROGATION**
The interrogation should take place immediately if the suspect is surprised or apprehended in the act of committing a crime. In all other instances, interrogation should be conducted only after sufficient information has been secured and the background of the suspect has been thoroughly explored. The purpose of interrogation of a suspect is to obtain an admission or confession of his wrongful acts and a written, signed, and witnessed statement, and to establish the facts of a crime or to develop information which will enable the investigator to obtain direct, physical, or other evidence to prove or disprove the truth of an admission or confession. A confession is an acknowledgment of guilt, whereas an admission is a self-incriminatory statement falling short of an acknowledgment of guilt. The securing of confessions or acknowledgments of guilt does not complete the investigation of a crime. A statement made by one conspirator during the conspiracy and in pursuance of it is admissible in evidence against his co-conspirators as tending to prove the fact of the matter stated. In interrogation, the investigator seeks to

learn the identity of accomplices and details of any other crime in which the suspect may have been involved.

20. PREPARATION FOR INTERROGATION
a. Preparation for interrogation should be thorough. The investigator should base his plan for interrogation on background data, information, or direct evidence received from victims and witnesses, physical evidence, and reconstruction of the crime scene. The plan, which should be written, should take into consideration the various means for testing the truthfulness of the suspect and for gaining a psychological advantage over him through the use of known facts and proper use of time, place, and environment. Unless the investigator interrogates a suspect immediately following the commission of a crime, or desires to question him without previous notification, he should be interrogated at criminal investigation headquarters, where recordings may be made or stenographic notes may be taken.
b. During interrogation, the subject should be seated in a plain chair placed where his movements and physical reactions may be observed easily. The interrogation room should be plainly but comfortably furnished, without items that may cause distraction. Recording devices, one-way mirrors, and similar equipment should appear as normal furnishings. Tables, desks, and other furnishings should be located where they will not impair the interrogator's observation of the suspect.

21. CLASSIFICATION OF SUSPECTS
Background information and the facts established in an investigation enable the investigator to classify persons to be interrogated as follows:
a. Known offenders, whose guilt is reasonably certain on the basis of the evidence available
b. Persons whose guilt is doubtful or uncertain because of the evidence or lack of evidence.
c. Material witnesses, accessories, and persons who have knowledge of the crime but may not themselves be guilty of a crime. Persons to be interrogated may be further classified as those readily influenced by sympathy or understanding; and those readily influenced by the use of an attitude of suspicion and obvious disbelief.

22. LENGTH OF INTERROGATION
No time limit is placed on the duration of interrogation except that it shall not be so long and under such conditions as to amount to duress. Questioning for many hours without food, sleep, or under glaring lights has been held to constitute such duress as to invalidate a confession. The suspect may be questioned at length in an attempt to break down his resistance, or he may be questioned for short periods daily as a test of his consistency. The interrogator should always consider the physical condition of the person being interrogated as well as his emotional stability. Once the suspect has begun to reveal pertinent information, the interrogator should not be interrupted.

23. **PERSONS AT INTERROGATION**
   An interrogation usually should be conducted in complete privacy. A person under interrogation is not inclined to reveal confidences to a public gathering. Witnesses to a confession may be called in to hear the reading of the statement and the declaration that it is the subject's statement, to witness the signing by the subject, and to affix their own signatures. Some investigative agencies advocate the presence of a witness at all times during an interrogation, particularly during the period of warning of rights and at such other periods when corroborative testimony might be needed or desirable. When a woman is questioned, the interrogator should provide witnesses, preferably women, in order to avoid charges of compromise which an unscrupulous woman may later interject a mitigating circumstance.

24. **INTERROGATION CHECKLIST**
   Before beginning an interrogation, the investigator should check his preparation against the following questions:
   a. Has the crime scene been carefully and adequately searched for real evidence?
   b. Have all persons known to have knowledge of the crime been questioned?
   c. Has all possible evidence been obtained?
   d. Has the person to be interrogated been searched?
   e. Have all files been checked for pertinent information?
   f. Is background investigation complete?
   g. Is the interrogation room properly prepared for the interrogation?
   h. Is the interrogation plan complete?
   i. Have the elements of legal proof been checked?
   j. Are all details of the investigation firmly fixed in the investigator's mind?
   k. What information should be elicited from the individual to be interrogated?

25. **INTRODUCTION OF INVESTIGATOR**
   Prior to any interrogation, the investigator may introduce and identify himself by presenting his credentials if the person to be interrogated questions the authority of the investigator. After the introduction, the person to be interrogated should be informed in general terms of the investigation being conducted. The investigator, however, should not disclose his knowledge of the case, nor should he prematurely disclose any fact of the case.

26. **RIGHTS OF PERSON BEING INTERROGATED**
   The investigator should begin interrogation by explaining to the person to be questioned his rights under the Fifth Amendment to the Constitution of the United States. If he is a civilian, and under Article 31 of the Uniform Code of Military Justice, if he is a military person. The person to be questioned is informed that he need not answer any question which may tend to incriminate him but that, if he chooses to answer any question, such answer may be used in testimony against him. Throughout the questioning the investigator must refrain from threats, violence, or promise of reward. In response to a request by the person being questioned for legal counsel, the investigator should courteously but firmly refuse and state that the Uniform Code of Military Justice does not provide for counsel prior to charges being preferred against a soldier.

27. **ATTITUDE OF INVESTIGATOR**
Because of the importance of admissions or confessions, the investigator must become skilled in the art of interrogation. He must master a variety of questioning techniques, learn to judge the psychological strength of weakness of others, and learn to take advantage of his own particular abilities in questioning any suspect or reluctant witness. He must not presume guilt of the persons being interrogated without sufficient proof. He must act as naturally as possible under the circumstances. If a suspect begins admitting criminal acts, the investigator must not become overeager or condescending. The interrogator should, when it is necessary to stir the emotions of another to confess a wrongful act, permit his own emotions to be stirred.

28. **TYPES OF APPROACH**
He adapts his approach to the character and background of the person to be interrogated, the known facts of the crime, and the real evidence available. The investigator may use any of the following type approaches or any combination of them:

a. The *direct approach* is normally employed where guilt is reasonably certain. The investigator assumes an air of confidence concerning the guilt of the offender and points out the evidence indicative of guilt. He outwardly sympathizes with the offender and indicates that anyone else might have done the same thing under similar circumstances. He urges the offender to tell the truth, avoids threatening words or insinuation, and develops a detailed account of the crime from premeditation to commission. He may ask questions such as the following: "Tell me all you know about this. When did you get the idea of doing it? Why did you do it? How did you do that? Where did you get the money?" In dealing with habitual criminals whose guilt is reasonably certain and who apparently have no feeling of wrongdoing, the investigator must convince them that their guilt can be or is established by the testimony of witnesses or available evidence. Investigators must never make promises of leniency or clemency as these promises might vitiate confessions obtained as a result of the interrogation.

b. The *indirect approach* is normally employed in interrogating a person who has knowledge of the crime. The investigator must proceed cautiously. He requests the individual being interrogated to tell all he knows about the incident. He then requires an explanation of discrepancies or distortions and endeavors to lead the individual being interrogated into admissions of truth. When facts indicative of guilt are developed, the investigator casually asks question to determine through the offender's reactions whether he will acknowledge or deny guilt. When guilt appears probable, the investigator reverts to direct questioning to obtain an admission or confession.

c. The *emotional approach* is designed to arouse any play upon the emotions of a person. Body actions may indicate the presence of nervous tension. The investigator points out these signs of nervous tension to the person under interrogation. The investigator may discuss the moral seriousness of the offense, emphasize the penalty, and appeal to the suspect's pride or ego, fear, like or dislike, or his hate and desire for revenge. This approach may lead to emotional breakdown and a confession.

d. *Subterfuge* is employed to induce guilty persons to confess when all other approaches have failed. Considerable care should be exercised in the employment of subterfuge. If the person to be interrogated recognizes the approach as subterfuge, further efforts to obtain an admission or confession may be futile. Examples of subterfuge are:

(1) *Hypothetical Story.* A fictitious crime, varying only in minute details from the offense of which the subject is suspected, is related to him. The investigator later visits the subject and asks him to write out details of the hypothetical story as related. If the subject is guilty, he often includes details of the crime under investigation, but not mentioned by the investigator in his fictitious story. When confronted with these inconsistencies, the suspect may make a confession.

(2) *Signed False Statement.* When evidence indicates, but is not conclusive, that a certain person may be guilty of a crime, he may be requested to make a sworn written statement. After he has made a false written statement, the discrepancies contained therein are pointed out to him in an attempt to gain a true confession.

(3) *"Cold Shoulder."* This term designates a technique of subterfuge keynoted by indifference. The person suspected is invited to come to the investigator's office. If he accepts the invitation, he is taken either to the office or the crime scene. The investigator, or those accompanying the person subject to this type of interrogation, say nothing to him or to each other, and await his reactions. This technique may cause the suspect to surmise that the investigator has evidence adequate to prove his guilt.

(4) *Playing One Suspect Against Another.* When two or more persons are suspected of having been involved in a crime, the person believed to have the weakest character is interrogated first. The others are interrogated separately and informed that their partner has accused them of the crime. A confession, shown to the others involved, may influence them to attempt to protect themselves by confessing.

(5) *Contrasting Personalities.* This technique employs two investigators, one determined and the other sympathetic and understanding. The interrogation is so arranged that the person under interrogation will play into the hands of one or the other.

29. INTERROGATION NOTES

The taking of notes during an interrogation may be essential in order to record all pertinent information; however, the effect of note-taking on the success of the interrogation must be considered. If notes are not taken during the interrogation, the investigator should record all pertinent data immediately after the interrogation.

30. SCIENTIFIC AIDS TO INTEROGATION

Scientific aids are available to the investigator to assist in the investigation of criminal offenses. These aids are normally employed to develop information from persons who are suspected of committing a crime. They may also be used to check the validity and completeness of information given by complainants, witnesses, and victims.

31. LIE DETECTING SET

Lie detecting set examinations can be conducted only by operators trained in the use of the instrument. The lie detecting set is an instrument which records the body changes that accompany emotions and is used to develop information, to determine if a person has knowledge of an offense, and to obtain an admission or confession of guilt. The provisions of Article 31, Uniform Code of Military Justice, and the Fifth Amendment to the Constitution of the United States apply to persons who are requested to submit to an examination by a lie detecting set. Investigators should obtain written consent from all persons subjected to lie detecting set examinations, acknowledging that they have been informed of their rights and that they agree to submit voluntarily to such an examination. A copy of this statement should be included in the case file folder. In general, graphs obtained during a lie detecting set examination are not admissible as evidence in court. However, the operator is usually permitted to testify relative to the questions asked, and the answers given. Oral or written admissions or confessions obtained as a consequence of the examination may be admitted into evidence, if they meet legal requirements.

32. **NARCO-ANALYSIS**

Narco-analysis is the term employed to define the questioning of a person under the influence of drugs (truth serums). Scopolamine, sodium amytal, and sodium pentothal are the drugs most commonly used. When properly administered, these drugs tend to overcome inhibitions. The use of narco-analysis as an investigative technique has not found general acceptance. Admissions or confessions obtained through the use of truth serums are not admissible as evidence in court. The information obtained may be used only to develop the investigation. The subject must be warned of his rights, and a written statement obtained wherein the subject acknowledges the warning and voluntarily agrees to the narco-analysis. *No person may be compelled to submit to such an examination. It must be conducted only when a qualified medical officer if available to administer the drugs and to witness the examination.*

www.ingramcontent.com/pod-product-compliance
Lightning Source LLC
Chambersburg PA
CBHW080932020526
44116CB00033B/2340